Social Movements and the Indian Diaspora

With the elevation of Islam and Muslim transnational networks in international affairs, from the rise of Al Qaeda to the revolutions in North Africa and the Middle East, the study of diasporas and transnational identities has become more relevant.

Using case studies from Fiji, Mauritius, Trinidad, and South Africa, this book analyzes the influence that the indentured Indian diaspora has on state nationalism and transnational politics. It explores the way in which diasporas are defined by themselves and by others, and the types of social movements they participate in, showing how these are critical indicators of the threat they are perceived to pose. The book examines the notions of national and transnational identity, and how these are determined by the placement of diasporas in the nation-state. It argues that the transnationality intrinsic to diaspora identities marks them as others in the nation-state, and simultaneously separates them from the perceived motherland, thus displacing them from both states and situating them in a transnational locality. It is from this placement that social movements among diasporas gain salience. As outsiders and insiders, they are well placed to offer a formidable challenge to the host state, but these challenges are limited by their hybrid identities and perceived divided loyalties.

Providing an in-depth analysis of Indian diasporas, the book will be of interest to those studying South Asian studies, migration, and diaspora studies.

Movindri Reddy is an Associate Professor in the Department of Diplomacy and World Affairs at Occidental College, USA.

Routledge Contemporary South Asia Series

Social Movements and the Indian Diaspora

Movindri Reddy

Routledge
Taylor & Francis Group

LONDON AND NEW YORK

First published 2016
by Routledge
2 Park Square, Milton Park, Abingdon, Oxon OX14 4RN

and by Routledge
711 Third Avenue, New York, NY 10017

First issued in paperback 2018

*Routledge is an imprint of the Taylor & Francis Group,
an informa business*

British Library Cataloguing in Publication Data
A catalogue record for this book is available from the British Library

Library of Congress Cataloging-in-Publication Data
Reddy, Movindri, author
  Social movements and the Indian diaspora / Movindri Reddy.
    pages cm. — (Routledge contemporary South Asia series ; 104)
  Includes bibliographical references and index.
  1. South Asian diaspora.   2. South Asians—Colonization.
3. Indentured servants—India—History.   4. Social movements—
History.   I. Title.
  DS339.4.R43 2016
  332.4089'91411—dc23
  2015024394

ISBN 13: 978-1-138-59295-7 (pbk)
ISBN 13: 978-1-138-90063-9 (hbk)

Typeset in Times New Roman
by Apex CoVantage, LLC

For my parents Jackie and Leela Reddy.

Contents

Preface

Growing up in apartheid South Africa during a period of intense resistance, I was ambivalent about asserting an Indian identity – being Black and African was far more compelling and urgent. Many years later, long after the euphoria of the transition had worn out, I visited the Narainsamy Temple built by my great-grandfather. I couldn't help but wonder how the millions of other indentured laborers had faired. They too must have their temples and mosques, their distinctive cuisine and language, and they too must have experienced the challenges of negotiating their diaspora and national identities. The isolation of the apartheid regime from the rest of the world led me to assume that the others in this 1.3 million diaspora must be in dialogue with one another and with India. My own experiences abroad in the 1980s made it patently clear that this was not the case – Indians from India related to its diaspora with a sense of bemusement bordering on disdain. Diaspora Indians themselves had scant knowledge about each other, and a vague understanding of history at best, was the norm. But most disturbing was the fact that everyone assumed I was Indian, no matter my attempts to define myself as Black and African. These experiences eventually led me towards embarking on an ambitious study in four disparate parts of the world: Mauritius where Indians are in the majority, Fiji and Trinidad where Indians make up close to half of the population (although this has changed in Fiji with emigration), and South Africa where Indians are a small minority but constitute the largest number in this diaspora. Nearly a decade later after an incredibly fulfilling and equally challenging experience, my findings and observations have culminated in this book. Apart from the specific conclusions I drew, it was clear that the indentured diaspora is diverse and resilient. Like all diasporas it defies generalizations but demands recognition. This book represents a small step in that direction.

This research project could not have been possible without the support of many. My interest in ethnic identity started with a Ph. D. at Cambridge University when I researched questions related to intra-ethnic conflict among members of the Zulu-based Inkatha organization in South Africa. Here John Lonsdale was an inspiring advisor especially as he was working on intra-ethnic tensions among the Kikuyu in Kenya. I continued to explore these questions in several post-doctoral fellowships at Yale, Princeton, and under a MacArthur Fellowship at the University of Chicago. Throughout this period I worked with a number of supportive colleagues including Colin Bundy, Archmat Davids, Susanne Rudolph, Rob Shell, and Leonard Thompson. The study of the indentured Indian diaspora was a move away from a concentration on inter- and intra-ethnic relations within nation-states to identities forged at the transnational level. Here I had the pleasure of conversing with Brij Lal, Tim Shaw, Jane Parpart, and many others. The John Park Young Grant at Occidental College generously funded my research trips.

Hospitable informants, supportive faculty colleagues, and encouraging family members assisted me throughout this process. My colleagues Larry Caldwell, Jane Jaquette, Derek Shearer, and Dale Wright have been steadfast in their support and encouragement. I could not have coped with the demanding teaching and service requirements of a liberal arts institution without my co-conspirators in CODE (The Coalition of Diversity and Equity) – Regina Freer, Donna Maeda, Martha Matsuoka, Paul Nam, and James Ford. My biggest thanks go to my informants, their warmth and graciousness was invaluable. Wherever I went wonderful people hosted me, Indians throughout this diaspora were infinitely engaging, informative, and had a terrific sense of humor. I thank my family: Mike, Akasham, and Shalini Pace, my brother Thiven Reddy, and all my relatives and friends who supported me through the years.

Introduction

In February 1942, 2 months after Pearl Harbor, President Roosevelt signed Executive Order 9066 that relocated 117,000 United States residents of Japanese descent into internment camps. After the September 11, 2001 attacks, the United States Department of Homeland Security Department instituted the "Special Registration" program that required male Arab and Muslim non-citizens (including those with permanent resident status) to register with the government; 85,000 were fingerprinted, photographed, and interviewed. In both these instances, the state reacted to international insecurity by targeting diaspora communities living within its national borders, and efforts were made to identify and isolate them from the general citizenry. Diasporas have historically come under attack when states experience external crises. What makes them such visible targets and why are they assumed to have divided loyalties? These are some of the questions explored in this book.

Studies of diasporas have generally focused on how their identities are constructed, or on specific case studies that offer insightful analyses of how diasporas function in the nation-state. In many respects these studies are inward-looking – focusing on identities and political activities from the perspective of the nation-state. Particularly in international relations and political science, the centrality of the state in defining notions of citizenship and identity have led to studies of diasporas that are confined to nation-states. For example, Shain and Barth focus on the dual identities of diasporas, those that are associated with home and host states to show how they influence politics in both states. Esman classifies diasporas as minority ethnic groups of migrant origin residing in and identifying with the state but continuing to maintain links with their land of origin.[1] Diaspora studies in these disciplines are relatively few in number, but in cultural studies and sociology they have grown exponentially. There still however remains a strong focus on the home-host trope, a dual territorial identity that impacts allegiances, citizenship, and rights.

The gaps in the literatures include a neglect of the transnational aspect of diaspora identities and the social movements they form. Most scholarship proposes that the reason for the perceived threat that diasporas pose for nationalism and sovereignty is their split state-centered identities. The role of the transnational side of diasporas is generally underplayed in the literature. Here, the way in which diasporas define themselves and are defined by others, and the kinds of social movements they participate in, are critical indicators of the threat they are perceived to present. This is the focal point of this book – it takes the perspective of diasporas from an insider's viewpoint (i.e.: from the point of view of how diasporas define themselves) *and* from an outsider's viewpoint (i.e.: how diasporas are defined by other ethnic groups and by the state) and attempts to understand these from the perspective of social movements. Theoretically it connects inward-looking identity-focused analyses with states and transnational relations.

The main argument made here is that the transnationality intrinsic to diaspora identities *mark* them as others in the nation-state (sometimes referred to as the host-state/nation) and simultaneously *separate* them from the homeland/motherland, thus displacing them from both states and situating them in a *transnational locality*. It is from this placement that social movements among diasporas gain salience. As outsiders *and* insiders, diasporas are well placed to offer a formidable challenge to the host-state, but these challenges are limited by their hybrid identities and perceived divided loyalties.

While this book explores the impact of diasporas on politics and nationalism as it pertains to all states, the case studies that are analyzed pertain to the South Asian indentured diaspora in Fiji, Trinidad, Mauritius, and South Africa. Even though the experiences of this diaspora are peculiar to these states, they are not dissimilar to other diasporas in their placement and identities within the states they reside. Notions of national and transnational identity have distinctive features but are more broadly determined by the placement of diasporas in the transnational locality – a placement that typifies all diasporas to a greater or lesser extent.

Challenges in diaspora and social movement literatures

Theoretical studies of diasporas have attracted diverse and interdisciplinary participants. This dynamic field is exemplified by the journal *Diaspora: A Journal of Transnational Studies* edited by Khachig Tölölyan, a multidisciplinary journal dedicated to publishing articles on history, culture, social structure, politics, and economics of the classical diasporas (Armenian, Greek, Jewish) and more contemporary diasporas like the African, Indian, and Chinese. The field engages high-level theoretical analyses (for example works by Stephen Dufoix, James Clifford, Stuart Hall), and numerous local-level fieldwork generated studies (for example those of William Safran, Robin Cohen, Peter Van der Veer). With the elevation of Islam and Muslim transnational networks in international affairs, from the rise of Al Qaeda to the revolutions in North Africa and the Middle East, the study of diasporas and transnational identities has become more relevant. My study adds to this field by engaging with it at the theoretical and empirical levels.

It critiques the home-host trope that is typical of many studies and situates diaspora identities in a transnational space that is also intrinsically localized. This perspective provides a compelling reason for why diasporas are usually considered threatening – they are never fully located within the confines of the nation-state. By their placement with respect to the nation-state (both the state from which they left, to the state in which they settled), they are marked as located in a trans-national locality. It is this placement that defines them as having identities that do not neatly fit into the nation of all the states they are associated with (home, host 1, host 2, and so on); they are seen as a threat by multiple states. Diaspora identities change over several generations, as does the degree of assimilation into the nation-state. This process is affected by their ancestral nationality, race, and ethnicity. But in terms of diasporas that are still considered as such within a nation-state, their placement always makes them more vulnerable to questions of loyalty and patriotism and makes them open to transnational mobilization. The home-host trope locates them in two states, the transnational locality locates them in a space beyond states but which is also linked to states – this allows for greater analytical flexibility. It elevates the transnational sphere that is seen as threaten-ing to state sovereignty, but that is also viewed positively by diasporas them-selves. The notion of belonging *and* dissociation from the nation can be a source of empowerment and a source of persecution from others.

Recognizing this placement opens up the possibility of illustrating why few generalizations can be made for any diaspora. Their distance/displacement from the motherland/homeland *and* their current home nations insinuates ambivalence into their identities. Over time they develop localized/nationalized/Creolized identities, but the perception that they have stronger and permanent ties with the nation-state they left behind interferes with the relationship they have with their current home-nations. Furthermore the nation-states they left change considerably through the generations of departure; notions of belonging are based on nostalgia, memories, and narratives/stories, all of which give the sense of a weak, ill-defined relationship. It is this objective lack of belonging that affects the subjective con-struction of identity.

Diasporas are consistently defined as others in a nation-state, they are consid-ered obvious security risks, and their bodies give meaning to nebulous notions of insecurity. They in turn have to come to terms with scrutiny and suspicions regard-ing their patriotism, allegiance, and loyalty to the nation-state. The prioritization of state borders in global politics and scholarship contributes to this ambivalence and to subjective feelings of otherness, displacement, and alienation. The increas-ing numbers of diaspora members (many first and second-generation immigrants) who join groups like the Islamic State (ISIS/ISIL) and other violent transnational organizations, to some degree reflect the ability of these organizations to offer an alternative identity that taps into the ambivalences associated with placement in a transnational locality. Here the quest for identity is motivated by national dis-placement and adherence to a transnational religious movement that defies state borders and ideological boundaries. The analysis in this book provides evidence for thinking about diasporas in terms of its placement in the transnational locality – this notion is relevant for understanding the success of contemporary transna-tional social movements in their recruitment drive for members from a diaspora.

At the empirical level this study adds to country-specific studies in a com-parative framework of the indentured South Asian diaspora, it is written from the perspective of a political scientist specializing in international relations and comparative politics. The emphasis on institutions, states, political engagement, and global interactions structure this analysis. This study also adds to the social movement literature and exposes instances that don't simply fit in the main theoretical perspectives. The field of social movements is robust with foundational theorists like Sidney Tarrow, Charles Tilly, Margaret Keck, and Kathryn Sikkink, expanding their analyses to seriously consider the role of transnational networks and associations. My analysis highlights how diasporas construct social movements and shows that while they participate and develop movements that are transnational in scope, they do not necessarily activate old (original) diaspora networks. For example, the indentured Indian diaspora does not activate diaspora networks that originated from India, but rather those who 'twice-migrate' to other host-lands like the United Kingdom, the United States, New Zealand, and Australia. Transnational linkages were weakened during British colonialism by the experiences of isolation and alienation from others in the diaspora, and further by independent India's ambivalence towards them.

Furthermore, social movements among this diaspora, like most in the Global South, are energized by the new possibilities brought about by globalization and technological innovations. However they are simultaneously marginalized because of their location in the Global South and heavy reliance on organizational resources from the Global North. In many instances too, these social movements operate in a space in which their states are undergoing democratic transitions and economic transformations at the same time. The neoliberal economic regimes that have come to be hegemonic in post-colonial states affect the kinds of social movements that evolve. Many have had to recalibrate organizational techniques to operate in the new globalized arena. The role of India in the post-colonial states in which the South Asian diaspora resides has changed considerably since it transitioned to an economy structured by neoliberal economic principles. Previously the indentured Indian diaspora was largely ignored by India, but with the new wave of more affluent Indians and prioritization given to the global reach of the subcontinent, this diaspora is now viewed as potential sources for global networking and investment. Transnational transactions, which have become the hallmark of this latest iteration of economic globalization, have also given rise to more cultural exchanges increasing the Indian presence in these regions. From investment in local temples, festivals, and other cultural exchanges, India has also begun to play a larger role in direct investment in economic infrastructure throughout the diaspora. Social movements in these regions have had to contend with local management who represent transnational companies. In this respect diasporas play a peculiar role; well placed to engage with the new neoliberal regimes but also more open to severe exploitation. This study adds to those that have argued that rather than focusing on political opportunities as the prime cause for the formation of social movements in the Global South, there is a need to once again focus on economic inequalities brought about by global capitalist demands, and state policies that facilitate greater international economic integration.

Social movements among diasporas are often considered threatening. It is assumed that cultural and religious organizations are the basis for more politically oriented organizations that will likely challenge the state given the diasporas divided loyalties. The Indian indentured diaspora, for example, has been considered a threat by the state and/or other ethnic and racial groups in every location and at various points in time. For example, in 1960 riots erupted in Durban, South Africa, when the apartheid state tried to forcibly move Africans out of Cato Manor, a designated Indian urban residential neighborhood. African residents and squatters retaliated against the municipal police, they also attacked Indian residents and destroyed and looted many of their homes and businesses. In Mauritius, ethnic tensions between Creoles and Indians have exploded in violent confrontations on several occasions – for example in 1965 during the run-up to constitutional amendments and independence, and again in 1999 over a soccer game. Ethnic clashes in Trinidad often make headlines during election campaigns where political parties representing different ethnic groups vie for support and power. Politicians can often manipulate low-level ethnic tensions. In post-independent Fiji, the presiding government was ousted four times (May 1987, September 1987, May 2000, and December 2006) resulting in coups and a deeply divided society. Ethnic tensions between indigenous Fijians and Indo-Fijians underlie political instability, with Indo-Fijians viewed most starkly as outsiders and temporary residents ever since they first entered the Island between 1879 and 1916. This study adds to theoretical discourses questioning why diasporas are viewed as threats to state security, and why diasporas themselves struggle to come to terms with their hybrid identities. Here participation in social movements clearly reflects these challenges.

Empirical bases for this study

This book is based on fieldwork done periodically from 2007 to 2012 among Indians in Fiji, Trinidad and Tobago, and South Africa. In the field I collected primary source data, conducted interviews, attended religious and political functions, and documented my observations using print and digital media (mainly photographs). The main perspective through which diaspora identity is gleaned is through social movements that are prevalent and the issues around which they mobilize. In South Africa for example, the role of Mahatma Gandhi in forming the Indian National Congress to mobilize Indians against segregation, formed the organizational repertoire for subsequent multi-racial, anti-apartheid organizations like the United Democratic Front. The strategy to make townships ungovernable had precedents in Gandhi's *satyagraha* movements against pass-laws. The more recent anti-eviction organizations formed in Chatsworth, a predominantly Indian area in KwaZulu-Natal, clearly reflects historical precedents in the way in which Indians navigate their minority status in post-apartheid South Africa.

In Mauritius, issues pertaining to national identity and vernacular educational training take the lead in many Indo-Mauritian organizations. Divided along the lines of religion and language, they have pushed for the teaching of ancestral languages in public schools. The majority speaks Mauritian-Creole and about a quarter of the population also speaks Mauritian-Bhojpuri, a language derived from the north Indian language of the Bihari group, the forefathers of many of the Hindus in Mauritius. English is the official language medium for education and the bureaucracy, and French is the main language used in the private sector and mass media. However Indians (Hindus are 52% and Muslims 16% of the population) who rarely speak Hindi, Tamil, or Telegu have been pushing for ancestral languages to be taught in schools. Patrick Eisenlohr succinctly shows how the language agenda is closely tied to the construction of diaspora identities that cement connections to India. Examples of organizations that mobilize among Hindus are the Arya Samaj, the Sanatan Dharm Temples Federation, and the Hindi Pracarini Sabha (Society for the Propagation of Hindi) and those that work with Tamils include The Tamil League, The Mauritius Tamil Temple Federation, and the Tamil Speaking Union.

In Trinidad and Fiji, cultural and religious organizations as well as more politically orientated movements proliferate. In post-independent Fiji, religious organizations also mobilized support for political parties. Ranging from the more orthodox Fiji Sanatan Dharam Pratinidhi Sabha (SDS) to the reformed Arya Pratinidhi Samaj (APS/Fiji) for Hindu's, separate organizations for South Indians (TISI Sangam for Tamils and Andra Sangam for Telegus) and Muslims (Fiji Muslim League), these disparate organizations show that Indians do not engage in politics as a coherent voting bloc. They are divided, religiously and regionally, representing varying articulations with a diaspora identity that consistently situates them as outsiders and temporary residents in a country that is defined by indigenous Fijian terms.

Indo-Trinidadians appear to be the most indigenized of all Indians in this study – they have fewer religious and regional divisions among them and share similar cultural and linguistic practices. While they have religious and political organizations similar to others in the diaspora (Sanatan Dharma Maha Sabha, Arya Pritinidhi Sabha, Trinidad Muslim League, etc.), they also have strong ties to Creoles; Indo-Trinidadian culture is visibly hybridized. Social movements span religious, trade, and political organizations, but mixed ethnic membership in political parties is slowly entering a new phase as Indo-Trinidadians attempt to engage with their status as Trinidadians linked to an Indian diaspora.

The South Asian indentured diaspora

Specifically for this diaspora, emphasis is placed on how social movements among them have influenced the construction of nations and states. Here relations between diaspora Indians and Creole or indigenous groups are important. Further relations with India bear some import on the kinds of social movements that have evolved. The study argues that Indians are categorized as "ethnic" Indian across the diaspora, in part because of their own desire to separate themselves from indigenous and local peoples on the basis of 'purity' and historical authenticity derived from India. But also in part because indigenous or Creole communities delineate *themselves* as belonging to the land, thereby claiming indigeneity or indigenous status and rights in relation to Indians. In other words Indians have attempted to establish *themselves* as the opposite of mixed/Creolized by continuing to emphasize ancestral ties to India; and indigenous or Creole communities use this trope to define themselves as insiders and Indians as perpetual outsiders and temporary residents. Indians are othered by host nation-states because of their perceived transnational identity (in this case, their Indianness), and they distance themselves from locals by emphasizing their ties to India but are also marginalized and seen as 'unauthentic' by the motherland (India). The history of indenture and the divisive relations that it set in place in the host-lands, also served to divide the diaspora itself by isolating them from each other. This occurred despite the fact that high-level British administrators and plantation owners had first-hand experiences throughout the diaspora and nurtured strong transnational networks. Under colonialism structures were set in place that cemented this isolation and hence transnational networks among this diaspora are very weak.

These identities influence the development and agenda of social movements – in this diaspora they are largely nationally based, focused on local issues with weak transnational linkages. However because of internationalism (spurred by a new wave in globalization), the leaders of social movements employ a cosmopolitan perspective to fight for local bread-and-butter issues. In sum, social movements in each of these states have not relied on diaspora ties but have reached beyond borders to places of second-migration that are mainly in the West. They rely on this diaspora for direct funding, international media coverage, and access to other global networks.

Overall several propositions are made:

- At the macro-level it is argued that diasporic identities, which are de-centered and constructed within the discursive framework of states *and* transnational relations, influence the ideologies and policies of nations and states.
- At a national level, it is argued that Indian diasporic identity is exemplified by the kinds of relations that exist between Indians and Creole or indigenous groups, and Indians and the "motherland," and that these relations influence how the nation is constructed.
- At a micro-level it is argued that Indians are marked as "*ethnic* Indian" across the diaspora because of their own desire to separate themselves on the basis of "purity" and historical authenticity and are marked as such by other ethnic/racial groups who attempt to demarcate *themselves* as belonging to the land claiming indigeneity or indigenous status and rights, and marking Indians as perpetual outsiders.

Some definitions

- ***Ethnic identity***: In the debate around definitions of ethnicity, I err on the side of seeing it as a constructed entity that is renewed, modified, and remade in each generation.[2] Ethnic solidarities derive meaning and are politicized through grievances with the larger political system or rival ethnic groups. In terms of diasporas, the notions of hybridity and indigenization are key concepts. The notion of *hybridity*, derived from biology, connotes the idea of mixing and became an important term for analyzing racial mixing. Appropriated by post-colonial studies this term also came to stand for theoretical discourses on cultural and identity mixing.[3] In my work, I use the term to challenge the notion of "purity" that is often propagated by diaspora Indians despite being three or four generations deep in former British colonies and despite being marginalized by India for most of their history. In a similar vein I use the term *indigenization* to reflect ways in which identities associated with India have been modified through generations to adapt to current homelands.

• *Transnational:* A term used to refer to relations that transcend states and to emphasize relations between non-government organizations, international business networks, and individuals sharing similar cultural and other allegiances and interests. This differs from inter-state relations, which refers to relations between states. Diasporas exhibit what Steven Vertovec calls a "triadic relationship" between globally disbursed but self-identified ethnic groups, the territorial state where such groups live, and the state from which such groups originated.[4] The transnationality of diasporas is of central import in this study and forms the basis of the arguments being made.

Specificities of the Indian indentured diaspora

Originating as a diaspora between 1833 and 1920 under the British system of indenture, Indians were employed as either a new source of cheap labor (as in Fiji and South Africa) or scab labor to replace freed slaves (as in Fiji and Mauritius). All four states differ vastly in terms of their political systems, economic size, and political and social histories, but all have the presence of a common "diasporic" community (historically and analytically). This comparison is structured by focus on two sets of variables in all four states.

• Relationships between Indians (majority/minority) and Creoles/indigenous communities. Here they are evaluated along a spectrum from antagonistic or prone to conflict, to compatible with a high degree of intermixing and cooperation.
• Relations with the motherland/India. These relations are evaluated in terms of whether they have strong and close connections, to whether they have weak and thin connections with India.

Both sets of variables are strongly influenced by the identity of Indians within each state, and this book assumes that over the three or four generations of settlement, Indian identity has been "indigenized" or "Creolized."

A puzzle that pertains to all four states is that despite the indigenization and Creolization of Indian identities, a generalized notion of "Indianness" and "otherness" prevails. While former slaves are considered Creolized, Indians continue to be essentialized as Indian. They tend to straddle the local (inward looking with respect to each state), and the global (outward looking and gaz-ing towards India). Using the two sets of variables outlined above to move the analysis across all four states, this comparison attempts to address this paradox of being "insiders" but also "outsiders." Some of the main questions asked are: why, despite the numerous differences in the experiences of Indians in these multiple locations, are they ascribed an ethnic (and not racial or other) identity? Why is it possible for other diasporas to earn a sense of indigeneity or belong-ing whereas Indians are always considered outsiders/temporary migrants? How have Indians contributed to this status as perpetual outsiders? If diasporas are linked to both India and local/indigenous networks, why are they not considered to belong, and what does belonging mean in different states? One conclusion is my argument about Indian and indigenous/Creole self-identifications with respect to one another.

There are two books that speak directly to this project: *The Domestic Abroad: Diasporas in International Relations* by Latha Varadarajan (2010), and *New Homeland. Hindu Communities I Mauritius, Guyana, Trinidad, South Africa, Fiji, and East Africa,* by Paul Younger (2010). Written from the perspective of interna-tional relations, Varadarajan highlights the relationship between the Indian state and its diaspora; she cogently analyzes the reasons for the shift from relative indif-ference to active engagement and even celebration. Younger studies the diaspora from the perspective of cultural adaptations, localized religious innovations, and continuities with India. My analysis fits well within this genre, but it is distinc-tive in that both authors take the "motherland" as the point of departure making the "external" the salient factor. Instead, I am looking at "diaspora states" with a sharp focus on the "internal" as it plays out across the diaspora. My objective is to investigate what it means to speak of Indianness (or a diaspora identity) from a place outside India. Here local nationalist struggles, culture, politics, econom-ics, geographies, etc. make a difference. My study then is different on a number of counts:

- A focus on diaspora states with an Indian minority/majority.
- A focus on the "messiness of identities" in terms of political, economic and social imperatives, and with respect to the range of possibilities across other social constructs like gender, class, and generation.
- The influence of the local context and dynamic changes on identity construction.
- The meaning of "indigenized" Indian identities as reflected in everyday speech, dress, art, and other cultural elements, as well as in political and eco-nomic participation.
- A focus on *differences* in Indian identities in each state, reflecting the theme that states make a difference to the way identities are constructed.
- A focus on the *sameness* of Indian identities, in terms of their common mark-ing across the diaspora in terms of ethnicity. Being Indian trumps categoriza-tion by race. This exemplifies the importance of transnational identities over state-determined identities.

Organization of the book

Chapter 1 sets up the historical framework for the comparative study making the primary argument that the international movement of labor, with antecedents in the transatlantic slave trade, occurred because of the strategic position of Britain, the pervasive ideology of racism, Western notions of superiority, and the subservient position of colonial subjects in the global economy of empire. The indentured labor system was initiated on the tailcoats of slavery mainly because estate owners desired cheap labor and were able to use their influential positions in Britain to make this possible. While this system was not slavery, there were lines of continuity between the two – indenture was a form of bonded labor: Indians were under contract in exchange for a small salary, housing, and rations. Like former slaves, they traveled in the same ships, lived in the same quarters, and worked under similar exploitative practices – but unlike the former system there were some checks and balances including short-term contracts, access to judicial processes, and some degree of labor protections. Yet the similarities in both systems attest to the prevailing ideologies of racial superiority and oppression of people of color. The call for majority rule, equal rights, and justice for all subjects, was still not part of the political rhetoric of the anti-slavery and other liberal organizations.

In all the colonies Indians were used to undermine the bargaining position of freed Africans or indigenous communities, and their position in the social hierarchy reinforced racial suspiciousness and divisions. Akin to scab labor, local people resented them for reducing wages and sustaining the exploitative plantation economy. They in turn suffered the numerous injustices of the colonial system and in the process created cultural perspectives and political organizations that enabled engagement and a degree of disengagement from the colonial and later, the post-colonial systems. These identities impacted the kinds of social movements that were formed. Relying on leaders who were cosmopolitan in their outlook, opposition was initially on an individualistic level. Later more coherent groups were created and the characteristics of political resistance formed the repertoire of contention for future opposition movements.

Chapter 2 is a theoretical exploration of diaspora theories and the challenges that a dual territorial perspective has for understanding the transnationality intrinsic to diaspora identities. Any definition that is based on the idea of a stable point of origin (homeland), clear and final destinations, and coherent group identities, do not neatly apply. Given the generational depth of South Asians in Fiji, Trinidad, South Africa, and Mauritius, there is little desire among current descendants to return to India and memories associated with the homeland have long died. The diaspora itself is divided along lines of class, gender, generation, ethnic and religious identity, language, and culture. Culture has been indigenized over time, and an entrenched feeling of belonging has developed, together with an increasing recognition of the possibility of moving and traveling (twice-migration is high). Religious and cultural practices have become more streamlined and have adapted to local conditions, differing markedly across the diaspora in relation to India. While racial and ethnic stereotypes become more significant during political upheaval or elections, relations with other ethnic and racial groups are not always tense or antagonistic.

How then can this sense of diaspora be theorized? The emphasis on states and the relegation of diasporas to a non-place, anarchical in-between zones, makes it difficult to understand the role that diasporas play within states. Diasporas further challenge the binaries of colonizer/colonized, White/Black, Western/ Eastern, developed/underdeveloped, state/nation, citizen/subject, and national/ transnational. Acknowledging the strength and reach of the state, this chapter suggests that there is a growing need to recognize the increasing salience, relative order, and significance of the in-between/outside state spheres. Strict divisions are not helpful; especially the neo-realist idea that states are ordered/controlled/ authoritative and the international arena is anarchic/disordered/uncontrolled. Borrowing from other disciplines, it is expedient to see identities as de-centered, constructed both creatively and continually within the discursive framework of citizenship and trans-state relations and interactions. While this does not detract from the capacity of states to control the movement of people, it does change the way in which states operate – their ideologies and policies are constantly challenged by civil society, unfettered in their communication capabilities by state controls and borders. In other words, states can no longer act in a narrowly defined sense of self-interest, the sheer weight and impact of the global sphere ensures that diasporic interests matter, in politics and in cultural identity. Notions of citizenship and nationalism have to change to meet new and more globally informed expectations and perspectives.

This chapter also provides a comprehensive overview of social movements and situates this study within that framework. The analysis of opposition and cultural movements among this diaspora has been localized and this study attempts to situate them more clearly in theoretical discourses.

Chapter 3 draws attention to the indentured South Asian diaspora in Fiji and Trinidad and analyzes why their similar colonial and post-colonial historical experiences led to different political outcomes. The argument put forth is that constitutional reforms that were adopted by Fiji were unsuccessful because of systemic conditions specific to the country. Sustained by structural features such as land rights, chiefly jurisdiction, and more intangible factors such as cultural identity and nationalism, ethnic identity is the lens through which most public discourse occurs. By contrast, Trinidad does not have these corresponding institutional structures. Furthermore, the existence of public spaces for the contestation of ethnic identities, together with the construction of hybrid identities at the local and national levels, have contributed to political stability. In terms of the larger comparative framework, relations between Indians and indigenous Fijians are hard (prone to conflict), while relations with India are soft (relatively weak). In Trinidad, the opposite is true; Indian-Creole relations are soft (less prone to conflict), and relations with India are relatively strong.

Chapter 4 explores the concept of nation as it is constructed by the Indo-Mauritian majority and evaluates its implications for Creole identity. From all the cases being highlighted, Mauritius is distinctive for its Indian majority as well its close connections with India. Specifically Hindu Mauritians have reinvigorated ties to India by prioritizing economic and cultural collaboration. The main argument made is that despite the strong connection pursued by Indo-Mauritians and India, the former activate these ties to bolster their hegemony in the Mauritian state. Through prioritizing cultural and historical connections to India, they also attempt to substantiate their claim in the nation against contested counter claims from Creoles and other minorities. Notions of citizenship and identity have become intricately tied to race, class, ethnicity, generation, and religion.

As a minority in a country that has recently transitioned to democracy, the place and identity of Indians in South Africa is dynamic. Chapter 5 focuses on resistance and argues that in the post-apartheid system Indians have largely closed ranks, becoming more insular and self-sufficient, constituting themselves as a separate but equal ethnic group. However in terms of their historical role in the politics of resistance, their significant place in the country's economy, and their role in the professions, Indians reflect their Africanness. Inter-racial tensions have erupted from time to time and low-level animosities persist, but collaboration and cooperation is normative. This chapter focuses on questions of race and ethnicity – identities that are lived and debated within the Indian community. It also looks at how Indians have reacted to their new minority status (under apartheid while Indians were a minority, they were treated as a recognized separate and equal ethnic group like "Coloureds" and "Africans"), by re-focusing on their distinctiveness, emphasizing their connections to India, celebrating their legacy of indenture (a hitherto neglected subject in the school curriculum), and supporting vernacular languages (the majority of Indians speak only English).

The cultural distinctiveness and hybridity of the indentured Indian diaspora is the focus of Chapter 6. Here the idea of a transnational identity and linkages with India is of significance. Looking at these issues from the perspective of the diaspora, emphasis is placed on indigeneity, hybridity, and Creolization. This chapter argues that the Creolization of cultural identities is at the basis for both resistance and adaptation to citizenship and nationhood. The following is highlighted: food (ex: "Doubles" in Trinidad, "Bunny Chow" in South Africa), religious places of worship (temples and temple architecture in South Africa- some of which are the oldest in the diaspora), music (Chutney-soca in Trinidad, banghra in Mauritius), religious ceremonies (Holi in Mauritius, Diwali in Trinidad) and local festivals (carnival in Trinidad, 150th anniversary of indentured laborers in South Africa). The objective of this chapter is to provide a glimpse of the dynamic cultural milieu that exists.

The concluding chapter returns to the argument made with respect to diasporas in general and the South Asian indentured diaspora specifically. The argument that diaspora Indians occupy a discursive space of the *transnational locality* is evaluated with respect to each of the cases that were analyzed. Of significance to this study is the current moment when globalization and the movement of goods, services, information, and people are persistent and exponentially greater than at any other time in the past. Here the ways in which social movements in this diaspora are navigating these new challenges and gateways, is of interest. The concluding remarks allude to some of the subjects that will make for fruitful further study.

Notes

1   Yossi Shain and Aharon Barth, "Diasporas and International Relations Theory," *International Relations Theory* 57, (2003); Milton J. Esman, "Diasporas and International Relations," in *Modern Diasporas in International Politics*, ed. by Gabriel Sheffer, (New York: St. Martins, 1986).
2   My Ph.D. dissertation and post-doctoral work centered on theories and case studies pertaining to ethnicity. See Movindri Reddy, "Conflicts of Consciousness: Zulu Ethnicity and Violence in Natal, South Africa," (PhD diss., Cambridge University, 1993); "Ethnic Conflict and Violence: South Africa and South Asia", in *Ethnicity and Governance in the Third World*, ed. by John Mukum Mbaku, Pita Ogaba Agbese, Mwangi S. Kimenyi, (England: Ashgate Publishing Company, 2001); "Challenging Democracy: Ethnicity in Post-Colonial Fiji and Trinidad," in *Journal of Nationalism and Ethnic Politics* 17, no. 2 (April-June 2011). I specifically look to the work of Clifford Geertz, Abner Cohen, Nelson Kasfir, Milton Esman, Jean and John Comaroff, and others.
3   Key works include Homi Bhabha, Néstor García Canclini, Stuart Hall, Gayatri Spivak, and Paul Gilroy.
4   See Steven Vertovec, *Transnationalism*, (Routledge, 2009).

1 Colonialism and indenture

Originating as a diaspora between 1833 and 1920 under the British system of indenture, Indians were employed as either a new source of cheap labor in colonies like Fiji and South Africa or scab labor to replace freed slaves in colonies like Trinidad and Mauritius. Over 1.3 million Indians were indentured over a period of 83 years. The system was abolished in 1914 but continued until 1920; the largest numbers of Indians were indentured to Mauritius (453,063), followed by Natal (152,184) and Trinidad (143,939), with Fiji (60,000) at the lower end of the scale. Currently Indo-Mauritians make up 68 per cent of the population of Mauritius, Indo-Trinidadians, and Afro-Trinidadians are somewhat equal in number, Indo-Fijians decreased in number through emigration from being close to half the population of Fiji to about one-third, and South African Indians are a small minority but are the largest in this diaspora. The implications of indenture on the social, political, and economic outcomes of former British colonies continue to be significant.

The objective of this chapter is to highlight the structural institutions and ideologies that enabled the passage of indenture. This is particularly relevant given that indenture was introduced immediately following the Slavery Abolition Act 1833 and abolition, which followed a year later. Slavery and indenture were intimately connected through two main points of intersection: the West Indian slave owner and planter interests, and the agendas, ideology and characteristics of the anti-slavery movements. Of relevance too were the elevated position of Britain in India, the new wave of imperialism and empire, and the role of global capitalism. This chapter argues that while the post-abolition period was defined by a new sense of British identity, one that was associated with a sense of high moral and Christian purpose, it continued to rely on the racially framed assumptions of non-Western and non-European people as inferior and unfit for Western values of democracy and equality. To some extent these assumptions explain why the British anti-slavery movements did not push for equal representation in Britain and majority rule in the colonies. The emancipation agenda did not include a call for the freedom for self-rule, restitution for former slaves, or judicial protections and rights for all citizens. Significantly the anti-slavery movements did not call for the abolition of *all* bonded labor. These ideological and strategic moves were relevant for anti-indenture movements. First, indenture was positioned midway between slavery and free labor, making it seem as if the institution was more benign than slavery especially as Indians appeared to join contractual labor voluntarily. Moreover indenture involved a contractual period that was temporary rather than the lifelong arrangement that defined slavery. These ambiguities regarding the exploitative and oppressive nature of indenture affected the ability of anti-indenture movements to mobilize substantial support. Second, the anti-indenture movements situated their rhetoric within the discourses articulated by the pro-indenture lobby – the merchants, plantation owners, bankers, and a host of others who had direct interests in colonial production. Priority was given to profit margins, the competitiveness of British products, and the growth and sustenance of empire. Protests against indenture focused more on protections and oversight over indentured workers rather than on abolition and rights of Indian workers in the colonies. Hence British protestors also emphasized the shortage of labor, the need for expanding sugar production, and the desire to maintain British economic and political competitiveness.

Of significance too is the fact that indenture as an institution was historically well developed in England. Husbandry in early modern England was an arrangement whereby young people from poor families typically entered into annual contacts with more prosperous farmers in exchange for wages, food, and lodging. A form of this system was later employed in British America with the indentured servitude of young English men and women. In Britain at the time there was ongoing contestation over labor rights, and the lines between free labor and bonded labor were fuzzy. In the colonies indentured servants, slaves, and convicts provided labor. As Northrup says we should focus on how free labor grew out of bondage rather than how bondage fell short of freedom.[1] David Eltis observes that during this period it was wage labor and not slavery that was the "odd institution."[2]

In the rapidly changing global arena during this period, states were continuing to construct themselves as nations, and competition among Western powers demanded access to novel and cheaper material goods. Production costs were lowered by using cheap labor in Europe and in the colonies, by growing and accessing raw materials, and by relying on rudimentary production processes in the colonies supplemented by machinery and factory-line mass production in the metropolis. The indenture of Indians to work in the colonies contributed towards cheapening the production process and enhancing profits.

Indians resisted this system both overtly and covertly. In the public realm they initially relied on individual and community petitions, later engaging the colonial authorities through more organized social movements. From the beginning although they appealed to the Colonial Office in England or administrators in the colonies and India, social movements concentrated on local issues – working conditions, laws regarding rights, and personal trials. In all the colonies, Indians were isolated from indigenous peoples and other settled communities, and they did not activate transnational networks despite the similarities they shared with others in this diaspora. This kind of mobilization that focused on parochial and national issues became a definitive characteristic of social movements amongst this diaspora; it became what Charles Tilly refers to as a 'repertoire of conten- tion' for mobilization and action.[3] Most social movements operated separately from other racial or ethnic groups increasing the distance between Indians and other oppressed groups. Covert resistance included a closing of ranks to outsiders, go-slows, and other surreptitious forms of resistance that were practiced on a daily basis in the workplace. Further they celebrated religious and cultural festivals despite the distance and forced dissociation from India. For example although caste segregation and observances were undermined from the very beginning with the passage in ships and in other communal spaces, indentured Indians adapted practices which had been largely caste and regionally specific in India. The inher- ently weak position of Indians under indenture was also exemplified by the help- lessness and despair they experienced – marital violence and suicides increased dramatically across the diaspora.

While the majority of indentured Indians who participated in social movements were focused on local issues, Indian leaders were keenly aware of the interests of Britain and India. This was particularly relevant in South Africa where the prom- inent South African Indian Congress (formed in 1923) represented the interests of the trader and professional classes, many of whom were non-indentured dias- pora Indians, while the Colonial-born Settler and Indian Association (which held its first conference in 1933) sought to represent the interests of those born in the colony, many of whom were in the working and agricultural classes. Accus- ing the Congress of consisting of a "few wealthy Mohammedans and banias" who "sold our rights in the name of the community for their sole benefit," the Colonial-born Indians strongly objected to the participation of Congress in the Colonisation Enquiry Commission. The main aim of this commission was to discuss the 1927 Cape Town Agreement, which included an assisted emigration scheme for Indians to voluntarily repatriate to India to reduce the population in the country.[4]

This chapter attempts to do several things. It will show that the international movement of labor with antecedents in English indentured servitude in the Ameri- cas and West Indies, the use of convicts, the trans-Atlantic slave trade, and the indenture of Chinese laborers, occurred because of the strategic position of Brit- ain, Western elite notions of cultural superiority, and the subservient position of colonial subjects in the global economy of empire. It will also demonstrate that while the anti-slavery movement garnered substantial support in England, they failed to mobilize similar support for an anti-indenture campaign as both the lead- ers and public were ambivalent about indenture and were still grappling with the concept of free labor. Further it illustrates that with the internationalism spurred by a new wave of globalization, prominent leaders of social movements of Indi- ans living in the colonies employed a cosmopolitan perspective to fight for local bread-and-butter issues, and this was to become a strong mobilization technique and strategy against strong and intransigent opponents. Rank and file Indians, however, continued to focus on local issues reflecting the growing long-term investment in their new homelands and further separating them from India and the diaspora.

India: the colonial state and indenture

Theoretical discourses on the British Empire have shifted from an emphasis on imperial economics and the official thinking behind British administrative decisions to a focus on knowledge. Bernard Cohn proposes that by defining and classifying space, British administrators constructed the nation-state of Indian subjects in a demarcated territorial place, with an official history and identity.[5] He contends that the "metropole and colony have to be seen in a unitary field of analysis;" the British entered India with some degree of knowledge that to rule they had to *know* the region, and the knowledge they gained during their 200 years in India was in turn used to consolidate the British state during the period of imperialism.[6] Tony Ballantyne sees empire as re-imagined not just as a "set of economic and political structures of dominance but as a cultural project."[7] Nicolas Dirks argues that colonial conquest was not only the "result of the power of superior arms, military organization, political power, or economic wealth," but was also made possible (and sustained and strengthened by) "cultural technologies of rule."[8] Colonial knowledge both "enabled conquest and was produced by it: in certain important ways, knowledge was what colonialism was all about."[9]

Ruling the vast and diverse regions as one country and from a centralized administrative system required a concerted effort, a multi-pronged set of strategies to codify and control. A cornerstone of this enterprise was the gathering of data – the census of 1881 solicited the help of 500,000 people to "list the names of what they hoped was every person in India but also to collect basic information about age, occupation, caste, religion, literacy, place of birth, and current residence."[10] In the process, as Dirks observes, caste "became a single term capable of expressing, organizing, and above all "systematizing" India's diverse forms of social identity, community and organization."[11] Although caste had existed prior to colonialism, it had been one category among many others that represented identity – "temple communities, territorial groups, lineage segments, family units, royal retinues" and so on.[12] The British were able to produce "caste as the measure of all things social" and standing for Indian tradition; it became the basis of knowledge and power.[13] Caste was constructed as more hierarchical and totalizing than it had been. Susan Bayley disagrees with this reading, instead seeing caste as preceding colonialism, having been "made and remade into varying codes or moral order over hundreds or even thousands of years."[14] For Dirks even the idea that the colonial state was a novel form of state rule is problematic. He argues that states were in fact "powerful components in Indian Civilization. Indian society, indeed caste itself, was shaped by political struggles and processes."[15] Such theories have been critiqued for silencing Indian agency and underplaying resistance. Furthermore there has been a tendency to undermine the role of pre-colonial class divisions and social and political systems.[16] All agree that under colonial rule, caste, class and other local identities were reconfigured, and the society was restructured, challenging the ability of Indians to survive at pre-colonial levels and forcing them into new labor markets or into unemployment. The mid-1800s was a time of dramatic economic change in India. Many Indians found themselves landless, superfluous in the new economy, and marginal to the production processes that revolved around cash crops and other products.

During the abolition debates slavery also existed in India. With a long history going back to 1000 and 1025 AD, Indian slavery included a diverse set of circumstances as Major explains: "Indian forms of slavery were varied, regionally and historically specific, and involved complex relationships of dependence and obligation."[17] The East India Company (EIC) had expanded its influence in India, coming under more direct parliamentary supervision in the 1790s. The administration that was set up was conducive to exploitation with priority given to "profits that could be made by controlling its internal markets and international trade, appropriating peasant production and, above all, collecting the revenue."[18] It was also assumed that Indian slavery and bondage did not fall under the rubric of anti-slavery legislation as people entered into it voluntarily during times of hardship. Major contends that this was in tandem with the "emerging orientalist tropes about the inherent passivity, indolence and lack of entrepreneurial spirit that supposedly characterized Hindus" predisposing them to "individual and collective subordination."[19] The debates in the British and Foreign Anti-Slavery Society (BFASS) Convention of 1840 show that even though attention was given to Indian slavery, the organization was reticent to recommend abolition in India. They believed that Indian cotton and sugar production, once India became a British colony and free labor was employed, would be so lucrative and central to the British economy that it would lead to an end of all slavery. When the BFASS tried to institute a ban on sugar produced by slave labor, some members chastised the leadership for discriminating against poor labor in Britain who relied on cheap sugar. They nevertheless pushed for free trade and free labor and even though indenture was not popular among the society, it was accepted as a way to prove the superiority of free labor over slave labor.

The British public had been actively mobilized in support of the abolition of slavery, and in the process their sense of moral and cultural superiority over people in the colonies was elevated. While English men and women had emigrated to America and the West Indies under indentured servitude, African slaves replaced them. After the abolition of slavery, the new groups that were indentured were mainly Indians and Chinese servants. This took place at a time when the English working classes were gaining more rights and engaging in more acts of rebellion and resistance. For the administrative elite, knowledge about Indians contributed towards a sense of power and by assuming to know the complexity and diversity that was India, they were able to rule the subcontinent as if it were a manageable coherent entity. When indentured labor was proposed, there was less public opposition and less attention given to this new system of bonded labor with its undertones of the slave system it replaced.

From slavery to indenture

England had experienced industrial revolutions in the 1790s, the 1830s, and the 1840s, and observers were still in awe of the new factory system.[20] The turmoil these new modes of production created in the countryside and the impact on towns and cities is well known. The working classes were in part created by industrial revolutions that reinvented and cheapened labor with the introduction of technology and machinery. Mass production of goods and the relative abundance of labor, mainly supplied by newly urbanized peasants fleeing the confines of the feudalistic countryside, spurred manufacturing capitalism and ignited the quest for raw materials. These periods saw shifts in the economy, a redistribution of wealth, and a changing social system that upset the established hierarchies.[21]

The growth of capitalism in England affected the way in which entrepreneurs set up shop in the colonies. While all observers praised the innovation and capabilities of new technology and machinery like the steam engine, the spinning jenny, and the power-loom, they lamented the implications the new system of mass production had for the English working classes. There was always the fear that a latent radicalism prone to violence and disruption lurked below the surface of the working people. Cooke notes: "As a stranger passes through the masses of human beings . . . he cannot contemplate these 'crowded hives' without feelings of anxiety and apprehension, almost amounting to dismay . . . There are mighty energies slumbering in these masses . . ."[22] The social system was messy and, in its formative years, threatening.

These fears were exacerbated by consistent organized as well as sporadic resistance throughout the country. E. P. Thompson shows that during this period the English working classes were beginning to challenge the system:

> Between 1811 and 1813, the Luddite crisis; in 1817, the Pentridge Rising; in 1819, Peterloo, throughout the next decade the proliferation of trade union activity, Owenite propaganda, radical journalism, the Ten Hours Movement, the revolutionary crisis of 1831–2; and, beyond that, the multitude of movements that made up Chartism.[23]

Industrial owners now faced challenges from homespun working class activism and increasing demands from liberal critics.[24] But the way in which the empire was perceived at home furthered the notion that Britain *should* have dominion over other lands and as Kathleen Wilson says, this conception of empire was "self-serving" and contributed towards "mystifying or obscuring" the brutality and exploitative nature of trade and colonization.[25]

To some extent the British public believed that what went on in the colonies was part and parcel of Britain's superior position, the details of slavery were largely unknown or considered unimportant. Yet within a few decades they went from viewing empire as a "Protestant, oceanic commerce and mastery of the seas"[26] with slavery as an integral and necessary part of that endeavor, to viewing empire as a Christian and moral enterprise that needed to spurn slavery for free labor.[27] Major shows that anti-slavery political campaigns ran in tandem with Protestant movements that lobbied to open India to missionary activity between 1793 and 1813 and to prohibit sati or widow-burning in 1829.[28] Further key anti-slavery proponents like William Wilberforce, Charles Grant, William Ward, and Claudius

Buchanan also had strong evangelical roots.[29] For example Grant used the term "Hindooism" to define the entire population of India, thereby adding to the evangelical discourses that saw Indians as alien and unenlightened.[30] Christian missionaries felt able to deal with the large masses in India who lived under these 'heathen' beliefs that kept them in ignorance. Wilberforce made a direct comparison between the need for missionary activity in India and the agenda of the anti-slavery movement in the West Indies. In his speech to parliament in 1813 he argued that Indians were absolutely different to the British and further that these differences could be traced to the influence of religion, which he regarded as 'one grand abomination.'[31] Wilberforce continued to paint a shocking and disturbing picture of Indian society, emphasizing polygamy, infanticide, sati, and idol worship, concluding that together they contributed towards the degraded moral character of Indians. He used this to preface his main argument that it was the duty of Christian Britain to change things: " . . . Must we not then be prompted by every motive, and urged by every feeling that can influence the human heart, to endeavour to raise these wretched beings out of their present miserable conditions."[32] This was the frame within which the slave trade was abolished, emancipation laws instituted, and indenture introduced. It is to this that we now turn.

Slavery

Between 1680 and 1786, over 2 million slaves were transported from Africa to British and American colonies.[33] In the seventeenth century, Britain rose as a naval power and leading slave trader while it continued to consolidate and expand its empire. The colonies and plantation economies were set up as suppliers of raw materials and other products with little attention given to political and social implications. As Drescher says in referring to the Caribbean: "Labor approached the status of a pure commodity more completely than anywhere in the world ruled by Europe."[34] As England in the seventeenth century moved towards a system of free labor at home, it continued to rely on coerced labor in the colonies all within a single economic and political system.[35]

The Slave Act entitled 'An Act for the Abolition of the Slave Trade' was passed in 1807, but while it abolished the slave *trade* it did not abolish slavery, which only ended 26 years later under the Slavery Abolition Act of 1833. Both these acts failed to prevent the abusive apprenticeship system or the establishment of indenture. The academic debate surrounding the passage of the Slave Act of 1807 is complex and deserves a thorough analysis, but for the purposes of this chapter only those themes that are relevant to the establishment of indenture as a replacement for slavery will be highlighted.

Abolition: slavery to indenture

Against a background of oligarchic politics and the strong presence of the West Indian planters, anti-slavery organizations pushed for political reform. Ultimately both the West Indian planters and the anti-slavery movement set the terms of abolition;[36] but while a number of forces led to the abolition of the trade and eventually slavery itself, exactly what those forces were is hotly disputed. Situating the slave trade at the center of an economic analysis, Eric Williams makes the argument that this trade was intrinsic to industrial transformation in Britain, especially in the important seaport of Liverpool.[37] For example in 1771, of the 190 slave ships that left Britain, 107 were from Liverpool.[38] Williams adds that profits from West Indian commerce went towards establishing the leading banks that financed the industrial revolution.[39] Hence slavery was only abolished after it was no longer profitable.[40] Eltis and Engerman disagree with these conclusions, instead arguing that slavery "formed a relatively small share of the Atlantic trade of any European power."[41] In essence, the slave trade equaled less than 1.5 per cent of all ships and less than 3 per cent of all British shipping tonnage and was far less lucrative than textiles, iron, and coal.[42] Further they see the impact of the Caribbean on eighteenth-century England as ideological rather than economical; Britain resorted to slavery outside its borders in order to continue the "celebrating of English liberties at home."[43]

The use of indenture was not limited to Indians. Indenture had roots in the English system of husbandry whereby prosperous farmers contracted young people annually. This system was transferred to the New World in part to provide credit for young men and women wishing to immigrate to British America, but who did not have the funds to make the trans-Atlantic journey. Between the 1630s and the American Revolution, about half to two-thirds of white immigrants who went to the American colonies went under indentured servitude. Contracted for a period of 1 to 7 years, young indentured servants provided labor in return for accommodation, food, clothing, and training and worked to pay off the debt of their travel costs from England and other European countries. Indentured servants were guaranteed release from bondage, unlike slaves, and their contracts and the person could not be bought and sold. About 500,000 Europeans were also indentured to the Caribbean (Trinidad and Tobago, French Guiana, and Surinam) before 1840. After the end of the indenture contract, the servant was paid "freedom dues," which was a usually a piece of land or a free laborer. Further, between 1701 and 1775 European indentured servitude included Irish servants, German redemptioners, and English convicts in America and the West Indies.

The reason for the transition from English indentured servitude to African slavery is a subject of debate. Using a quantitative analysis, David Galenson offers a strong argument for concluding that it was not the "inherent characteristics of blacks that made slavery a necessity for the Southern colonial regimes," but rather the economic conditions (example: shorter terms, higher freedom dues, more demands) that made "slavery the economic solution for planters."[44] Russell Menard concurs arguing that the reason the Chesapeake planters abandoned indentured servitude was because of a "decline in the traditional labor supply" which forced them to "recruit workers from new sources, principally but not exclusively from Africa."[45] Others have emphasized the threat of rebellion from indentured servants as a possible cause, and the fact that slaves slotted into a system that was already in existence but worked for a lifetime of servitude rather than a fixed term.

Chinese indenture to the West Indies was initially unregulated, relying on Chinese "crimps" who worked on a commission basis to recruit laborers immediately following the abolition of slavery. Legalized in 1851 by the British, Chinese indentured workers were recruited under a contract that bound them to work for a specified number of years. Between 1838 and 1918, about 500,000 indentured laborers went to the British West Indies, about 3 per cent of these were Chinese, mainly Cantonese and Hakka.[46] After the Kung Convention in 1873, more regulations were imposed on West Indian colonies regarding re-indenture (example: free passage home, re-indenture for only a year), leading to the demise of the system. Chinese indenture ended in Hawaii by the turn of the century and in Cuba by 1898. However, 60,000 Chinese were indentured to the Transvaal between 1902 and 1904, representing 40 per cent of the unskilled workers in the gold mines. By 1907, a repatriation program left few Chinese in South Africa.[47] Chinese indentured laborers went to Australia, New Zealand and the South Pacific Island, Mauritius and other areas in the Indian Ocean, to South Africa, and the Americas.[48]

The British also used convict labor in South Asian colonies. Anand Yang shows how the Poligar rebels, who were chieftains, lords, or "little kings" in south India, were punished by perpetual banishment to Penang in 1802. At Penang, which had become a penal colony since its inception as a British settlement in 1786, they joined 600 convicts (mostly from Bengal, but also Bombay and Madras).[49] The British considered banishment a strong form of punishment among Indians and as a "weapon of tremendous power" because it involved transporting Indians across the "black waters" that "many Hindus were believed to be fearful of doing because of their religious beliefs."[50] Banishment away from India and transportation across the oceans was considered part of the deterrence and punishment regime of the British. The convicts in Penang were used as cheap labor to build and maintain the region. Several decades later, this was to be a systematized arrangement for over a million Indians indentured to work in the colonies.

Those arguing for the salience of economic interests as causal variables that led to abolition also emphasize the increasing prominence of slave owners in British economic and political systems. As absentee landlords leaving plantation management to resident managers, these men were able to support a comfortable lifestyle in Britain and gained more political leverage in the House of Commons and House of Lords. They opposed abolition through the Planter's Club, formed in 1740, and later the West India Committee. As Williams observes, absentee landlords considered the sugar colonies as a "sort of infernal region, a purgatory, through which they must occasionally toil to enjoy the Elysian fields of Scotland or Mary-le-bone."[51] Even though the West Indian planters themselves were relatively small in number, nine in parliament between 1784 and 1790, a larger group of merchants, lawyers, creditors, and others with West Indian interests constituted thirty-six members in parliament.[52]

The structure of the colonial administration contributed towards the power of the planter oligarchy. The level of control that the English government had over the colonial branches varied from tenuous to strong, and the governing mechanisms were cumbersome. West Indian Affairs for example were administered through four geographically determined departments of the Colonial Office, each with its own set of civil servants and administrative structures. As a result colonial legislation was slow, impeded by multiple levels of consultation and administrative hurdles. The capabilities of the Colonial Office depended to some extent on the capabilities of the Colonial Secretary. But as Green states: "By no stretch of the imagination did the Colonial Office rule the empire. Power was diffuse between Westminster and the dependencies."[53] The bloated and cumbersome administration left room for increasing neglect and poor understanding of colonial developments and allowed for the infiltration of planters and planter interests into key areas of power. In the 1790s, there were thirty West Indian MPs in the House of Commons, by 1828–1832 there were fifty-six.[54] They influenced legislation regarding slavery, the terms of abolition, and later the passage of laws that led to the indenture of Indians.

Others propose that even though economic factors played a role, they were not the definitive reason for abolition. For example, Drescher sees the impact of "overproduction, structural weakness, and imperial insignificance" as important.[55] The slave trade was first questioned in the English Parliament in 1774. Although rejected, in 1783 the Quakers expanded a bill in the House of Commons that prohibited the servants of the African Committee from becoming slavers to include a call against the entire system of slavery. Prior to the formation of a national committee to abolish the slave trade in 1787, which was supported by Quakers in England and America, there was little public interest in slavery. This changed, as some have argued, because of cultural shifts in England.[56] Foremost was the influence of Enlightenment thinkers who emphasized the idea of progressive social change based on innate human capabilities.[57] Protestant theologians added to these debates questioning the doctrine of original sin, while secular critics of Christianity viewed it as detrimental to an optimistic and progressive society.[58] Enlightenment thinking did not lead effortlessly into an anti-slavery stance, in fact there were ideological differences that had to be resolved. As Davis explains:

> At the risk of gross oversimplification, it can be said that the Enlightenment was torn between the idea of the autonomous individual and the ideal of the rational and efficient social order . . . (between) some notion of individual liberty with some notion of a rationally functioning state. Negro slavery dramatized the difficulties of any synthesis; antislavery provided an illusionary means of resolution.[59]

For Gyan Prakash, it was the post-Enlightenment notions of individualism and capitalism that influenced discourses on slavery and freedom.[60] Enlightenment thinking ran parallel to the tenets proposed by the Anglican Church in England and other Protestant sects including Quakers, Baptists, Presbyterians, Methodists, Unitarians, and Independents. Prominent leaders of the anti-slavery movement like Wilberforce were Anglican evangelists who were supported by Quakers, Methodists, and Baptists. These dissenting sects had few political and religious rights and were excluded from universities and military service; their experiences placed them in a good position to empathize with the conditions of slaves.[61] But their beliefs were not without paradoxes. Quaker opposition was linked to the belief that every individual could inwardly and directly experience God, and together with evangelical Protestantism, they also believed in Britain's imperial Christian mission. As Midgley observes: ". . . it combined a belief in black humanity with a conviction of African cultural inferiority."[62] English women were actively involved in the anti-slavery movements but stopped short of empathizing fully with enslaved women; the slogans and visual images they used exemplified black powerlessness and portrayed black women as victims of physical punishment.[63] This tension between the desire to end slavery and to keep the racial (and gendered) hierarchies intact influenced legislation pertaining to both slavery and indenture.

Another important cultural shift related to the economic turn from mercantilism to capitalism. Here Adam Smith made a definitive impact on public thinking by denouncing sanctioned monopolies, price fixing by states, and royal control over the economy. He was a proponent for the unfettered operation of the open market, pricing based on supply and demand, and the rise of the independent owner and consumer.[64] It was within this broader critique of mercantilist production that Smith evaluated slavery. Arguing that the motivation for all labor to work was self-interest, Smith saw slavery as inherently inefficient in that slaves lacked the individual motivation to work and relied on their overseers' to support and provide them with supplies. In contrast, it was in the interests of free labor to work hard and pursue higher salaries in order to support themselves and their families and to procure a higher standard of living.

This was also a period that was influenced by three revolutions: American (1776), French (1789), and Haitian (1791). Together they served to convince the English that Britain could not continue indefinitely with slavery.[65] Mobilization against slavery was gradual; social movements were just beginning to develop given that "National extraparliamentary associations . . . were unknown in 1750, novel in 1780, commonplace in 1830."[66] Trade organizations and religious societies were already petitioning the government, but the new anti-slavery movements "were pioneers in forging a central tool of modern civil society."[67]

Williams proposed that slavery was "originally established on economic not moral or religious grounds. . . . An economic system is overthrown only when it ceases to function."[68] He contended that with a decline in the economic standing of Britain after American independence, British economic policy shifted from imperial monopoly to laissez-faire economics. Arguing against elevating the significance of changing international capitalist relations and the role of slavery, critics nevertheless look to a "combination of humanitarian ideology and political economy to explain the rise and triumph of abolitionism."[69] In particular, Drescher shows that abolition was the conversion of a market-oriented sanction to a criminally defined act, and the reasons for this shift in policy cannot be found in a clean causal model.

Between 27 June and 29 July, 1814, more than 600 petitions were submitted to support global abolition.[70] In 1823 a number of veteran abolitionists established the Society for Mitigating and Gradually Abolishing the State of Slavery Throughout the British Dominions. The Society was able to identify 220 local societies who supported their call and presented parliament with 1499 petitions and 168,000 signatures.[71] In 1830 the Anti-Slavery Society was re-founded, and its leaders were surprised by the overwhelming support for immediate abolition expressed by its supporters. The increasing dissatisfaction of the British working class toiling under exploitative working conditions and poor social welfare, added to the overall popular call for abolition. A wave of labor revolts swept across the country; a workers demonstration in October 1831 organized by The Union of the Working Classes in London attracted 70,000 supporters. The rapid growth of radical labor unions and the violent repression that followed fueled the call for parliamentary reform and universal suffrage.

A pivotal event that propelled the movement for emancipation was the Jamaican revolt in December 1831. Acting on rumors that the King had granted emancipation but that planters had refused to comply, between 20,000 and 30,000 slaves revolted. By the time it ended in February 1832, 200 slaves were killed and 312 were executed, twelve to fourteen Whites were killed, and property damages amounting to about £1,500,000 were reported.[72] The revolts were spurred in part by the Baptists who had encouraged slaves to conduct their own church services. These became the places where action against slavery was mobilized. Baptist churches and missionaries were specifically targeted, and this fact was widely publicized in journals and other print media distributed in England. Green suggests that "It was the Jamaican rebellion, not the new vigor of the anti-slavery movement, that proved the decisive factor in precipitating emancipation."[73] The widespread oppression of missionary work was viewed as an attack on Christianity. A campaigner for emancipation clearly articulates why 26 years lapsed between the end of the slave trade and abolition:

> . . . from the year 1823 forward, many events contributed to awaken the slumbering conscience of the nation as to the guilt of slavery . . . most of all, the furious persecution of the missionaries, displayed by the destruction of their chapels, their wanton imprisonment, or expulsion from the islands . . . [74]

Why did the anti-slavery movements not push for greater freedoms for former slaves, or for the abolition of all bonded labor? Swaminathan proposes that part of the reason may lie in the debate that evolved around slavery – both the anti-slavery movement as well as the West Indian landowners influenced the rhetoric adopted by each side, and despite their differences both believed in a few fundamental tenets.[75] Both sides agreed that Africans (and all people of color) were inferior to Whites (albeit for different reasons), both shared a pride in the nation, and both had a strong sense of Britain holding a singular position in the world. While pro-slavery groups referred to the biological and innate weaknesses of Blacks, anti-slavery groups shifted the emphasis to society by using 'racial historicism' that viewed African society as less developed. As Swaminathan says: "Viewing Africans as a less advanced civilization allowed abolitionists to maintain racial superiority in a manner that did not question the inherent humanity of the African."[76] This also allowed anti-slavery groups to call for abolition *and* to push for missionary work to uplift Africans while still supporting British imperialism and colonization.

Pro-slavery groups acknowledged that slavery was a flawed institution; they pushed for regulation rather than abolition and framed the debate with a focus on Britain's national and international economic position.[77] They also tried to deflect attention away from slavery in the colonies to the plight of the poor back home, particularly the adverse economic impact that abolition would have on industries and workers associated with the trade.[78] This is clearly explained by Thomas Irving: "The British empire is a vast body composed of a multitude of fragments, of which our marine is the general cement. Destroy this cement, the empire is destroyed; and its last citadel, namely, this island itself, is no longer safe."[79] While Swaminathan argues that British identity was reworked through an "amalgamation of the abolitionist and regulationist positions," Colley sees abolition itself as forming "the vital underpinnings of British supremacy in the Victorian era" offering proof that "British power was founded on religion, on freedom and on moral caliber, not just on a superior stock of armaments and capital."[80] Both agree that with abolition, the British public viewed colonialism in a new light – British identity was now associated with a sense of moral Christian pride and a mission that called for the expansion of empire. Notions of the West as being racially superior, developed, and Christian, were constructed in opposition to African and Indian natives who were considered racially inferior, underdeveloped, and heathen.

Another path that favored India and hence Indian labor over the West Indies was the way the anti-slavery debate was framed around the strategy of sugar boycotts – the main crop of the West Indies and produced by slave labor. India was strategically located as the alternative supplier of sugar that could be produced by free labor. But as Drescher observed, the abolitionists knew "from the beginning that the least controversial way to end both the slave trade and the slave system of production was to supply sugar grown by free labourers *at a cheaper rate*."[81] Indian labor was considered cheap, and this was apparent from the Orientalist assumptions of Indian passivity, laziness, inward-looking and backward spirituality, and the caste system. It was assumed that Indians would never work to accumulate luxuries, and their lifestyles required few conveniences.[82] The anti-slavery arguments then presented India as a free-labor substitute for West Indian slavery, but stopped short of problematizing what 'free' labor meant in the colonies. Moreover it was only in 1843 through Act V that slavery in India was delegalized, but this was also the year in which indenture to Mauritius and the West Indies was reopened.

The Abolition of Slavery Bill that was introduced by the Colonial Secretary Edward Stanley in May 1833 passed with larger majorities in both houses and received royal assent at the end of August 1833. While endorsing the abolitionist agenda, it also met the needs of slave owners – gradual change and compensation for monetary and labor losses. The bill put into place a 6-year apprenticeship and £20,000.00 compensation to be paid in government bonds at a standard rate for each slave according to age and sex. These measure were designed to relieve the losses experienced by planters through direct compensation and indirectly through apprenticeship. During this period while planters had to provide food, clothing, lodging, and medical care, slaves had to work an unpaid 45-hour week with few checks and balances. A body of 100 magistrates created to oversee the conduct of all parties had little success in preventing abuse. The harshness of punishments, ineffectiveness of the magistrates to monitor the system, and the "incorrigible intransigence of colonial whites," led to the passage of the second Emancipation Act by which all slaves were unconditionally freed at midnight on 31 July 1838.[83]

The impact of abolition and the termination of apprenticeship had a dramatic effect on the economies of the colonies. The majority of emancipated Africans left the plantation system, many choosing to subsist on small farms and in independent villages. For example in Trinidad in 1849 there were 7000 small holdings as opposed to a small fraction during slavery.[84] Workers also began to seek employment only when they needed to, some worked for a few days or weeks per month. They began to demand higher salaries and better working conditions, striking in some cases.[85] In 1838 when the apprenticeship period ended in Mauritius, 16,000 remained on the plantations, but by 1839 only 4000 to 5000 former slaves agreed to contract work for 1 year, and by 1847 only 1890 worked on the estates.[86] In British Guiana the estate workforce decreased from 88 per cent of the working population to 43 per cent.[87] After experiencing the violent and dehumanizing system of slavery and apprenticeship and receiving no economic compensation or restitution, Blacks were convinced "that the best and safest guarantees of their welfare lay in self-employment and in the maintenance of minimal contracts with the world of the bosses."[88]

In 1839 a large proportion of the sugar crops in the British West Indies rotted in the fields.[89] Sugar production fell as prices rose with Britain losing its competitive edge against Cuban, Brazilian and American planters, all of whom still relied on slave labor.[90] This was also the period when British protectionism ended, the Sugar Duties Act of 1846 stopped protections for West Indian sugar and made way for increasing price competition among international sugar producers. The situation was exacerbated by an economic depression that spread throughout Europe, reducing the demand for sugar and speculative buying. This directly affected the West Indian merchant houses in England, and forty-eight were bankrupted.[91] Planters were no longer able to redeem bills drawn in exchange for products already shipped and suffered losses. Local banks in the West Indies had difficulty providing cash payments leading to plummeting estate values. The Attorney General of Trinidad described the situation in 1848 as follows: "64 petitions of insolvency have been filed . . . many estates have been abandoned from the inability to raise money on the faith of the coming crop . . . "[92] Forty estates collapsed in Trinidad by 1850, and seventy-two in Guyana.[93] It was during this economic crisis that the sugar industry began to recover.

In 1836 the Calcutta shipping agency Gillanders, Arbuthnot & Co. responded to John Gladstone's inquiry regarding 2000 Indians they had already transported to Mauritius. Assuring him that they could themselves recruit Indian labor for his needs, they also recommended the kind of labor best suited for the colonies, couching their evaluation in prejudicial ways:

> The tribe that is found to suit best in the Mauritius is from the hills to the north of Calcutta, and the men of which are well-limbed and active, without

prejudices of any kind, and hardly any ideas beyond those of supplying the wants of nature, arising it would appear, however, more from want of opportunity than from any natural deficiency, of which there is no indication in their countenance, which is one of intelligence. They are very docile and easily managed, and appear to have no local ties, nor any objection to leave their country.[94]

The quest for new sources of labor was driven by the desire to maintain profitable production and the assumptions that prioritized Indian and African labor over their humanity. Throughout the discourses on indenture these assumptions prevailed, pro-indenture constituencies pushed for favorable policies while attempting to mask the exploitation and violence that defined this new source of contracted labor.

While plantation owners lobbied heavily for other sources of cheap labor, premising their argument on the notion that there was a severe labor shortage after abolition. This was, however, not an accurate reflection of the situation. Firstly, in most colonies although there was a large pool of potential laborers available, colonial employers found it difficult to recruit people to work under highly exploitative conditions. At the height of slavery, there were 311,070 slaves in Jamaica, 82,824 in Demerara, 67,619 in Mauritius, and 20,657 in Trinidad.[95] After abolition the vast majority continued to live in these countries constituting a potential source of labor. Secondly, in some colonies the indigenous people were self-sufficient and uninterested in taking up employment in colonial enterprises. In South Africa white plantation owners could not get Zulus to work for them; many were closely aligned with the independent and powerful Zulu Kingdom. In Fiji colonial administrators chose to protect rather than recruit from indigenous Fijian communities. They recognized the challenges that other colonies experience when indigenous communities were destroyed and/or undermined. Thirdly, colonial landowners were reluctant to increase wages or change their labor practices to meet the demands made by free labor. They were also fearful of the possibility of a more organized labor force. Instead they resorted to procuring other sources of cheap labor, arguing that to remain competitive with other slave-dependent sugar producing countries, they had to maintain very low production costs. Apart from cheap labor, they relied on British tariffs to protect sugar monopolies at home and low-level technology and production costs. They also deliberately pushed for indenture in order to lower the wages of freed people. As Look Lai said: "It was the freedman's newfound bargaining strength on the labor market, rather than his absolute disappearance from that market, which troubled the West Indian plantocracy."[96] The Stanley Commission of 1842 was very clear that the objectives of immigration policy were to "introduce a fresh laboring population whose purpose would be to act as a competitive element against the black labor force and thereby to depress wages to what the plantocracy would consider manageable and reasonable levels."[97]

In their arguments to end slavery, abolitionists used economic criteria to show that slavery was less productive than free labor and that the British government was in fact subsidizing sugar produced under slavery. Arguments against slavery were more ambivalent when it came to moral, social, and cultural criteria, leading them to shy away from considering Black majority rule in the colonies. For example, James Stephen, like some of his fellow abolitionists, worried about the moral implications of abolition. For Stephen, if freedmen were allowed to do as they liked, they were likely to be "distracted" by immoral pursuits like "basking in the sun" or nurturing an appetite for "pork and Rum" and other finery of their former masters' households.[98] Lord Howick argued that in order to keep freedmen in the labor market and to prevent their reversion to a subsistence economy, it was useful to make land expensive to provide them no option but to sell their labor. Stephens agreed, but wanted to make this policy less obvious by imposing a discriminatory land tax making land acquisition impossible for freedmen, giving the owners a monopoly on food and other production. For the former then, the "dread of starvation is thus substituted for the dread of being flogged."[99] Yet Stephen was also a strong critic of indentured immigration and advocated for political rights for qualified freedmen. With the failure to keep freedmen laboring on the plantations, abolitionists were caught between citing the moral success of emancipation but simultaneously ignoring the implications of indenture. Unable to deal with the exodus of freed people from the plantations, abolitionists and others gained a "tolerance of new forms of coercion for unprogressive peoples."[100] Or as Davis concludes, "the absolute ownership of one person by another has become as rare as Wilberforce, Buxton, or Garrison" would have wanted, even though other forms of exploitation continued to exist and flourish.[101] The period following abolition was also difficult for the abolition movements; planter and merchant claims of labor shortages, the economic priority to remain competitive, and the growing necessity for cheaper goods largely determined their analyses and agenda.

During the last few years of emancipation and following the end of slavery, West Indian planters began making their argument for a new source of cheap labor. In the "Resolution of the Commons Committee on the West Indies, 1842," the committee made their case:

4. That the principle causes of this diminished production and consequent distress are, the great difficulty which has been experienced by the Planters in obtaining steady and continuous labor, and the high rate of remuneration which they give for the broken and indifferent work which they are able to procure.

7. That this state of things arises partly from the high wages which the insufficiency of the supply of labour, and their competition with each other, naturally compel the Planters to pay; but is principally to be attributed to the easy terms upon which the use of land has been obtainable by Negroes.

11. That one obvious and most desirable mode of endeavouring to compensate for this diminished supply of labour, is to promote the immigration of a fresh laboring population, to such an extent as to create competition for employment.[102]

West Indian planters emphasized the ability of former slaves to sustain themselves because of access to fertile land, their power to bargain for higher wages given the short supply of labor, and their propensity to work for short periods and whenever they found it necessary. These challenges constituted the basis for the system of indenture. While the anti-slavery movements continued to argue against indenture, they were nevertheless caught between their support for the empire and the demands made by planters and merchants. They were, however, initially successful in halting the indenture system for a few years, from May 1839 to 1842, after which it was resumed in Mauritius and in 1845 in British Guiana, Jamaica, and Trinidad. The BFASS argued that indenture, like slavery, involved violations against families, human rights, and Christianity and that "enlightened self-interest" was a better incentive to work than "physical or contractual coercion."[103] While they did not oppose all labor immigration, they did oppose indenture from Africa and Asia on the basis that local conditions made exploitative recruiting practices highly probable and that workers from these countries were incapable of demanding better wages and working conditions, thereby depressing the wages of freed peoples. This rationale was questioned on the grounds that nothing made Africa and Asia unique and that their demands prevented British free labor from enjoying the comforts of cheap products. Further, by situating indenture between slavery and free labor, they saw the system as *both* a new form of slavery and also an example of free labor that required better contracts – men and women voluntarily chose to enter into these contacts. These contradictory positions undermined the arguments and ability of anti-indenture movements to mobilize mass support against indenture.

Indenture as bonded labor

Indentured labor replaced slavery or in some cases provided a new source of labor. The intentions behind indenture were clear: the provision of alternate sources of labor: to provide another cheap and pliable labor force and to undercut wage demands made by emancipated Blacks. Expressing the sentiments of plantation owners, John Gladstone articulated this succinctly when he said: "It is of great importance to us to endeavor to provide a portion of other laborers, whom we might use . . . [to] make us, as far as is possible, independent of our negro population."[104] North-Coombs adds: "Racism reinforced coercive traits in the planters' character and fostered an unwillingness to bargain with laborers."[105] And Huge Tinker says: "Slavery produced both a system and an attitude of mind, in which the product determined everything, not the people."[106] Indians were considered docile, hardworking, and trustworthy, albeit inferior.

Slavery had been associated with the ideas of the European "civilizing mission" and "scientific theories" of racial superiority based on the notion of inherent genetic differences. The indenture of Indians was also framed as such. "Scientific racism from the eighteenth century", says Ania Loomba, "calcified the assumption that race is responsible for cultural formation and historical development."[107] During the abolition debates an underlying assumption was the superior and progressive attitudes of Europeans and the modern civilizing force of Britain. In 1833 when slavery was abolished, there was some ambiguity about the definitions of slavery. It was recognized that slavery was the "perpetually heritable condition of legal bondage."[108] Freedom was in effect the "absence of the legal conditions that characterized servile status."[109] Given these broad parameters it is possible to see why indenture might have been condoned.

Stuart Hall makes the point that despite a slave not owning his or her labor-power; a slave is nevertheless tied to the global capitalist system and actively contributes towards its sustenance.[110] Throughout the period of slavery and beyond, global capitalism began to grow stronger through increasing networks facilitated by better transportation and technological innovations. Sugar production serves as a good example to illustrate this early global economic connectedness. Colonialism introduced the British public to a host of new products, sugar, and the taste for all things sugary grew exponentially in Europe and elsewhere. In Britain sugar consumption per capita increased rapidly, for example from 1820 to 1860 sugar consumption in Britain doubled from 16.8 pounds per capita per annum to 34.8 pounds,[111] and production increased from 300,000 tons in 1790 to 10 million tons in 1914.[112] With the increase in demand came increasing competitiveness and a drop in the price of sugar. New sugar plantations blossomed in South East Asia, Australia, Hawaii, and Southern Africa due in part to better land and knowledge about agricultural successes, and by 1900 they produced more sugar than the West Indies and the Macarena's.[113] New technology like the horizontal rollers powered by steam engines to crush cane to extract juice and the vacuum-pan process to boil the juice into a syrup, increased efficiency and production making some areas more competitive than others.[114] David Northrup argues that the reliance on Indian indentured labor was not necessarily more efficient but it allowed for greater control of the workforce.[115] Britain was a key player in this global economy, well placed to manipulate the production process to remain competitive.

Hugh Tinker views indenture as a "'new system of slavery" in that it was a labor system that was largely based on the oppressive political, economic, and social institutions it replaced.[116] Immediately following the Act of Abolition in 1833 and during the apprenticeship period, the indenture of Indians was underway. In 1838, 437 Indians left on the Whitby and Hesperus for British Guiana and took up employment and residence on the same plantations as their predecessors. Even prior to the end of slavery, influential plantation owners were looking for other sources of labor, and India and China emerged as lucrative possibilities. In Mauritius by the time the apprenticeship period came to an end in 1839, there were 25,000 resident Indians.[117] The British parliament made indenture a policy through Act V of 1837 whereby a number of regulations were put in place to provide for its legal basis. These included procedures for recruitment (that the emigrant had to appear before an officer designated by the Government of India and an emigration agent who provided a written statement of the terms of the contract), the length of service (5-year terms renewable for a further 5 years), end of indenture requirements (example: payment of return passage), transportation regulations (in terms of space, dietary requirements, medical provisions, etc.), and institutions to oversee the system (the superintendent of police was charged with carrying out the duties under the act). An investigation into the conditions of the indentured system in 1838–1839 exposed high levels of misrepresentation and coercion by recruiters and severe exploitation in Mauritius. The Government of India suspended indenture until further review. New regulations were passed including the appointment of Protectors of Emigrants at the Calcutta, Madras, and Bombay ports. Indenture resumed and on 23 January 1843, the Emerald Isle docked in Port Louis in Mauritius with 233 adults and 3 children. After 48 hours (the new rules required that Indians could not enter into contract service until they had been 48 hours on the island), all were engaged for 1 year at $2.50 per year on three estates.

What are the main differences between slavery and indenture? Moses Nwulia succinctly concludes that: "The Immigrant workers were not slaves as the blacks once were, but their working conditions and the administration of the system of indentureship made them unfree rather than free workers."[118] They were many significant differences in the two systems; most important was the fact that Africans were 'purchased' as commodities for their entire lifespan while Indians were contacted for a period of time. Slaves could be sold, loaned, inherited, transferred to pay off debts, and counted towards owned property, whereas indentured workers were considered only as laborers. However, covert and overt violent oppression continued through both systems. Ex-Chief Justice Beaumont criticized indenture because he clearly saw the similarities:

> This is not a question of more or less, of this or that safeguard . . . it is that of a monstrous, rotten system, rooted upon slavery, grown in its stale soil, emulating its worst abuses, and only the more dangerous because it presents itself under false colors, whereas slavery bore the brand of infamy upon its forehead.[119]

Major Fagan, a "Coolie Magistrate" in Trinidad from 1846 to 1848, was sharply critical of the indenture and described the system as

> more recklessly cruel than what obtained in the times of slavery when the Negro, if unable to work from age or sickness, had to right to be maintained by his owner, and could not, like the coolie, be driven to perish by the roadside.[120]

Although the indentured labor system included more checks on employee abuse, once Indians were on the sugar estates there was little colonial oversight.

The way Indians were recruited to engage in the indentured system did not always appear to be based on voluntary action. Further, the same shipping companies that once transported slaves were again used to transport Indians. While conditions were better, the mortality rate on each vessel was high as were the levels of illness. For example, of the 324 passengers bound for Trinidad in March 1858, more than one-third (120) died en route.[121] In the colonies Indians were contracted to work for 5 days a week and 7 hours a day in Demerara, 280 9-hour days in

Trinidad, 6-day weeks in St. Lucia, Grenada, and Jamaica, and in Mauritius, 9 hours for 6 days a week and 2 hours on a Sunday.[122] Contracts were for 5 years and renewable for a further 5. Absences from work were punishable, estate managers could meter out punishment when they desired, and the court systems were difficult to navigate. The many roadblocks preventing access to judicial process is best captured by a deposition made by Hureebhukut on 10 February 1877 in Natal:

> I was at that time just entering my hut when he (the white man) caught me by the neck, and struck me three times on the back with a stick (two marks shown) after which I snatched away the stick and ran into the cane. I went to Verulam court on Monday morning and at 9 a.m. I met the Indian constable there who said the magistrate is not here today, come tomorrow, and on Tuesday when I went to the court house, the same Indian constable told me that the magistrate would not be in that day also, and said try and come again tomorrow. I went the next day and made my statement to the interpreter of the court, after he had taken down all that I had to say, he told me to go back to my master's estate. I said I would not go back till my case was settled, and if I did not get proper satisfaction I would go to the Protector of Immigrants at Durban [,] which I have done.
>
> I have been twice during the Christmas month to complain at the Verulam court, and the first time the interpreter would not take down my complaint but he did so the second time I went with a large mark on my left shoulder.[123]

One-third of indentured servants returned to India, while two-thirds remained in the colonies. Indentured Indians "described themselves as *bound*, and they were portrayed in folk art with hands bound behind their backs. Those out of indenture were known as *khula*, 'opened' from bondage"[124] or as a South African Indian put it, they were "dogs without mouths."[125] Pay rates were standardized in each colony and absences or sickness led to pay cuts. Failure to complete a task resulted in the loss of a day's pay and planters were often in arrears with their paychecks. Indians were housed in the quarters vacated by former slaves and were managed by 'coolie-drivers.' They were also confined to the estate and only allowed to leave with a pass. Divisions between emancipated Africans and Indians, or as in Fiji and South Africa, between indigenous peoples and Indians were reinforced. Freed Africans saw plantation work as "coolie work," and the 1897 West Indian Commission found that they regarded Indians as "Coolie Slaves."[126]

Colonial administrators and entrepreneurs viewed Indians as industrious and hardworking but lazy and prone to idleness and promiscuity. Europeans had a superficial understanding of the people they hired from abroad. As an observer incorrectly notes: "The Hindoos have no regular place of worship, and it may be affirmed, without exaggeration, that the great mass of the 130,000 Indians in the colony are without religion of any kind."[127] Such conclusions could more readily be made at a time when there were few contesting views and the overall perspectives of progress, modernity, and civilization were associated with Europe and the West.

Indenture and labor

During the period following abolition, influential sugar estate owners like John Gladstone made a concerted effort to pressure the British government to allow for the widespread indenture of labor from India. Gladstone had the support of plantation owners, nearly 800 petitioned for relaxation of indenture restrictions after India suspended further indenture to Mauritius in 1838. Prior to the use of Indian labor, planters had also attempted to recruit labor from the United States and surrounding regions. The British government initially did not want to sanction indenture from Africa because it undermined British foreign policy. But by 1842 public sentiment had shifted, and they were prepared to allow the recruitment of freed Africans to the West Indies. The reasons for this shift are complex, but a few can be isolated: the increasing price of sugar, the consistent demands made by the plantation elite, the negative impact that emancipation had on the plantation economy, the growing public desire for abundant and cheaper sugar, and changing political leadership in Britain. Most Africans refused to leave Sierra Leone, only 4000 emigrated between 1843 and 1846, and once again attention moved to Indian labor.[128] The argument for a new system of labor based on cheap, subservient, and contractually bonded labor made economic sense only to some degree.

Sugar estates were progressively consolidated among fewer owners. For example while there were 206 plantations in Trinidad in 1838, by 1859 there were only 5.[129] This allowed for the streamlining of production with predictable production costs, supply lines, and profit margins. But despite this growing concentration of ownership, the methods of production still depended mainly on labor. The most dramatic change was the replacement of the common process with the vacuum pan process. This led to the centralization of production replacing smaller plants on each estate. Apart from this, sugar production continued to rely on rudimentary tools and bonded labor. The estate owners were reluctant to invest in innovative technology and machinery that would have reduced their reliance on large numbers of laborers. Colonization engendered a feeling of the impermanence of Empire and fearfulness that with increasing local resistance and nationalist demands coupled with liberal pressures at home, the system would ultimately collapse. The colonies were exploited for raw materials with little thought given to the longevity of production or the consequences of colonial policies on the local political, economic, or cultural landscape.

Recruitment in India and colonial demand

Since 1834 Indians were indentured to Mauritius, then to the West Indies and the French colonies, and finally Natal and Fiji. The system was suspended in 1838 for a few years until the passing of Act XV of 1842 when it was resumed. An emigration agent for Mauritius was appointed in the main Indian ports, and 30,000 Indians were indentured that year.[130] Of the many regulations and acts that were subsequently instituted, the 1871 Act VIII was all encompassing. It stipulated that immigration agents were to be paid a fixed annual salary and were to be approved by the government of India. Further, a protector of emigrants at each of the three authorized ports of Calcutta, Madras, and Bombay was to be appointed to oversee and license recruiters. Indentured workers also had to register with the magistrates of their home districts before leaving. The act included mandatory medical examinations, inspection of transport ships, and regulations regarding space, separate accommodation for women and children, fuel and water.

Indians joined the indentured labor system for a number of reasons. India itself had undergone significant changes under colonial rule, and the peasantry was adversely affected. As is expressed in a report for the 1871 Emigration Commission:

> ... it cannot be denied that as a general rule Indian emigrants improve their condition very much by emigration to the West Indies. In their own country their wages, even at the best are very low; their employment is uncertain; they are exposed to privations which from time to time assume the dimensions of wide-spread famines, and they are without the prospect, or even the possibility, or improving their material or social condition. . . .[131]

Other reasons for indenture include, as Carter notes: "chance encounters, trickery, and traditions of labor mobility in defining causative factors."[132] While labor mobility at the time had increased, there is also ample evidence that many Indians were unaware of their destination or they were sent to colonies that they had not chosen. A fellow passenger on the *Salsette* that sailed from Calcutta to Trinidad in 1958 observed: "out of the 324 Coolies who came on board, I do not believe five, at most, either know where they are going, or what is to be their occupation."[133] Gopinath Pandey, a headmaster of the village school in Uttar Pradesh, wrote to the Government of Bengal on 26 March 1905 saying that his son had been tricked into joining the indentured laborers heading for Natal. He writes as follows:

> . . . 2. That when on the occasion of attending to some ceremonies at his maternal uncle's house he was decoyed and criminally misrepresented by some recruiters of professional roguery at Cawnpur to join the Coolie Depot preparing emigrants for the Colonies. . . .
>
> . . . 4. That I need not state that I have already struggled hands and feet in applying to the District Officer at Cawnpur, who again wired the occurrence to the Protector of Emigrants at Calcutta, who in his turn furnished me with the information referred to herein. . . .
>
> . . . 6. Under the circumstances I am constrained to reach your honour in the sanguine expectation of your being gracious pleased of adopting prompt measures for stopping the said Gyapershad my son at any of the intervening stations available to the S.S. *Pongola* in transit from Calcutta to Natal and for taking him back to Calcutta to me and for thus saving his old parents' critical life.
>
> P.S. It is sickening to hear that I am a Brahmin and my son Gyapershad has been misrepresented to be Rajput (Thakur) for sheerly serving the evil purposes of the recruiter.[134]

A number of factors induced Indians to engage in indenture, like the increasing rents and taxes imposed by the British. As the Commissioner of Chota Nagpur wrote:

> The country is capable of supporting a very much larger population than it contains, but in bad season the Ryots are unable to meet the heavy rent demand in some parts of it and reduced to poverty . . . they are in that condition easily persuaded to accept the tempting offers of the Agents of the Emigration Companies. The Subordinate Agents for those Companies have no scruples about suiting these offers to the wishes of the Ryots, always recruiting for whatever place they are most likely to agree to go to . . .[135]

In India whenever a labor force was needed, it was mobilized through the institution of *begar* – obligatory labor for the state or landlord.[136] It was also not uncommon for peasants to move off the land because of crop failure caused by natural disasters, famine, or invasions. From the middle of the nineteenth century onwards, the growing movement of people from the rural areas to urban informal neighborhoods was a byproduct of a rapidly changing economy. During the period of indenture this 'surplus' population was available for recruitment. In addition there were a few educated individuals who saw the colonies as a source of upward mobility. For example Robert E. Somasundram, a teacher, enquired in a letter dated 3 June 1891 whether the Protector knew of any vacancy.

> The undersigned begs to bring the following few lines to thy honour's presence hoping thereby not to intrude into thy honour's precious time. I am an Indian young man who came over to Natal from Madras by the S.S. Umtata in April 1890. I was educated in the Wesleyan Mission College in Madras up to the university matriculation standard. I have passed my middle school examination and hold a government certificate to that effect. I am now employed in the Point school as a teacher but I have informed my superiors that I would leave school because it does not suit my convenience. I would be very thankful if your honour would be pleased to remember me (thy humble servant) if any vacancy should occur under your honour's superintendence. I enclose my certificate given to me in Madras.[137]

The system of indenture was institutionalized on a large scale. Abolished in 1914, it continued until 1920 with around 1.3 million Indians having left India to work abroad.

Leaders and social movements

Gandhi arrived as a lawyer in South Africa in 1894 and returned to India in 1914 as a potential political leader with strong organizational experience and deep spiritual insights. His most significant mobilization technique was "satyagraha," a concept that he first called "passive resistance" but chose later to move away from that notion completely. For Gandhi satyagraha was:

> Truth *(satya)* implies love, and firmness *(agraha)* engenders and therefore serves as a synonym for force. I thus began to call the Indian movement 'satyagraha', that is to say, the Force which is born of Truth and Love or non-violence, and gave up the use of the phrase 'passive resistance' in connection with it . . .[138]

Such resistance seemed to connote the absence of access to weapons and was a weapon of the weak.[139] But for Gandhi, Indians in South Africa would have used *satyagraha* even if they had possessed arms or the franchise. In 1894, he created the Natal Indian Congress and became its first secretary, and in 1903 he founded the British Indian Association as well as the newspaper "Indian Opinion." Gandhi was criticized by the colonial born Indians who accused the Congress of representing the interests of traders and merchants, many of whom were free passengers (those who voluntarily entered the country) and were of a wealthier class. Like Gandhi they continued to maintain strong ties with India and many still observed caste distinctions. The Congress didn't make a concerted effort to represent the vast majority of Indians who had moved aware from caste identities and whose cultural practices had been indigenized. These were the Indians who were part of the large working classes, agricultural subsistence farmers, and the poor in South Africa. The Congress also failed to push for the termination of indenture from India. Finally, both Gandhi and the Congress separated the Indian struggle for rights from the Black majority who were engaged in similar forms of resistance. After he left the country, a new group of Indian leaders who were more attuned to the struggles of all people of color under apartheid, embarked on a political agenda that was more connected to larger resistance movements. The differences in the experiences of indentured laborers and passenger Indians were reflected in the kind of leadership that evolved.

The pivotal legislation against which Gandhi took a leadership role was the Draft Asiatic Ordinance of 1906, which was amended in the Transvaal in 1907 [the Asiatic Law Amendment Act 2/1907 – also known as the Black Act]. All Asian males over the age of 8 were to be registered and fingerprinted, and these identity documents had to be carried at all times and were to be shown to police on demand. Failure to have these papers was punishable with imprisonment. It also limited where Indian traders could work and live. At a mass meeting in 1907, Transvaal Indians met and agreed to use *satyagraha* to protest these unjust laws. This led to a 7-year struggle and culminated in a compromise made between General Jan Christiaan Smuts and Gandhi.

Gandhi left South Africa for India in 1915 where he started his *satyagraha* campaign in the Kheda district in the state of Gujarat. The region was also the birthplace of another leader of diaspora Indians, Amabalal Dhyabhai Patel (known as A.D. Patel), who arrived in Fiji from London in 1928 having trained as a barrister and graduating the bar. Following in the footsteps of S.B. Patel, who had been sent to Fiji by Gandhi to deal with Indian issues, A.D. Patel soon became one of Fiji's most formidable leaders, mainly mobilizing among Indo-Fijians but having broad ideological and political objectives for all Fijians. His biographer, Brij V. Lal, describes him as "an uncompromising . . . advocate of social and political equality of all people within Fiji, and of democracy and independence for Fiji itself."[140]

Like Gandhi, Patel was a cosmopolitan leader, educated in India and England, who used this knowledge to mobilize social movements to oppose colonial laws and rule. In London he mixed with many future leaders of India, Pakistan, and Ceylon all of whom were deeply influenced by Gandhi. But Patel was more deliberate about fighting for the higher goals of all Fijians irrespective of race or ethnicity and moved beyond sectarian Indian interests. As he wrote:

> We believe in freedom, justice and human dignity as the birthright of mankind. It shall therefore be our duty to fight and resist imperialism, exploitary colonialism, racialism and such other natural enemies of the fundamental rights of human beings. It will be our duty to preserve and promote mutual understanding and respect for the rights of the individual and to spread the light of knowledge and culture. We seek your support and co-operation in this noble cause.[141]

One of Patel's most passionate objectives was to ensure that independent Fiji had a common voters' roll that carried the possibility of undermining the ethnic and racial divisions fostered during colonialism – he strongly opposed the communal system that was supported by indigenous Fijians and Europeans:

> Of all the people, Indians are bitterly against communal representations because they have seen its painful results in the course of time. It may not be very serious now, but as time goes on, once people get used to the idea of racial separation, racial attitudes harden and people start thinking in racial terms and racial interests which leads not to one nation but, in the course of political developments, it leads to claims of several nations.[142]

To this end, and for the tenant farmers exploited by the Colonial Sugar Refining Company (CSR), Patel organized social movements, trade unions, and political parties.

Colonial born leaders began to emerge during colonialism and in the countries being studied, they became prominent and influential. From Pandit Vishnu Deo, Parmanand Singh, and James Ramchandar in Fiji, to Yusef Dadoo and Monty Naiker in South Africa, Indians mobilized for rights. These leaders too were very aware of the nature and characteristics of colonialism, and they fought consistently for equality in the colonies.

Resistance by Indians took the form of active social movements as well as individual petitions and appeals. In the political realm, while Indians had no direct representation, they lobbied for direct and indirect representation through political organizations and parties. On the economic front, trade unions and other worker associations pushed hard for higher salaries, better working conditions, and for policies and rules that were less exploitative and harsh. Indians also actively participated in religious organizations, which became centers for religious and cultural practices and places where people mobilized and coalesced support around particular parties or issues. These organizations also became places from which ethnic identities and separateness were reinvented. These social movements and organizations will be explored more thoroughly in the following chapters.

Conclusion

The indentured labor system was initiated on the coattails of slavery mainly because the estate owners desired cheap labor and were able to use their influential positions in Britain to make this possible. The fact that Britain had colonial ownership of India also made it possible to move people around the empire. While the indentured system was not slavery, there were clear lines of continuation between the two systems. Indenture was a form of bonded labor, Indians were contracted for a certain period of time to individual estate owners, and they received a small salary, housing, and some rations in exchange for their services. The main differences included protections from abuse (albeit not always effective) and a limited contract (5 to 10 years). The entire systems of slavery and indenture fell within the overarching ideology of racism and oppression of people of color. The call for majority rule, equal rights, and justice for all subjects was still not part of the political rhetoric of the anti-slavery and other liberal organizations.

In the pursuit to maintain low production costs, Indians were used to undermine the bargaining position of freedmen and women, and their slot in the social hierarchy of the colonies reinforced racial suspiciousness and divisions. Akin to scab labor, they were resented by the local working classes for reducing wages and for maintaining the economic basis of colonialism. They in turn suffered numerous injustices of the system, but in the process created a culture that had its own internal hierarchies and ideologies of exclusion in terms of race, class, and religion.

The system of indenture changed the demographic composition of the colonies. The dominant ideology of the time that prioritized products over humans undermined a consideration of the ramifications of these demographic shifts. It was only when Indians began to make political demands that the implications of immigration on the local political and economic system began to surface. By then decolonization was fast becoming a reality, and the status of Indians, who constituted a large minority or majority of ethnic groups in newly independent states, was left in the hands of post-colonial authorities and social movements that organized for more rights.

Notes

1 David Northrup, "Free and Unfree Labor Migration, 1600–1900: An Introduction," *Journal of World History*, Vol. 14 No. 2, (2003), pp. 125–130.
2 David Eltis, "Slavery and Freedom in the Early Modern World," in *Terms of Labor: Slavery, Serfdom, and Free Labor*, ed. by Stanley L. Engerman, (Stanford: Stanford University Press, 1999), p. 36.

3 Charles Tilly, *The Contentious French*, (Cambridge: Harvard University Press, 1986), p. 10. This is explained in greater detail in Chapter 2.
4 Moonsamy Naidoo, Natal Mercury, 18 March 1927, in *A Documentary History of Indian South Africans*, ed. by Surendra Bhana and Bridglal Pachai, (Stanford: Hoover Institution Press, Cape Town & Johannesburg: David Philip, Publisher, 1984).
5 Bernard S. Cohn, *Colonialism and Its Forms of Knowledge. The British in India*, (Princeton: Princeton University Press, 1996), p. 3.
6 Ibid., p. 4.
7 Tony Ballantyne, "Colonial Knowledge," in *The British Empire: Themes and Perspectives*, ed. by Sarah Stockwell, (Victoria: Blackwell Publishers, 2008) p. 177.
8 Nicolas B. Dirks, *Castes of Mind*, (Princeton: Princeton University Press, 2001), p. 9.
9 Nicolas Dirks, *Castes of Mind*.
10 Ibid., p. 8.
11 Ibid., p. 5.
12 Ibid., p. 13.
13 Ibid., p. 8.
14 Susan Bayley, *Caste, Society and Politics in India from the Eighteenth Century into the Modern Age*, (Cambridge: Cambridge University Press, 1999), p. 25.
15 Nicholas B. Dirks, *Castes of Mind*, p. 11.
16 See Rosalind O'Hanlon and David Washbrook, "After Orientalism, Culture, Criticism, and Politics in the Third Word," *Comparative Studies in Society and History*, Vol. 34 No. 1, (1992); Lata Mani, "Cultural Theory, Colonial Texts. Reading Eye-Witness Accounts of Widow Burning," *History Workshop Journal* p. 30 (1993); Sheldon Pollock, "Deep Orientalism? Notes on Sanskrit and Power Beyond the Raj," in Carol A. Breckenridge and Peter van der Veer, eds., *Orientalism and the Postcolonial Predicament: Perspectives on South Asia*, (Philadelphia: University of Pennsylvania Press, 1993).
17 See Andrea Major, *Slavery, Abolition and Empire in India, 1772–1843*, (Cambridge: Cambridge University Press, 2012), p. 34.
18 Ibid., p. 45. Also see Sudipta Sen, *Empire of Free Trade: The East India Company and Making of the Colonial Marketplace*, (Philadelphia: University of Pennsylvania Press, 1998).
19 Andrea Major, *Slavery*, p. 56.
20 E. P. Thompson, *The Making of the English Working Class*, (England: Penguin Books, 1963). p. 208.
21 Ibid. Also see Margaret R. Hunt, *The Middling Sort: Commerce, Gender, and the Family in England 1680–1780*, (Berkeley: University of California Press, 1996), Kathleen Wilson, *The Sense of the People: Politics, Culture and Imperialism in England, 1715–1785*, (Cambridge: Cambridge University Press, 1998), Kathleen Wilson, *A New Imperial History: Culture, Identity and Modernity in Britain and the Empire. 1660–1840*, (Cambridge: Cambridge University Press, 2004).
22 W. Cooke Taylor, *Notes of a Tour in the Manufacturing Districts of Lancashire*, (1842), pp. 4–6. Quoted in E. P. Thompson, *The Making of the English Working Class*, p. 209.
23 Thompson, *The Making of the English Working Class*, p. 209.
24 See David Armitage, *The Ideological Origins of the British Empire*, (Cambridge: Cambridge University Press, 2000).
25 Wilson, *A New Imperial History*, p. 157.
26 Armitage, *The Ideological Origins*.
27 Srividya Swaminathan, *Debating the Slave Trade. Rhetoric of British National Identity, 1759–1815*, (England, New York: Ashgate Publishing Company, 2009), p. 213.
28 Major, *Slavery*, p. 9.
29 Ibid., 233.
30 Ibid., 253.

31 William Wilberforce, Substance of the Speeches of William Wilberforce, Esq. On the Clause in the East India bill for Promoting the Religious Instruction and Moral Improvement of the Natives of the British Dominions in India, on the 22[n]d of June, and the 1st and 12th of July, 1813, (London: John Hatchard; J. Butterworth; T. Cadell and W. Davies, 1813), p. 53. Quoted in Major, *Slavery*, p. 257.

32 Quoted in Major, *Slavery*, p. 258.

33 Eric Williams, "The Golden Age of the Slave System in Britain," *Journal of Negro History*, Vol. 25, No. 1, (Jan, 1940): p. 66.

34 Seymour Drescher, *Econocide. British Slavery in the Era of Abolition*, (Pittsburgh: University of Pittsburgh Press, 1977), p. 3.

35 See Sidney Mintz, *Sweetness and Power*, p. 44.

36 Dale H. Porter, *The Abolition of the Slave Trade in England 1784–1807*, (US: Archon Books, 1970), pp. 140–143.

37 Williams, "The Golden Age," p. 78.

38 Ibid., p. 68.

39 Ibid., p. 77.

40 See Eric Williams, *Capitalism and Slavery* (1994, reprinted New York, 1996); *From Columbus to Castro: The History of the Caribbean, 1942–1969*, (New York, 1970). See also Ragatz who shares this opinion. Lowell Ragatz, *The Fall of the Planter Class in the British West Indies, 1763–1833*, (New York, 1928, reprinted in 1963).

41 David Eltis and Stanley L. Engerman, "The Importance of Slavery and the Slave Trade to Industrializing Britain," *Journal of Economic History*, Vol. 60, No. 1, (2000): p. 129.

42 Eltis et al., "The Importance of Slavery," p. 129.

43 Ibid., p. 140.

44 David Galenson, *White Servitude in Colonial America: An Economic Analysis*, (New York: Cambridge University Press, 1981), p. 64.

45 Russell R. Menard, *Migrants, Servants and Slaves. Unfree Labor in Colonial British America*, (Burlington: Ashgate Publishing Company, 2001), p. 65.

46 Jessie G. Lutz, "Chinese Emigrants, Indentured Workers, and Christianity in the West Indies, British Guiana and Hawaii," *Caribbean Studies*, Vol. 37 No. 2, (2009).

47 Jessie Lutz, "Chinese Immigrants," p. 147.

48 Walton Look Lai, "Chinese Diaspora: An Overview," *Caribbean Quarterly*, Vol. 50 No. 2, The Chinese in the Caribbean, (2004).

49 Anand A. Yang, "Bandits and Kings: Moral Authority and Resistance in Early Colonial India," *Journal of Asian Studies*, Vol. 66 No. 4, (2007).

50 Ibid., p. 884.

51 Cynric R. Williams, *Tour through the Island of Jamaica from the Western to the Eastern End, in the Year 1823*, (London, 1827), pp. 136–137, quoted in William Green, *British Slave Emancipation. The Sugar Colonies and the Great Experiment 1830–1865*, (Oxford: Clarendon Press, 1976), pp. 62–63.

52 Dale H. Porter, *The Abolition of the Slave Trade in England 1784–1807*, (Hamden, CT: Archon Books, 1970), p. 17.

53 Ibid., p. 90.

54 Robin Blackburn, *The Overthrow of Colonial Slavery 1776–1848*, (London, New York: Verso, 1988), p. 437.

55 Drescher, *Ethnocide*, p. 136.

56 See David Brian Davis, *The Problem of Slavery in Western Culture*, (Ithaca: Cornell University Press, 1973), *The Problem of Slavery in the Age of Revolution*, 1770–1823, (Oxford: Oxford University Press, 1984), *Slavery and Human Progress*, (Oxford: Oxford University Press, 1984).

57 See David Spadafora, *The Idea of Progress in Eighteenth-Century Britain*, (New Haven: Yale University Press, 1990).

58 See David Davis, *Slavery and Human Progress*.

59 David Davis, *The Problem of Slavery*, p. 263.

60 Gyan Prakash, *Bonded Histories: Genealogies of Labor Servitude in Colonial India*, (Cambridge: Cambridge University Press, 1990).

61 Edith F. Hurwitz, *Politics and the Public Conscience. Slave Emancipation and the Abolitionist Movement in Britain*, (London: George Allen & Unwin LTD, 1973), pp. 80–81.

62 Clare Midgley, *Women against Slavery. The British Campaigns, 1780–1870*, (London and New York: Routledge, 1992), p. 200.

63 Midgley, *Women against Slavery*, pp. 204–205.

64 Adam Smith, *Wealth of Nations*, [first published in 1776], (Blacksburg, VA: Thrifty Books, 2009).

65 See Linda Colley, *Britons, Forging the Nation 1707–1837*, (New Haven: Yale University Press, 2009), C. L. R. James, *Black Jacobins: Toussicont L'Overture and the San Domingo Revolution*, 2nd ed., (New York: Vintage Books, 1989).

66 Adam Hochschild, *Bury the Chains. Prophets and Rebels in the Fight to Free an Empire's Slaves*, (Boston and New York: Houghton Mifflin Company, 2005), p. 106.

67 Hochschild, *Bury the Chains*.

68 Eric Williams, "The Golden Age of the Slave System in Britain," *Journal of Negro History*, Vol. 25. No. 2. (Jan, 1940): p. 93.

69 Seymour Drescher, "Eric Williams: British Capitalism and British Slavery," *History and Theory*, Vol. 26, No.2, (May, 1987): p. 195.

70 Bernard H. Nelson, "The Slave Trade as a Factor in British Foreign Policy 1815–1862," *Journal of Negro History*, Vol. 27, No. 2, (April 1942): p. 194.

71 Robin Blackburn, *The Overthrow of Colonial Slavery 1776–1848*, (London, New York: Verso, 1988), p. 422.

72 Green, *British Slave Emancipation*, p. 113, Blackburn, *The Overthrow of Colonial Slavery*, p. 432–433.

73 Ibid., p. 112.

74 "Statement by Joseph Sturge on the delay between abolition and emancipation," in *Slavery, Abolition and Emancipation. Black Slaves and the British Empire. A Thematic Documentary*, by Michael Craton, James Walvin and David Wright, (London and New York: Longman, 1976), p. 290.

75 Swaminathan, *Debating the Slave Trade*.

76 Ibid., p. 186.

77 Ibid., pp. 196–199.

78 Ibid., 201–202.

79 Remarks upon the evidence given by Thomas Irving, Esq., Inspector General of the Exports and Imports of Great Britain, before the Select Committee appointed to take the examination of witnesses on the slave-trade, (London: Printed in the year 1791), 11. Quoted in Ibid., 202–203.

80 Ibid., p. 205, Colley, *The Britons*, p. 359.

81 Drescher, "Abolitionist Expectations: Britain," p. 47.

82 Marshall, *The Moral Swing*, p. 80.

83 Craton et al., *Slavery, Abolition and Emancipation*, p. 326.

84 Blackburn, *The Overthrow of Colonial Slavery*, p. 463.

85 Green, *British Slave Emancipation*, p. 195.

86 Moses D. E. Nwulia, *The History of Slavery in Mauritius and the Seychelles, 1810–1875*, (New Brunswick, Associated University Press, 1981), p. 182. Walton Look Lai, *Indentured Labor, Caribbean Sugar. Chinese and Indian Migrants to the British West Indies, 1838–1918*, (Baltimore, London: The Johns Hopkins University Press, 1993), pp. 5–6.

87 Lai, *Indentured Labor. Caribbean Sugar*, p. 6.

88 Nwulia, *The History of Slavery*, p. 234.

89 Ibid., p. 20.

90 Northrup, *Indentured Labor*, p. 22.

91 Green, *British Slave Emancipation*, p. 234.

92 Ibid., p. 235.

93   Lai, *Indentured Labor, Caribbean Sugar*, p. 10.

94   Quoted in Kale, *Fragments of Empire*, p. 16.

95   Hugh Tinker, *A New System of Slavery. The Export of Indian Labour Oversees. 1830–1920*, (London: University of Oxford Press, 1974), p. 15.

96   Lai, *Indentured Labor, Caribbean Sugar*, p. 5.

97   Ibid., p. 12.

98   James Stephens, "6 July 1832, The Grey Papers," in Davis, *Slavery and Human Progress*, p. 218.

99   Quoted in Davis, *Slavery and Human Progress*, p. 226.

100 Ibid.

101 Ibid., p. 320.

102 "Resolution of Commons Committee on the West Indies, 1842," in *Slavery, Abolition and Emancipation*, Michael Craton et al., pp. 343–344.

103 Kale, *Fragments of Empire*, p. 107.

104 Madhavi Kale, "Projecting Identities: Empire and Indentured Labor Migration from India to Trinidad and British Guiana, 1836–1885," in *Nations and Migration: The Politics of Space in the South Asian Diaspora*, ed. by Peter van der Veer, (Philadelphia: University of Pennsylvania Press, 1995).

105 North-Coombs, 1984, p. 85.

106 Tinker 1974, p. 19.

107 Ania Loomba, *Colonialism/Postcolonialism*, (London and New York: Routledge, 1998), p. 118.

108 Madhavi Kale, ""When the Saints Came Marching In": The Anti-Slavery Society and Indian Indentured Migration to the British Caribbean", in *Empire and Others. British Encounters with Indigenous Peoples, 1600–1850*, ed. by Martin Daunton and Rick Halpern, (Philadelphia: University of Pennsylvania Press, 1999), p. 335.

109 Ibid.

110 Stuart Hall, "Race, Articulation and Societies Structured in Dominance", in *Sociological Theories, Race and Colonialism*, (Paris: Unesco, 1980), pp. 305–345.

111 Tinker, *A New System of Slavery*, p. 28.

112 Northrup, *Indentured Labor*, p. 30.

113 Ibid., p. 31.

114 Ibid., pp. 31–32.

115 See Ibid.

116 Tinker, *A New System of Slavery*, p. 19.

117 Northrup, *Indentured Labor*, pp. 61–62. Tinker, Ibid, p. 63.

118 Moses D.E. Nwulia, *The History of Slavery in Mauritius and the Seychelles, 1810–1875*, (London and Toronto: Associated University Press, 1981), p. 235.

119 Quote from Beaumont's The New Slavery: An Account of the Indian and Chinese Immigrants in British Guiana, quoted in Lai, *Indentured Labor; Caribbean Sugar*, p. 138.

120 Lai, *Indentured Labor*, p. 159.

121 Quoted in Kale, *Fragments of Empire*, p. 135.

122 See Carter, *Voices From Indenture*.

123 Surendra Bhana & Bridglal Pachal, *A Documentary History of Indian South Africans*, (Stanford: Hoover Institution Press, 1984), pp. 4–5. *Source: I.I./l/3, 20/1877, Natal Archives.*

124 Hugh Tinker, "Into Servitude: Indian Labour in the Sugar Industry, 1833–1970," in *International Labour Migration. Historical Perspectives*, ed. by Shula Marks, (Middlesex: Great Britain, Maurice Temple Smith Limited, 1984), p. 80.

125 Bhana et al., *A Documentary History*, p. 2.

126 Quoted in Tinker, "Into Servitude," p. 81.

127 Reverend Patrick Beaton, *Creoles and Coolies. Five Years in Mauritius*, (New York and London: Kennikat Press, 1859), p. 182.

128   Green, "Emancipation to Indenture", p. 103.
129   Kale, *Title*, 1998, pp. 56–57.
130   Marina Carter, *Voices of Indenture. Experiences of Indian Migrants in the British Empire*, (London and New York: Leicester University Press, 1996), 22.
131   Quoted in Carter, *Voices of Indenture*, pp. 32–33.
132   Ibid., pp. 40–41.
133   Jane Swinton, widow of the captain of the *Salsette*, quoted in Madhavi Kale, *Fragments of Empire*, p. 135.
134   From Bhana et al., *A Documentary History*, pp. 20–21. Source: I.I./2/7, 207/1905, Natal Archives.
135   Quoted in Carter, *Voices of Indenture*, p. 44.
136   Tinker, *A New System of Slavery*, p. 39.
137   Bhana, *Documents from Indenture*, p. 12. Source: I.I./1/134, 738/91, Natal Archives.
138   M.K. Gandhi, *Satyagraha in South Africa*, (Ahmedabad: Navajivan Publishing House, 1928 (2008)), p. 109.
139   See James Scott, *Weapons of the Weak. Everyday Forms of Peasant Resistance*, (New Haven: Yale University Press, 1987).
140   Brij V. Lal, *A Vision for Change: A. D. Patel and the Politics of Fiji*, (Canberra: The Australian National University, E Press, first edition 1977, 2011), accessed online October 18, 2015, pages not numbered.
141   A. D. Patel, 1953. Quoted in Brij Lal, *A Vision for Change*.
142   Ibid.

2 Transnational locality

Theories of diasporas and social movements in relation to indentured Indians

Figure 2.1 Hanuman statue, Carapichaima, Trinidad

The prestige of attaining the political premiership in the post-colonial state reflects, to a considerable degree, the political ascendency of indentured Indians. In May 1999, 120 years after the first Indians landed in Fiji, Mahendra Chaudhry became the first elected Indo-Fijian Prime Minister; a year later, he was ousted through a civilian coup led by George Speight, an Indigenous Fijian. The Fijian military imposed martial law, suspending the constitution; this was the third coup since independence in 1970. Similarly in 1995 in Trinidad, and a 150 years after the first Indians arrived on the island in 1845, Basdeo Panday, an Indo-Trinidadian, broke the monopoly of the Creole-dominated People's Nationalist Movement to become Prime Minister. And 9 years later, Kamla Persad-Bissessar of the People's Partnership Coalition became the seventh – and first female – Prime Minister. In Mauritius where Indians are the majority ethnic group, they have occupied the office of Prime Minister for all but 2 years (between 2003 and 2005 when Paul Berenger held the office) since independence in 1968. In South Africa, while Indians are a small minority and have never made it to the premiership, 1983 marked the year that they became part of the tripartite parliamentary system under the 'reformed' apartheid regime; this also led to increasingly progressive coalition building among Indians to oppose reforms and ultimately to overthrow the regime.

All these national gains were due to the committed and relentless work of Indian leaders and organizers who mobilized and pushed for more rights, greater political participation, and additional economic support. Initially appealing to the British through petitions and letters, they soon developed more direct and collective forms of resistance that spanned a variety of organizations and social movements. Perhaps the most well known of all the leaders in this diaspora was Mahatma Gandhi, an Indian barrister who arrived in Durban in 1893 and left in 1914 to lead the Indian revolt against British colonial rule. Gandhi developed his philosophy of resistance during his 21 years in South Africa; he also founded the Indian National Congress (1894), which influenced the formation of the African National Congress and other influential anti-apartheid organizations. The vastly different political outcomes among this diaspora are extraordinary given their shared historical experiences of indenture. This chapter aims to situate these differences in the theoretical frameworks of diasporas and social movements. While the empirical cases are specific, the implications for both theoretical perspectives are broad.

The main argument throughout is that the transnationality intrinsic to diaspora identities *marks* them as others in the nation-state and simultaneously *separates* them from the homeland/motherland, thus displacing them from both states and situating them in a *transnational locality*. This space is objectively and subjectively defined and includes the interplay of at least three dimensions. At the transnational level, diasporas have identities that are associated with like communities dispersed from the same point of origin and who share similar cultural foundations regarding language, religion, and customs. At the trans-state level, by maintaining (or presuming to retain) an association with a homeland (as myth or reality), they are distinguished as having dual identities. At the level of the nation-state, diasporic identities are localized, indigenized through generations, but nevertheless continue to represent difference, an otherness that contributes toward definitions of nationhood, but that also challenges it. The significance of each level of diasporic identities is dependent on factors such as the reasons for leaving the homeland (economic, political, social, through coercive means, or voluntarily), the generational depth of each diaspora, the degree of acceptance and assimilation in the host-lands, the character of relations with the motherland/homeland, and the strength of connections among the diaspora. The *transnational locality* encapsulates their indigenization *and* transnationality.

It is from this placement that social movements among diasporas gain salience. As outsiders *and* insiders, diasporas are well placed to offer a formidable challenge to the host-state (the state to which they have moved), but these challenges are limited by their hybrid/mixed/indigenized identities and perceived divided loyalties. In this study, emphasis is placed on how social movements among diasporas have influenced the construction of nations and states. Specifically for the Indian indentured diaspora, relations with creole or indigenous groups are important. Further relations with India, the motherland, influence the kinds of movements that developed. It is argued that Indians are categorized as "*ethnic* Indian" across the diaspora because of their own desire to separate themselves from indigenous and local peoples on the basis of "purity" and historical authenticity derived from the motherland (India). But also because indigenous or Creole communities delineate *themselves* as belonging to the land, thereby claiming indigeneity or indigenous status and rights in relation to Indians. In other words Indians have attempted to establish themselves as the opposite of mixed/Creolized by continuing to emphasize ancestral ties to India, and indigenous or Creole communities use this trope to define themselves as insiders and Indians as perpetual outsiders and temporary residents. Their perceived transnational identity (in this case, their Indianness) others them from the nation-state, and they distance themselves from locals by emphasizing their ties to India. However indentured Indians have also been marginalized and seen as 'unauthentic' by the motherland, although this perspective has changed more recently. India introduced dual citizenship legislation and ministries were set up for non-resident Indians (NRI) and persons of Indian origin (PIO). The history of indenture and the divisive relations set in place in the colonies served to further divide the diaspora itself by isolating them from one another; most Indians in this diaspora are only vaguely aware that other such communities exist. This placement (both subjectively and objectively defined) has led to Indians being viewed as conservative, insular, and at times, racist/prejudiced, and also progressive, radical, and outward-looking, open to pushing for more substantive changes in their new homelands. Unlike the indentured laborers, high-level British administrators and plantation owners had common first-hand experiences throughout the empire. They were able to influence British policies regarding the abolition of slavery and the institution of indenture, and they learned from their experiences in each colony. Colonial structures cemented the isolation of diaspora Indians in the various colonies and from India, and this led to weak transnational networks among them.

These identities influenced the development and agendas of social movements – in this diaspora they are largely nationally based, focused on local issues, with weak transnational linkages. However the leaders of such movements have used a cosmopolitan perspective, a product of colonial and global industrial relations of production, to fight for local bread-and-butter issues. Further, social and political organizations in each of these states have not relied on old diaspora networks (indeed, few if any, exist), they have instead reached beyond borders to places of second-migration like England, New Zealand, Australia, Canada, and the United States, to bolster support for movements back home through direct funding and to publicize these battles on the international stage.

Some of the broader questions that this chapter explores pertain to social movements among diasporas in general. Are such movements distinctive, and how do they inform and challenge dominant perspectives? How do social movements in diaspora communities challenge ideas about the state, the nation, and nationalism? How do the transnational identities of diasporas intersect with global and or transnational social movements? Significantly, how do the kinds of social movements formed among this diaspora differ from *transnational social movements* that rely on diaspora connections? Part 1 focuses on theories of diasporas with specific attention given to the home-host trope, the nation-state and state sovereignty, questions of identity (hybridity/indigenization) in the nation-state and transnational communities, and issues pertaining to globalization and transnational connections. This section aims to situate the Indian diaspora in the broader theoretical framework of diasporas.

Part II focuses on theories pertaining to social movements among diasporas. It starts with an overview of the theoretical perspectives and concepts that pertain to social movements in general, and then moves to conceptions relating to transnational organizations and globalization. This part aims to do two things: first, to place the study of social movements among the Indians indentured diaspora in a theoretical framework that best exemplifies their experiences. Second, it uses the case study of the Indian indentured diaspora to interrogate the dominant perspectives in this field.

Part 1: Diasporas and identity

In diaspora studies, the home-host trope is a strong current that tends to overlay the idea that identities are primarily associated with states. This dual territorial model, very much a dual-state model, elides the complexities of diaspora identities that traverse a transnational space, but which are nonetheless indigenized/localized in certain places. Another theme in discourses on diasporas is about the hybridity of identity. Even though it takes us further in understanding the complexities of diaspora identities, it is also limiting in that it provides a name for mixed identities without providing clearer definitions of what this entails. What it does highlight is that a pure form of identity does not exist anywhere, nor can nations and nationalism be associated with identities that are considered coherent and driven only by states. Instead we find that diaspora identities challenge state borders and nations by straddling multiple locations. They impact state identities and strengthen transnational communities. Finally, in line with increasing challenges to state sovereignty by globalization and transnational networks and organizations, an emphasis on states and a de-emphasis on the transnational is shortsighted.

Diasporas challenge the binaries of colonizer/colonized, White/Black, Western/ Eastern, developed/underdeveloped, state/nation, citizen/subject, and national/ transnational. The indentured Indian diaspora adds further layers of complexity. Given the generational depth of South Asians in Mauritius (indentured from 1834 until 1912), Trinidad (1845–1917), South Africa (1860–1911), and Fiji (1879– 1916), the relationship with the motherland generally lies in the realm of myths and stories kept current through travel, cultural exposure, or business engagements. A yearning for a homeland hardly exists. It is a diaspora that was created through indenture; displacement and disjuncture are abiding markers of identity, as is the prevalence of a transnational identity of "Indianness."

But this diaspora challenges broad definitions in that it is divided along the lines of gender, class, generation, ethnicity, religion, language, and culture. There are also differences in how individual states categorize Indians and how Indians categorize themselves. Culture has been indigenized over time, so has language and custom, differing markedly across the diaspora and in relation to India. An entrenched feeling of belonging to the host land prevails. And even though racial and ethnic stereotypes become more significant during political upheavals or elections, relations with other ethnic and racial groups are not always tense or antagonistic. In sum, this diaspora is embedded in the host states – their Indianness reflects what it is to be identified as Indian outside India, the homeland that at first neglected their existence but over time has begun to support a more cordial and inclusive relationship.[1]

The term diaspora is used extensively in academic writing yet is neither well defined nor historically specified. Generally the reader is reminded of its early usage, a Greek term tied to the forced movement of Jewish people in 586 BC from Jerusalem.[2] Diaspora came to be associated with dispersion, displacement, and exile. This definition fails to capture variations among the millions of groups it attempts to define that range from forced expulsion to voluntary movement. James Clifford adds a more nuanced perspective by viewing it as a "signifier, not simply of transnationality and movement, but of political struggles to define the local, as distinctive community, in historical contexts of displacement."[3] My research suggests that the term should assume movement, but this need not be forced movement. Nor should the term be associated with identities that are constructed around the idea of exile and longing for return. Hence as a *signifier* diaspora suggests a community that has moved and travelled, either forcibly or voluntarily, and a community that has an identity embedded in local as well as in transnational formations.

While individual states in each of the cases (Fiji, Trinidad, Mauritius, and South Africa) play an important role in framing the identities of Indians, other factors are significant. Mostly the transnational identity of "Indianness" – an identity that transcends state borders hovering in the space "above India" yet completely different to Indian identity; equally prevalent above individual nation-states yet indigenized and Creolized in each. This *is* a transnational identity – operating beyond states, appropriating a space associated with otherness, attached to an Indian (India) identity but far removed from it. The historical way in which *inter*-racial/ethnic and *intra*-racial/ethnic relations have been constructed, the subjective consciousness of group identities, and the notion of traveling/impermanence, are all tied to this concept of Indianness.

Diasporas and the state

Many theories about diasporas place emphasis on the state and view it as the main frame of reference. The centrality of the state in defining citizenship and identity is particularly prevalent in disciplines like international relations and political science. Many of the foundational ideas of realism, a strong theoretical perspective in both these disciplines, are to be found in a particular reading of Machiavelli's *The Prince*: the separation of power and ethics, the notion that power is of central importance in politics, and the idea that self-interest is the prime motivator for leaders. Further using Hobbes and treating relations between men as analogous to relations between states, realists see states as distrustful, fearful, diffident, and competitive. Relying on theories that were essentially historically and subject specific, any analysis of the character of states and relations between them proves difficult when there are unchanging characteristics assigned to both.[4]

Neorealism took these ideas further: they argue that states are the main actors in world politics, that they are homogenous units acting in their self-interest, and that they are rational actors engaging in an international arena of anarchy whereby no governing body exists and conflict is inevitable. During the Cold War these perspectives were well placed to explain and provide causes for the nuclear arms race, the reasons for relative peace, and the persistence of international tensions. However with the proliferation of *intra*-state ethnic conflicts in the post-Cold War period and increased activity by non-state actors, the margins of neorealism changed. New analytical endeavors looked at the impact and character of domestic politics, the prevalence and reach of trans-state networks, and the influence of identity, culture, and citizenship on the actions of immigrants, diasporas, exiles, and others. With respect to the diaspora in question, analysts had to grapple with the fact that South Africa transitioned into a democratic system, and the post-apartheid era exposed previously suppressed inter- and intra-ethnic divisions; Mauritius increased economic ties with India because of the realignment of global politics; and Fiji experienced increasing emigration after a series of coups, affecting subsequent political outcomes.

To capture some of these new developments, John Mearsheimer for example, saw "hypernationalism," the assumption that other nations are inferior as well as threatening, as a source of increasing tensions between states.[5] Here too, even though nationalism was given more attention, the emphasis on state self-interest, power, and international anarchy retained primary importance.[6] *Critical* theorists began to emphasize the social basis of international politics, and the impact of these structures in shaping the identities and interests of actors. No longer were culture and identity seen as fixed or natural but rather as constructed, not as unitary or singular but contested and polymorphic, and not as static and essence-like, but interactive and process-like.[7] Alexander Wendt for example, supports key neorealist assumptions, but his main point of departure is that "state interests are an important part constructed by systemic structures, not exogenous to them; this leads to a sociological rather than a micro-economic structuralism."[8] Furthermore, unlike the neorealists who maintain that structure is made of the distribution of material capabilities, *constructivists* see it as made of social relations.[9] Peter Katzenstein emphasizes "the cultural-institutional context of policy on the one hand and the constructed identity of states, governments, and other political actors on the other."[10] Using concepts of norms, identity, and culture, identity in international relations became a "shorthand label for varying constructions of nation and statehood."[11] As a theoretical orientation "constructivist research illuminates the sources of both conflict and cooperation."[12]

These theories in some ways attempt to answer the critical question put forth by John Ruggie: "Accepting that the international polity, by definition, is an anarchy, that is, a segmented realm, on what basis is it segmented?"[13] Even though the centrality of the state was retained, new perspectives began to draw attention to relations, culture, and identity. The Post-Positivist perspectives, which include critical theory, historical sociology, feminist critiques, postmodernism, constructivism, and post-constructivism, go beyond states, re-centering the analysis around global citizenship, transnational and diaspora identities. For example, Barry Buzan and Lene Hanson propose that by relying on the realist and neorealist Hobbesian notion of a contract between the state (which provides security) and individuals (who acknowledge this sovereign authority), the state is made immune from criticism.[14] Empirical evidence suggests that many states have not been able to offer its citizens a sense of security, they have in fact acted to persecute, oppress, and subordinate them. National security then cannot be assessed in terms of the dangers a nation confronts, but rather as a process through which a nation comes to produce and reproduce a particular identity.

R.B.J. Walker highlights the implications of state-centered approaches in international relations in that the inside (self – state sovereignty) is considered secure and authoritative, and the outside (other) becomes anarchic, decentralized, and the arena of competition and conflict.[15] The latter is also a "realm in which others can be turned into Other, and the Other may be subjected to the familiar practices of projection, negation, orientation and obliteration."[16] Moreover, since state sovereignty is viewed as a permanent and relatively unchanging territorial space, Walker proposes that "to claim sovereignty is already to know what lies beyond," the horizon is dark, filled with the horrors of war and the unknown, as opposed to 'home', which is associated knowledge, power, and belonging.[17] To talk of new trends in globalization like movement, acceleration, or speed, it becomes necessary to "confront state sovereignty as the discourse of limits in time and space that the theory of international relations reproduces in such a domesticated way."[18] Walker interrogates the idea of states as the primary locus of power in international relations, and he challenges what has become the center of international relations theory.

When attention is moved away from the primacy of states as unitary, closed, and all-powerful actors, what do we replace it with? The emphasis on states provides a powerful structural frame of reference, but it falls short of offering perspectives to understand the complexity of diaspora identities.

Diaspora and theoretical ambiguity

Stéphane Dufoix writes: "Modern societies, which are characterized by a belief in reason, progress, universality, and stability, are confronted by emerging post-modern societies dominated by doubt, fragmentation, the end of great narratives of truth and Science, racial mixing, and fluid identities." [19] Diasporas are at the center of this emergent post-modern society and have spurred many interdisciplinary discourses that focus on disjuncture and severance. I have divided the general fields into an emphasis on territorial duality (home and host), state sovereignty, and questions of identities and notions of hybridity/indigeneity.

Home and host

James Clifford highlights a theme that resonates through most theories on diaspora; that these are cultures that "mediate, in a lived tension, the experience of separation and entanglement, of living here and remembering/desiring another place."[20] A dual identity exists – longing for a homeland while living in a host-land. In reviewing multiple discourses on diasporas and the ideas associated with the home-host duality, I propose that despite its relevance, an intrinsic element in definitions of diasporas is the notion of travel/movement and identities forged in the transnational locality – neither associated exclusively with home or host, but situated in another place that is *both* transnational and localized.

The home-host duality is often used in descriptions of the Jewish and African diasporas. In both these cases, diasporas were formed through violent forced removals, terrifying journeys to unknown lands, a complete rupture from former identities, and the presence of an abiding desire for return from exile. In the case of the South Asian indentured diaspora, indenture was not forced but voluntary (albeit under coercion in some cases), and it was considered a temporary, short-term contractual arrangement.[21] Once the decision was made to stay beyond the terms of the contract, because of economic necessity and/or the desire to remain as 'free' residents, discourses shifted to settlement, immigration, and permanence. Over generations, while continuity with the homeland in terms of a reconstructed cultural identity was maintained, the yearning for return was not. This is exemplified by the post-coup periods in Fiji when Indo-Fijian emigrated to Australia, New Zealand, and Canada; few expressed the desire to settle in India.

A key concept is the way in which some diasporas are 'othered' in that no matter how many generations live in the hostland, they are always considered outsiders; racial and ethnic divisions are re-established in each generation.[22] Indians in Fiji, South Africa, and Trinidad are 'othered' in terms of ethnicity – they are marked as "Indian" (a national identity associated with India) across the diaspora,

yet other ethnic groups *become* Creole or mixed and indigenized over generations. Indo-Trinidadians, for example, have a Creolized culture in terms of communication, language, music, dance, and dress; but they are categorized as East
Indian – meaning non-Creole and immigrant, while Creoles, mainly the descendants of slaves from Africa, are categorized as if they were indigenous to the land.
Furthermore, Indo-Trinidadians distinguish themselves from Creoles in terms of
an abiding Indian identity, and even *douglas* (mixed race) define themselves as
belonging to either of the two main ethnic groups. Finally, India did not initially
welcome diaspora Indians. After independence Jawaharlal Nehru made it clear
that Indians living aboard could either choose to return to India or accept nationality in other countries and remain marginal to India.[23] It was only in the 1990s
when a wealthier and professional class of Indians began to immigrate in larger
numbers and the Indian economy was more globally oriented, did policies toward
the diaspora change to encourage economic investments and cultural linkages
with India.

For the Black diaspora, Africa as home is significant. Drawing on the W. E. B.
Du Bois' theory of "double consciousness," Paul Gilroy explores the indelible
impact that Africa has on diaspora identity.[24] Dubois wrote in *The Souls of Black
Folk*: "One ever feels his twoness,-an American, a Negro; two souls, two thoughts,
two unreconciled strivings; two warring ideals in one dark body whose dogged
strength alone keeps it from being torn asunder."[25] Gilroy takes this to refer not
just to the Black American experience, but also to post-slave populations in general.[26] He "breaks the primary connection" of Black Americans with Africa and
instead draws attention to experiences of movement, forced displacement, and
identity formation among the post-African diaspora.[27] Recognizing the historical
connection of the term diaspora to Jewish experiences of displacement and exile,
Gilroy sees the common themes of suffering, tradition, temporality, and the social
organization of memory in response to modernity. He sees in this the "ability to
pose the relationship between ethnic sameness and differentiation: a *changing
same*."[28] He shows that Black diaspora culture cannot be reduced only to a nation-
state or ethnicity, but must be understood within a discursive space, changing
while retaining historical and transnational connections.

Gilroy's propositions illustrates the differences between slavery and indenture –
the experience of slavery had the effect of destroying and subverting an African heritage, and it was so violent that it led to racial schisms in every society
where Africans settled. While indenture was highly exploitative, it was premised
on being a temporary engagement – after the end of the contract, Indians could
return to India. Indenture replaced slavery or in some cases provided a new source
of labor. In the colonies, Indians kept salaries low, they undermined the bargaining position of freed labor, and they sustained high profits for plantation owners –
they were positioned as competitive and inferior. Hence the trans-Indian diaspora
does not neatly parallel the trans-Atlantic diaspora. But Indians experienced similar
disjuncture and they too were severed from their families, communities, and culture. They were transported on ships that were originally used for the slave trade,
and these wretched journeys destroyed their caste, religious, and geographical

moorings. They too were defined as "non-white" and othered across the diaspora – they too became a '*changing* same.'

What are the distinctions, if any, between an ethnic group and a diaspora? Theorists tend to conflate both terms, but this undermines a key distinction between them: all diasporas are associated with movement, but all ethnic groups are not.[29] A foundational debate regarding the definition of ethnicity revolves around whether these identities are primordial or instrumental. If it is believed that all members of an ethnic group are of the same blood, of the same family, then it can be inferred that individuals will be held together by moral obligations that are tied to primordial affinities.[30] Primordial relations are said to explain the allegiance individuals have to one's own people,[31] and the identity to which one is born. For Clifford Geertz primordial relations are based on attachments that stem from the "givens," the "ties of blood, speech and custom."[32] These are the connections that link members of a "tribe"; these biological bonds become "sociologically real kinship."[33] The instrumentalist perspective emphasizes the constructed character of ethnicity, the renewal, modifications, and remakings of identities in each generation.[34] Nelson Kasfir outlines the steps that constitute the process of creating an ethnic group and further recognizes objective indicators (like historical experiences, language, religion) of common ancestry and subjective articulations of them (like the sense of belonging and common interests).[35] He also highlights the notion of ethnic entrepreneurs, self-proclaimed leaders who employ ethnicity to mobilize a political base.[36] These debates have expanded to include diasporas, immigrants, migrants and others

Milton Esman sees diasporas as minority ethnic groups of migrant origin that continue to maintain links with their land of origin.[37] While recognizing movement, his emphasis on a minority status clearly does not apply to some diasporas, like the majority ethnic group in Mauritius (Indo-Mauritians). Walker Connor however, sees fewer differences between the two categories and instead treats all ethnic groups as diasporic, given that most states as homelands depend on the myth of ethnic exclusivity. Connor suggests that a working definition of diaspora should be "that segment of people living outside the homeland."[38] Further "members of a diaspora can therefore never be at home in their adopted homeland. They are at best sojourners, remaining at the sufferance of the indigenous people."[39] This definition ignores generational depth (three or four generations for the Indian indentured diaspora) and the subjective identity constructions of diasporas themselves, especially for those born in the diaspora having no first-hand experiences of the motherland that their parents left behind. Virinder Kalra et al. make a clearer distinction between diasporas and ethnicity; they associate the latter with the nation-state, while they see the former as including ethnicities that are multi-locational.[40] These distinctions make sense, but a key question is left unanswered: when does a diaspora become an ethnic group? In looking at identity, the conflation of discourses of ethnicity and diasporas are inevitable, diasporas have strong claims to ethnicity, which can be defined in terms of local level communities, nations, or transnationalism. Yet in naming the two categories as different it seems appropriate to recognize the differences between them, for surely intrinsic to the notion of diaspora is movement and displacement. While Indians in each of the states in question have an ethnic identity like other groups constituting the nation, Indians are a diaspora because of their history of indenture from India.

Using yet another thread to define diasporas, William Safran emphasizes a homeland orientation as *the* major element distinguishing a diaspora from other immigrant communities.[41] Providing a list of criteria that best describes a diaspora, Safran concludes that "Most diasporas . . . are characterized by an overlapping double orientation: towards two cultures and two states (but not necessarily two *political* allegiances)."[42] Sudesh Misra correctly says that Safran conflates an imagined relationship with the homeland with actual political and economic relations, thereby ignoring the subjective constructions and imaginings of identity. Moreover his taxonomical justifications are "elusive" and "unquantifiable" making his definition problematic.[43]

Like Safran, Robin Cohen provides a descriptive taxonomy for diaspora characteristics. He proposes a table with nine common features including dispersal from an original homeland (due to trauma, for work/trade), a collective memory and myth of the homeland, development of a return movement, ethnic group consciousness, and a troubled relationship with the host country.[44] Moving away from ethno-national groups, his categories are victim (Jews, Africans, Irish, Armenians, Palestinian), labor (Indians), trade (Chinese, Lebanese), and imperial (British). The overarching frame remains dependent on ethno-national units, and it relies on a dual-territorial framework. Further, the list attempts to be all encompassing but doesn't clearly suggest what is essential for a diaspora.[45]

Directly challenging the association of the term diaspora with a home-host trope, Edward Said pointed to the experiences of the Palestinian diaspora who are exiled in their own homeland – displaced and deterritorialized. There is little doubt that they constitute a diaspora, yet the notion of home and host does not capture their experiences or identity. Said preferred the Arabic terms *shatat* (dispersion), *ghurba* or *manfa* (exile), and more specifically dispossession.[46] Another way of making sense of migrations is what Peter van der Veer calls the "dialectics of "belonging" and "longing." Here belonging opposes "rootedness to uprootedness, establishment to marginality." And longing includes the desire "for change and movement, but relates this to the enigma of arrival, which brings a similar desire to return to what one has left."[47]

This book adopts the instrumental perspective for ethnicity seeing it as constructed and re-established in each generation. Diasporas exhibit strong ethnic identities, but these are navigated through the lens of their transnational locality. The notion of perpetual displacement and identities associated with the *changing* same, particularly for diasporas from the Global South, form a crucial part of diaspora identity.

The dual territorial framework can be limiting especially if the concept of "home" is assumed to be stable and unchanging, or is imagined as frozen at the time of departure. In most cases people left the homeland because of economic, political, and social upheavals, and during their time away, the homeland inevitably changed. Indians were available for indenture in India because it was under colonial rule and because political and economic transformations led to the crea-tion of a large superfluous population, unemployed and unemployable. While the diaspora took root in the rest of the world, India gained independence and the sub-continent was partitioned. In time the diaspora encountered an India that was foreign and far removed from the everyday reality of their daily lives.

There is continuity in culture, religion, and language, but here too change and reconfigurations have occurred. For example, Fiji-Hindi and Trini-Hindi are indi-genized and Creolized versions of Hindi. While caste allegiances are mostly dead in the diaspora, some categories still retain a semblance of caste-based taboos: Brahmins in Trinidad and Mauritius, Vaish in Mauritius, and Gurajati caste mem-bership with some adaptations have remained. In all these instances, framing the analysis using dualistic reference points undermines the impact of other subjec-tivities. It also gives the impression that diasporas are coherent blocks, and this is far from reality. Intra-ethnic divisions along the lines of religion and class, gen-eration and gender, and ethnicity prevail. These divisions have affected politics in all the countries under review. In Fiji for example divisions between Muslims and Hindus, and in the latter category, between Hindi, Tamil, Telugu, and Gujarati speakers, have influence political allegiances. Indians do not always vote as a bloc and have instead supported different political parties at different historical junctures.

The home-host trope does not offer a compelling explanatory framework for Indian diaspora. More can be gained from theories that deal with the messiness associated with identity, political consciousness, and citizenship. Across the dias-pora, Indians are defined according to ethnicity irrespective of their citizenship – always Indian, always othered, and always assumed to be associated with India. Subjectively, "Indianness" is constructed to maintain a sense of community against marginalization. Indianness has also been employed to assert difference from other racial and ethnic groups. In Mauritius for example, where Indians are in the majority, Indian identity is constructed so as to elevate it in terms of Creole hybridity. Building closer ties with India, Mauritians have projected their identity as an "African tiger" analogous to an "Asian tiger" in the African continent. Yet in Trinidad, Creole identity is elevated in national discourses – East Indians are con-sidered to have a lower place in the racial/ethnic hierarchy. Indianness carries with it connotations of inferiority and marginalization – an identity that is ascribed and in part, subjectively constructed. Indo-Fijians are considered outsiders (temporary residents/visitors) with respect to indigenous Fijians. In South Africa, Indian iden-tity has changed as Indians shifted from being treated as a separate ethnic group under apartheid – where they were categorized as one of four "racial" groups, the others were Coloreds, Whites, and Africans – to a small minority in the post-apartheid system with rights like any other group, but having a minority status.

In terms of theory, the home-host trope has considerable resonance with dias-pora identities, but it also has shortcomings. It is the kind of distinction that best overlays state-centered paradigms, especially in international relations where states are largely seen as *the* sovereign and coherent blocs that define the interna-tional realm. Hence the home-host duality in diaspora identities can be assumed to be a state-to-state relationship. But my work suggests that the dual-allegiance assumptions do not capture the complexities and messiness associated with diasporas. Their identities are not clearly aligned with states, but can best be understood by recognizing that they inhabit a transnational locality. States then (be it homeland or host-land) are one of a multiple set of institutions that affect diaspora identity.

State sovereignty

The presence of diasporas challenges ideas associated with state sovereignty, especially since this concept is so closely tied to nations and nationalism. How has sovereignty been defined? To some extent it specifies a politics of spatial containment that resolves the disjuncture between the universal and the particular, self and other, space and time; that to some extent appears as natural.[48] State sovereignty has been associated with civilian consent to state domination,[49] and is sometimes viewed as a social construct.[50] It contributes to the sense of centralized state control exemplifying state power and providing a bounded frame of reference for citizens to imagine the nation. Over time national security (which merged security of the state *and* nation) came to mean international insecurity, with the threat of violence centered in the international (danger associated with external threats) rather than the domestic realm.[51] The place beyond states came to be considered the dangerous zone – where anarchy prevailed. This is precisely the place where diasporas gain their identity; to see it as anarchic and dangerous is to undermine its impact on identity and constructions of the nation. The fact that diaspora identities are to some extent constructed outside states challenges state sovereignty. In international relations diaspora identities are placed in two or more states, the transnational space is largely ignored. The concept of "Indianness" or being "Indian" outside India is difficult to grasp in this framing.

Sovereignty is closely tied to nation. Separate from states, nations are defined subjectively and psychologically – there is little objective reality to the term.[52] As Anderson sees it, nations are an "imagined political" community – "imagined as both inherently limited and sovereign."[53] The issue of definitions is further complicated by terms such as transnationalism and postnationalism, and there is little light shed on what exactly is being "surpassed" in the former or transcended in the later.[54]

For Arjun Appadurai, the nation was never perfectly contained within the state, even less so now that nationalism is itself diasporic. In the minds of the highly mobile populations, it is increasingly "unrestrained by ideas of spatial boundary and territorial sovereignty." [55] As he sees it, the nation-state is in crisis and has an increasingly "violent relationship" with its "postnational Others."[56] In all the states under review, diaspora Indians played a significant role in constructions of the nation – even where their presence in the national arena is not made apparent. In Fiji for example, even though indigenous Fijians have maintained a strong imprint on national identity, the very presence of Indians has led to political instability. In Trinidad, even though the nation is constructed as Afro-Creole,

Indians have pushed national identity toward a multi-cultural, multi-ethnic framing. In all four countries, a transnational identity is exemplified by increasing movement away from new homelands, not to the 'motherland' but to other places of second-migration: South Africans to the United Kingdom, Mauritians to India and the United Kingdom, Fijians to New Zealand and Australia, Trinidadians to the United States and Canada. Yet this process is not as complete or as all-encompassing as Appadurai would have us believe. Indo-Fijians, Indo-Trinidadians, Indo-Mauritians and South African Indians also have strong nationalist identities. They are *not* Indian Indians – they have nationalist identities and citizenships in vastly different nation-states. *Their* Indianness is located outside India, in both the transnational space *as well as* in the nation-state – in the *transnational locality*.

From another perspective, diasporas play an important part in constructing the nation – their presence influences how a nation is defined. Yasemin Soysal for example, sees guest workers and migrants as representing a time when "national citizenship is losing ground to a more universal model of membership, anchored in deterritorialized notions of person' rights."[57] The *postnational* moment reflects a time when migrants and other non-citizens are conferred rights regardless of their historical or cultural ties to the community. Even though these rights are not equivalent to those of citizens, they nevertheless exist, and it is this that defines post-national citizenship. But if the nation is premised on the notion of some kind of ethnic authenticity, then migrations, mixing, hybridity, and Creolization undermine this sense of nationalism. As Peter van der Veer argues, "Nationalism needs the story of migration, the diaspora of others, to establish the rootedness of the nation." [58] The sense of self, nationalism, and nationhood gains meaning with respect to the other: migrants, immigrants, aliens, and the undocumented.

Taking the notion of difference further, Pnina Werbner et al. see the tension in modern society as being between the politics of difference and the totalizing project of the nation-state: "between the drive towards integration, on the one hand, and the individualization and differentiation, on the other." [59] These tensions contribute towards enhancing national solidarities, and simultaneously weaken national bonds as more communities are alienated. There is also much disagreement on whether the emphasis on globalization, transnationalism, and diasporas imply that the state is 'withering away.' Instead Ulf Hannerz suggests that it is the nation and not the state that can wither away. The big question will be " . . . what can your nation do for you that a good credit card cannot do?"[60] To some extent, movement, displacement, and discontinuity have replaced the historical rootedness of nationhood. The state, however, continues to operate as a powerful entity albeit in an environment where global relations and transactions have altered its boundaries.

Roxanne Doty argues that by treating states as primary units, realists in international relations have undermined the distinction between state, nation, and sovereignty.[61] Hence questions of national identity and its impact on sovereignty can be dismissed. In focusing on how the inside/outside boundary of the nation-state is constructed, Doty sees it as a function of the state's discursive authority – its ability to impose fixed stable meanings on who belongs (the insider) in the midst of uncertainty and ambiguity. Along these lines, Homi Bhabha questions the representation of the nation as horizontal and homogenous, and as a linear narrative starting with origins and ending in the present. He sees the concept of "the people" in conceptual "double-time" whereby

> the people are historical 'objects' of a nationalist pedagogy giving the discourse an authority that is based on a pre-given, or constituted historical origin *in the past;* the people are also the 'subjects' of a process of signification that must erase any prior or original presence . . . to demonstrate . . . contemporaneity: as that sign of the *present* through which national life is redeemed and iterated as a reproductive process.[62]

These theorists highlight the difficulty in clearly separating state and nation, both sets of institutions are closely intertwined. Herein lies the challenges of theoretical observations versus the reality on the ground. Hall suggests that states have reacted to increasing globalization and erosions of sovereignty by becoming more xenophobic.[63] Here the experience of Indo-Fijians is insightful. As they have become more influential in national politics, some indigenous leaders have reacted by drawing tighter boundaries around conceptions of Fijian citizenship and nationhood. The nation has come to stand for indigeneity. The first coup in 1987 took place after the formation of a multiracial coalition government, the 2000 coup followed the victory of the Fiji Labor Party and the appointment of the first Indian prime minister, the 2006 coup occurred after the narrow victory of indigenous Fijians and the formation of a multiparty cabinet. While the coups were politically motivated, ethnicity has always been available for mobilizing support, and the nation continues to be reproduced as the land of indigenous Fijians.

The notion of sovereignty adds a sense of certainty, physical distinctiveness, internal coherence, and logic. Yet with the increasing presence of diasporas, immigrants, migrant workers, travelers, undocumented immigrants, and illegal residents, overlaid on internal divisions that have longer histories, the idea that the inside is clearly defined and united is largely unfounded.

Identity and hybridity

Diasporas are exoticized, celebrated, or disdained and in each instance it is their hybrid identities that are the source for these reactions. Exploring this, Virinder Kalra et al show how diasporas have come to be articulated in terms of subverting state-centered identity.[64] Seeing hybridity as a power-laden and asymmetrical term, they focus on how it has been intertwined with racialized assumptions and are sometimes used to avoid confronting racial inequality. To define individuals or a community as having hybrid identities assumes that the opposite (pure/single origin) exists. Discourses of racial/ethnic inferiority are intrinsic to the term hybrid, including mixed, Colored, Creole, Mestizo, and Dougla.

If hybridity assumes that something is pure and in terms of identity nothing can be assumed to be pure and hence everything must be hybrid, the term is rendered unhelpful. Furthermore as Kalra correctly states: "it does not offer an adequate language to discuss even the mundane exchanges of cultural difference in so-called 'postmodernity', let alone come to grips with contemporary social, political and economic conditions."[65] But how does one move beyond hybridity? Paul Gilroy suggests that by finding a new "idiom" that doesn't just invert the notion of "loss, dilution, and weakness" we might be able to conceive of "transcultural mixture' and the assumptions about alterity that it promotes, as a phenomena without any necessary or fixed value at all.[66] He suggests that "viable notions of civic reciprocity" will make obsolete narrow definitions that prioritize racialized differences. Yet as Kalra et al. argue, it is somewhat impossible to get of out this conundrum – in this particular instance, reciprocity implies debt and obligation as well as theft and extortion.[67] They conclude that:

> The drive to define and fix definitions is just what makes useless the categories of so much social science: caught in stasis, the closed character of analysis can only replicate itself, unable to attend to dynamic and contradictory processes in capitalism and social life as lived.[68]

Hybridity sometimes appears to mean a celebration of cultural mixing irrespective of political, economic, and social inequalities.[69] But a celebration of hybridity in the form of art, music, fashion, and even hiring practices also includes the oppression of hybridity in other contexts like anti-immigration policies, detention camps, police profiling, anti-hijab dress codes, and so on. For the term to encapsulate these various meanings and interpretations, it has to be contextualized. By labeling a group as hybrid, there is a tendency to undermine intra-group divisions, which can be significant with respect to strong or weak group coherence. For the cases being analyzed, such divisions have impacted political allegiances at the national political level – as is the case with middle-class Indian support of the African National Congress in post-apartheid South Africa, but working class support for the conservative National Party, or the divisions among Indo-Trinidadians that have contributed to the need for political party coalitions and multi-ethnic appeals. Throughout the diaspora religious distinctions along the lines of Muslims and Hindus, and further, between Hindi/Bhojpuri-speaking and Tamils (and Telegus), also influence political party allegiances and national political outcomes.

Despite the definitional fuzziness that prevails, it can be assumed that the identities of Indians in the indentured diaspora are hybrid. They are Creolized, and this is reflected in their culture, language, rituals, food, and so on. Take for example the fast foods that are popular among this diaspora: the popular *bunny-chow* in South Africa is a hollowed-out loaf of bread filled with curry (usually mutton, chicken, or beans), *doubles* in Trinidad are two bara (fried flat bread) filled with curried chick peas, *roti rolls* in Fiji are roti filled with potato curry, and *gateaux pimento* in Mauritius are spicy deep fried lentil balls. Officially only specific sub-groups are considered hybrid: *Douglas* in Trinidad, *Creoles* in Trinidad and Mauritius, and *Coloreds* in South Africa. In fact in many instances, a play on 'Indianness' as pure and unmixed, is often invoked.

In terms of the nation and national identity, the notion of hybrid identities presents a challenge. How do nations evolve to include and represent these identities?

What happens when then don't? How do such identities translate in the political arena? The experiences in Fiji is indicative of situations where nations marginalize diasporas, and this leads to serious divisions in civil society and the ruling elites. The 2006 coup, for example, led by Commodore Bainimarama of the Republic of Fiji Military Forces ousted a government voted into office by four out of every five indigenous Fijians. Despite the fact that chieftainship, communal land ownership, and the Methodist Church serve to unite the community, divisions along the lines of class, clan allegiances, generation, and urban and rural dwellers, have all come to play a defining role in the politics of the hegemonic indigenous Fijian community.

Globalization, transnationalism, and diaspora

Globalization theory often forms the backdrop to discussions about diasporas. One of the main problems with this is the "contemporary, presentist nature of the analysis" when the field should in fact start even before British colonialism.[70] Another challenge is the frequent and loose use of terms like globalization "to describe just about any process or relationship that somehow crosses state boundaries."[71]

Arjun Appadurai argues that the "nation-state as a complex modern political form is on its last legs."[72] He views diasporic public spaces as the 'crucibles' of the post-national political order.[73] Walker adds that the world is continually shrinking and states are losing their primacy,[74] and Susan Strange proposes that state authority has weakened in terms of quality (not quantity).[75] I agree with the latter view that state power has been reconfigured and because other powerful actors ranging from private corporations to independent terrorist networks constantly challenge it, its purview over some areas has shrunk but has become more concentrated in other areas. Hence while globalization entails the strengthening and increasing reach of corporate companies, states still retain the power to enable or impede that growth.[76]

Another analytical strand has been about globalization and culture – arguing against the notion of a McDonaldization of the world (global cultural homogeneity); theorists have highlighted difference, contestation, and the indigenization of global cultural exports.[77] While there is a new kind of globalization that differs from past incarnations in that it is pivoted around a global mass culture that is largely dominated by America, it is nevertheless still centered in the language of the West and it is very much part of the march of capitalism and modernity.[78] But exactly what this language entails is contested. While some theorists speak of a global-human condition,[79]others suggest that dynamic cultural strategies cannot be structurally contained in a secondary role.

The definitional challenge is made more complex when the term 'transnational' is introduced. Transnationalism covers multiple institutional movements – from the movement of digital images across state borders at breakneck speed, to the complex identities of people who are able to move across multiple state borders more frequently and regularly. Several theorists posit that the term refers to identities forged through movement and are constructed by linking societies of origin and settlement.[80] Peter Manderville, writing on the transnational Muslim *umma*, coins the term "translocality" to reflect the fusion of locality and move-ment, which focuses on ethnic nationhood and political 'otherhood'.[81] Ulf Han-nerz moves away from the term and instead uses the Greek *ecumene (oikoumene)*, which alludes to the "interconnectedness of the world. By way of interactions, exchanges and related developments, affecting not least the organization of cul-ture."[82] Diaspora identity is closely tied to the location of diaspora communities; they inhabit a *transnational locality*, giving them real or imagined ties at the local and international levels.

Part 2: Social movements

Resistance movements as well as social and cultural organizations are prolific across this diaspora. Theoretical perspectives associated with social move-ments are helpful in framing these processes. By looking at social movements that mobilize among diaspora communities, it is possible to understand some of the complexities associated with diaspora identities and their placement in the global arena. What follows is a theoretical overview of the main historical trends within this paradigm. The main propositions are that the existing perspectives are more suited to analyzing social movements in the global north rather than the Global South. In the latter region, while social movements mobilize when political opportunities become available, as the dominant theoretical perspectives highlight, they also mobilize around economic issues. Debates within the litera-ture on social movements revolve around whether a global civil society exists and if transnational networks challenge state sovereignty. This is relevant to organiza-tions among diasporas, but it still doesn't capture the distinctive features of the location that such communities inhabit – the transnational locality, which gives rise to social movements that are simultaneously localized and transnationalized. This section makes a connection between diaspora identities and the kinds of social movements they develop.

Theorizing social movements

While there is no definitive theorist or moment that lays claim to the concept of social movement, Charles Tilly suggests that it can be traced to a particular way of pursuing public politics that started in the later eighteenth century and combined three elements: "campaigns of collective claims on target authorities," a wide range of "claim-making performances," and "public representation of the cause's worthiness, unity, numbers, and commitment."[83] These themes are prevalent in most theories about social movements. Theorists who focus on *New Social Move-ments* (NSMs), those movements that developed from the mid-1960s during the postindustrial period, are of particular relevance to the study of this diaspora given its historical roots in colonialism and the period following independence. Theo-rists like Manuel Castells, Alain Touraine, Alberto Melucci, and Jurgen Habermas were reacting to the inadequacies of Marxist theorists to offer explanations for the kinds of social movements that were proliferating. Shifting attention away from class conflicts to political, social, and cultural conflicts in postindustrial systems, NSMs focused on collective action that addressed new relations of domination.[84] For them, the state and market framed and rationalized the private sector, giving rise to new social movements that reflected "the silent and arbitrary elements of the dominant codes" and publicized "new alternatives."[85] NSMs emerged out of the "crisis of modernity and focus on struggles over symbolic, informational, and cultural resources and rights to specificity and difference."[86] Despite wide variations among these writers, they all recognized the 'newness' of the social movements that evolved in the postindustrial period, and they were criticized precisely for attempting to define a break from 'old' social movements.[87] As Steven Buechler says: "the term new social movements inherently overstates the differences and obscures the commonalities between past and present movements."[88]

Critics of the NSMs approaches pointed out that the mere existence of discontent did not clearly explain how, when, and why specific organizations arose. Reacting to this model, a *resource mobilization* and a strategy-oriented paradigm began to emerge, with attention on 'entrepreneurs' who mobilized resources and organized grievances.[89] But in this interest-group perspective, the subjective feelings of camaraderie and solidarity were ignored; success was evaluated on the basis of whether policy objectives were achieved.

Another group of scholars began to write about *political opportunity structures*. Tarrow explained it as follows: "Movements are produced when political opportunities broaden, when they demonstrate the existence of allies and when they reveal the vulnerability of opponents. By mounting collective actions, organizers become focal points that transform external opportunities, conventions and resources into movements."[90] Those writing within this perspective looked at the historical cycles of movements and conflicts that occurred at similar and different times in the same region.[91] Critics felt that this model marginalized issues pertaining to identity, gender, and culture. Further the social construction of political opportunity structures itself were underplayed, and its broadly defined parameters included just about anything pertaining to social movements but lacked particular explanatory power.[92] This paradigm came to occupy a dominant position in the field of social movements.

Various aspects of this paradigm were expanded and re-articulated. Political opportunities, for example, came to include moves toward reform, shifts in the ruling alignment, the opening up of different avenues of power, exposure to new possible allies due to divisions among the ruling elite, and so on. Charles Tilly introduced the concept of a *"repertoire of contention"* in an effort to interrogate how a social movement formed or spread.[93] He proposed that they grew out of three kinds of factors: the daily routines of a population and their internal organization, their prevailing rights and system of justice, and the accumulated experience and knowledge of their history of collective action and contention. It also includes the existence of shared meaning prior to mobilization, and offers a range of symbols, rituals, and worldviews that can be accessed.[94] Tarrow added that from the late eighteenth century, similar forms of collective action spread throughout the world – strikes, petitions, demonstrations, barricades, and urban insurrection – and he called this a "modular repertoire."[95] The role of *social networks*,[96] community structures and history were highlighted,[97] as were investigations into the reasons for individuals joining a social movement.[98] Furthermore, cultural *framing* was underscored, viewed as enabling more sustainable, long-lasting collective action.[99]

One of the main criticisms of political opportunity approaches was the inherent structural biases and undermining of subjective constructs. Goodwin and Jasper proposed a social constructionist approach to understand emotions, personal perceptions, and the meanings that actors attribute to collective action.[100] They contend that the notion of political opportunity structures is too rigid and undermines particular contexts. In other words, an

> extraordinary large number of processes and events, political and otherwise, potentially influence movement mobilization, and they do so in historically complex combinations and sequences. . . Such opportunities, when they are important, do not result from some invariant menu of factors, but from situationally specific combinations and sequences of political processes – none of which, in the abstract, has determinate consequences.[101]

Replying to these criticisms McAdam, Tarrow and Tilly proposed a more "relational" perspective in which "interpersonal networks" are central to mobilization.[102] They emphasized agency and changing structures with respect to mobilization, framing, and repertoires of contention. The model was complex and attempted to encapsulate a changing dynamic that was both situation specific and also fit within broad thematic trends. Criticism included the vaguely defined distinction made between processes and mechanisms and a general weakness in terms of explicating how these two concepts functioned.[103] The model was also criticized for continuing with classical categories, albeit adjusted and re-formulated in novel ways.

How can these perspectives be used to analyze social movements in the Global South, where all the countries in this study are located? The results have been less promising. As Edelman observes, they are less appealing "because it was difficult especially under authoritarian regimes, to imagine political opportunity as a significant explanatory category," and in those instances where they were used, theoretical frameworks were understated.[104] Some of the early adopters of these perspectives were analysts in or studying social movements in Latin American. They tended to adopt the new social movement perspectives, and with the uprising of the Zapatista movement in Chiapas, they began to study the role of social media and transnational networking.[105] In general the gaps in the social movement literature with respect to understanding organizations in the Global South include the study of peasant and right-wing movements. Most significantly, instead of an emphasis on political opportunities that seem more relevant in Europe and other Western democracies, there remains a need to analyze the impact of economic inequalities for organizations and movements.[106] This provides a more fruitful way of getting to grips with issues pertaining to indigenous groups, barrio dwellers, street children, and other economically marginalized populations – these are the subjects of collective action that fall outside the purview of politics but lie at the center of economic policy and (in)action. Once again class, the basis of Marxist analyses, rather than other social and political cleavages had more explanatory power and instead of a steadfast attachment to new social movement theories, Latin American specialists began to speak of 'popular' movements.[107]

Those theorists who study Africa and the Middle East have shown that classical social movement theories are not applicable to states where authoritarian rule make few, if any, political opportunities available. Social movements form within a context of scarce resources and rely on informal family and community connections employing "innovative repertoires to mobilize."[108] The perception of threats or the subjective feeling of being under attack often leads to collective action – political opportunities are not clearly visible or in fact available.

The way in which actors mobilize resources and the kinds of resources they access also differ in the developing world.[109] Some have argued for a need to focus on informal networks, social movement communities, social and political histories, and contemporary circumstances.[110] However this can lead to an under-appreciation of the discontinuities and fragile consensus that exist within such social movements. Moreover, the emphasis on visible social movements under-plays hidden forms of resistance that are rife and consistent in the Global South.[111]

Joel Beinin et al. add that under many authoritarian states in North Africa and the Middle East, people do not necessarily mobilize to take advantage of political opportunities but rather because they are reacting to threats, when they "feel their sense of justice and morals, their basic rights, or the possibility of offering decent living conditions to their children, are being attacked."[112] While they draw from social movement theory, they emphasize the role of informal networks for everyday survival as well as for collective mobilization. [113] This also highlights how "undercurrents of anger and dissatisfaction" can be mobilized, the conditions under which such mobilization is made possible, why mobilization is an "episodic phenomenon" that is not sustained over long periods of time, or that when social movements are mobilized, they might not articulate "common strategic objectives."[114] Significantly many networks of former political activism have adopted a human rights platform that is tolerated by oppressive states, and rely on a repertoire of contention that provides the basis for further mobilization and survival.

In their work on the Iranian revolution in 1979 several theorists added elements to social movement theory that recognized the special circumstances of movements in the Global South. Misagh Prasa proposed that a structural explanation for the revolution was viable – especially the role of the state in determining petroleum prices, the direct role it played in creating the conditions for revolt, and the important part played by mosques in mobilizing social movements.[115] Charles Kurzman drew attention to agency and perceptions of contention by using a social constructivist perspective. He showed that while reforms did not offer new political opportunities, it didn't stop participation in social and political organizations. Actors engaged in social mobilization despite adverse conditions – he called this an anti-explanation.[116] Finally Mansoor Moaddel emphasized the "broad episodic context" in which revolutionary discourses emerged and the specific character of revolutions as modes of mobilization.[117]

Analysts are also beginning to recognize the peculiarities of many countries in the Global South where democratic transitions and globalization have occurred simultaneously. The adoption of a neoliberal economic model and the consequent increased integration with the global economy frame the politics of nascent democratic states. This is exactly how the post-apartheid South African economic system has been set up. The economy is conducive to global investors and a wealthy sector of the population, while the political system tries to address the social inequities that prevailed under apartheid.[118] Hence while the majority Black population enjoys more political rights, they continue to be economically marginalized. This has given rise to social movements that mobilize around the privatization of services, inflated prices for food and other commodities, and high levels of unemployment and poverty. Theorists analyzing social movements have begun to recognize some of the limitations of theories that were constructed mainly for the Global North. A few of these challenges remain when these theories are modified to capture the transnationalization of social movements.

Transnational social movements

In 1993 Richard Falk coined the phrase 'globalization-from-below' to capture the transnational forces instigated by concerns over the environment, rights, neoliberal economics, multinational corporations, oppression, and violence.[119] Social movements mobilized around key global events and meetings that represented globalization-from-above: for example, the global women's meetings sponsored by the United Nations in the 1980s and 1990s, the 1992 Earth Summit, and Non-Government forums held when the World Bank, International Monetary Fund, and Group of Seven met.[120]

A number of analysts began to focus on the characteristics of these transnational movements. Risse-Kappen shows how international governance structures support and legitimizes transnational activism.[121] Smith et al. relate contemporary transnational activism to earlier discussions about collective action and global governance.[122] Waterman uses old working-class transnational solidarities to discuss emerging trends.[123] Keck and Sikkink focus on transnational advocacy networks to elaborate on the depth and reach of transnational social movements.[124] What is distinctive about transnational movements in general is that they are "Acephalous, horizontal, loosely networked alliances."[125] This makes them particularly difficult to analyze.

Terms like transnational movements, coalitions, and networks refer to different instances of transnational organization, but the definitional boundaries are unclear.[126] Other concepts are equally fuzzy. Some authors disagree with the notion of a global civil society for example – this idea proposes a coherence among transnational movements that doesn't exist, and it pre-supposes a weakening of states and the institutionalization of international norms.[127] Moreover in the current moment, cleavages and tensions among activists operating simultaneously at the transnational and local levels, challenge notions of a global civil society.[128]

A example high-profile diverse coalition of forces against corporate power was the Seattle demonstrations of 1999 against the World Trade Organization. This represented the new wave of demonstrations and transnational organization against global neoliberal policies that affected states worldwide.[129] While the challenges of sustaining such organizations are high, transnational activists have become brokers who relay organizational techniques and mobilization tactics for national and local struggles. Opposition movements now have access to international funding and expertise to fight local battles. With new technology and the increasing impact of global economic networks, social movements have become more transnational, and yet they face the same old challenges in terms of group cohesion and dynamics. A growing distance between a small cabal of leaders and other members, the distancing of leaders and their followers, tensions among the leadership about goals and objectives, the lack of buy-in from various sectors of the groups, dealing with or ignoring social divisions like class, race, identity, gender, and region, and the myriad other problems that all social movements experience. With our lenses focused on trying to get to grips with the expansion in transnational social movements, or the ways in which all social movements are to some extent transnationalized, attention has moved away from studying the real challenges, disjunctures, and fissures that affect all these movements – we give them a coherence that does not necessarily exist.

For Sidney Tarrow, while globalization provides the "incentives and themes for transnational activism," it is *internationalism* that "offers a framework, a set of focal points, and a structure of opportunities for transnational activists."[130] Further Tarrow sees internationalism as having a triangular structure that includes states, international institutions, and non-state actors; states retain formidable power despite globalization and non-state organization.[131] Transnational activism is framed by internationalism that provides individuals the opportunities to engage in collective action at different levels of the system.[132] Of particular importance in transnational activism is the role of 'rooted cosmopolitans' – "individuals and groups who mobilize domestic and international resources and opportunities to advance claims on behalf of external actors, against external opponents, or in favor of goals they hold in common with transnational allies."[133] Mahatma Gandhi was such an activist, while being rooted in the context of South Africa, he used transnational networks and knowledge to mobilize support and make his case to British colonial administrators.

Social movements among the Indian indentured diaspora

What is interesting about social movements among the Indian indentured diaspora is the lack of transnational networking *between* members of the diaspora. Social movements across this diaspora have not engaged in coalition building or sustained engagement. The focal point of their identity remains India, and the foci for internal mobilization has been the domestic state. Why were diaspora linkages, clearly visible during colonialism and potentially constituting a powerful mobilizing force, not activated by Indian activists in their quest for more rights? The answer might lie in the very way in which indenture operated – Indians from the same region were separated into different ships and transported to the colonies, many losing all ties with India and the rest of the diaspora. While the colonial administrators were coordinating their efforts, Indians experienced the ruptures that Gilroy talks about, a separation from their former families with all the traditions, caste practices, and cultural mores that defined those communities. As scab labor in colonies where they replaced emancipated slave labor as in Trinidad and Mauritius, or as cheap labor in those colonies where indigenous peoples refused to work on plantations as in South Africa, or where they were prevented from working through protective British policies, as in Fiji, Indians were in a compromising position. They were forcibly separated from other communities and were seen as inferior, subordinate, temporary, and workers who undermined the bargaining position of free labor and helped to prolong the domination and power of the colonizers. Given the turmoil and cultural flux that followed, their efforts to separate themselves from what they saw as Creolized (and hence mixed) local communities further defined their place in their new homelands. Finally thinking of themselves initially as temporary residents and only later becoming more settled, Indians did not feel the need to reach out to others in the diaspora.

How can theoretical perspectives frame social movements in this diaspora?

- Organizations and movements among this diaspora are transnational, but they do not activate old diaspora networks. Instead they rely on networks of nationals who have immigrated to other host-lands. The majority of social movements focus on local and national issues. For example, Fijian labor organizations and cultural groups rely on support from Fiji immigrants in New Zealand and Australia. The African National Congress in South Africa and other anti-apartheid movements relied on support from exiles that had settled in England and other European countries. Trinidad cultural groups get support from Trinidadian immigrants to the United States and Canada.
- As Ballard et al. argue, social movements in all these countries are both energized by the new possibilities offered by globalization and transnational networks, *and* marginalized because of their location and heavy reliance on resources and the political ambitions of activists in the global north. This is especially relevant in an environment where neoliberal economics have become the norm and social movements deal with political and economic issues that transcend state borders. Moreover many countries in the Global South are undergoing democratic and economic transitions at the same time, and this impacts the kinds of social movements that evolve, perhaps requiring other theoretical explanations.
- In all these former colonies, there are many examples to show that Indians reacted to political opportunities by mobilizing their forces. In states where Indians are the majority, as in Mauritius, whenever there was a change in leadership, strong linguistic movements formed to push for greater support for Indian culture and language training. The South African Constitution of

1983 introduced a Tricameral Parliament that was to include Indians and Coloureds into a reformed apartheid state. Community organizations and trade
unions used this occasion to launch one of the biggest and most effective anti-
election campaigns; in the process they created the United Democratic Front
(UDF), which was a coalition and front for the exiled African National Congress (ANC). The UDF soon became one of the most effective organizations
to move the country towards a democratic transition. In the 1999 elections
in Fiji held under the reformed constitution of 1997, Indians responded by
organizing support for the Indian-dominated Fiji Labor Party, which lead to
the appointment of the first Indian prime minister. The South African example goes against the view that authoritarian states are unlikely to offer political opportunities. On the contrary, such states generally attempt to institute
reforms, and these can often provide political opportunities for social movements to organize.

• A large part of the resistance that occurs amongst this diaspora takes place
behind the official scenes in informal networks and through hidden forms.
Indians have maintained their identities through cultural organizations, music
groups, religious gatherings, and other organizations. These organizations
and informal networks offer a space to recalibrate and reinforce identities
that can lead to greater insularity (and conservatism) or progressiveness and
the recognition of hybridity/indigenization of culture.

• Rather than a focus on political opportunities that are more relevant to the
West, in this diaspora a focus on economic inequalities also offers compelling explanations for the kinds of social movements that evolve and the types
of resources they access. Throughout, class differences overlay religious/
linguistic differences and are crucial to understanding the movements that
developed. The anti-eviction organizations in post-apartheid South Africa,
for example, are grassroots organizations located mainly in poor neighborhoods. More interesting are the networks and alliances that these groups are
forging across racial and ethnic divisions. In Fiji, class and religion have
played a big role in elections, often dividing the Indian vote.

• Diaspora activity reinforces the notion of a repertoire of contention, specifically in the South African case where early struggles for more rights from
colonial administrators paved the path for the anti-apartheid struggles and
contemporary organization against the post-apartheid government. There is
a strong reliance on non-violent forms of resistance and Gandhi's notion of
satyagraha. This was the repertoire employed by the UDF and ANC in exile
when it called to make the townships ungovernable, and these are the tactics that are used by contemporary movements to protest rental increases and
energy prices. Non-payment and refusal to vacate their properties are resistance techniques that are connected with Gandhi's tactics of resistance. In Fiji
mobilization for greater parliamentary representation has framed activism –
the push for political representation, constitutional changes that ensure that
Indians have a chance of gaining political leverage, the drive for strong
participation in political parties and elections. These are the repertoires of

contention that frame resistance, as are organizations that insulate Indians from the indigenous Fijians – social movements that concentrate on religion, cultural festivals, and other social markers of Indian identity.

Conclusion

This chapter argues that diasporas inhabit a *transnational locality* that places them in a position whereby they identify with multiple locations, but recognizing their embeddedness in the local and their engagement with the transnational. Diaspora identities are decentered, constructed with respect to transnational allegiances and state citizenship.

In terms of the colonial indentured Indian diaspora, we find that definitions associated with forced dispersion and exile, as in its usage to describe the Jewish and African diasporas, do not neatly apply. The host-land/homeland trope has some degree of traction in that members of this diaspora are still culturally associated with India, but through generations they have become more localized in terms of ethnicity and nationalism. The idea of a hybrid identity is somewhat relevant, but here too, it is both proscribed as well as self-consciously determined – state definitions as "Indian" or "Asian" sit alongside individual identities that are constructed in relation to place, gender and generation, and ethnicity and citizenship. This diaspora occupies a space that is neither entirely tied to India nor disconnected from the states they inhabit – they are culturally associated with the diaspora, but politically and socially part of the nation.

How does their location affect the kinds of social movements they organize and participate in? This study suggests that Indians throughout the diaspora have strong cultural/religious organizations, sometimes associated with specific temples and mosques or with different religious schools like the Arya Samaj, Sai Baba, the Divine Life Society, and the Hari Krishna movement, which are active in all four states. All these institutions are derived largely from the motherland, India. Many of these organizations are fairly insular and tend to maintain divisions with the local/indigenous non-Indian peoples. Here the notion of Indianness is exemplified providing a source of security from the perceived feeling of cultural erosion and mixing, and serves to separate Indians from other hybrid cultures. It reinforces the notion of being tied to a classical culture with roots in India, despite the reality that Indianness in the diaspora is hybrid, Creolized and indigenized.

This location has also given rise to social movements that are internationally oriented. Access to twice-migrants living in the Global North provides a powerful source of funding and support for domestic movements. In some cases, like Mauritius, India has become a valuable ally and economic partner. The leadership in many of the social movements associated with this diaspora is 'rooted cosmopolitans' with strong and prolonged experiences abroad, but with roots in the domestic area. They include leaders who mobilized Indians against colonial exploitation, like Mahatma Gandhi in South Africa, A. D Patel in Fiji, and Dr. Maganlal Manilal from Mauritius (who was also active in Fiji). More contemporary leaders include

Mac Maharaj of the African National Congress and Jay Naidoo of the Congress of South African Trade Unions, Jai Ram Reddy in Fiji, Sir Seewoosagur Ramgoolam in Mauritius, and Bhadase Sagan Maraj and Dr. Rudranath Capildeo in Trinidad.

Social movements are indigenized – they focus on the local/domestic issues experienced by Indians in a place outside India. They cover a wide range of ideological perspectives from very conservative (insular, sectarian/religiously focused) to progressive and radical (and outward-looking, aiming to make cross-ethnic and racial allegiances). The main focus is local, even if networks beyond borders are activated. These networks tend to be those who have twice-migrated to countries like the UK, Canada, the US, New Zealand, and Australia. This study maintains that only when this diaspora is viewed from the perspectives of their distinctive location – the transnational locality – can their identity and the social movements that evolve be understood.

Notes

1 See Latha Varadarajan, *The Domestic Abroad. Diasporas in International Relations*, (Oxford: Oxford University Press, 2010).
2 Robin Cohen, *Global Diasporas: An Introduction*, (London: UCL Press and Seattle: University of Washington Press, 1997), p. 3.
3 James Clifford, "Diasporas," *Cultural Anthropology*, Vol. 9, No. 3, (1994), p. 308.
4 See R. B. J. Walker, *Inside/Outside: International Relations as Political Theory*, (Cambridge: Cambridge University Press, 1993).
5 John Mearsheimer, "Disorder Restored," in *Rethinking America's Security*, ed. by G. Allison and G. F. Treverton, (New York: W. W. Norton, 1992).
6 For a critique of Mearsheimer's propositions, see Yosef Lapid and Friedrich V. Kratochwil, *The Return of Culture and Identity in IR Theory*, (Boulder: Lynne Rienner, 1996), p. 112.
7 See Ibid., p. 8.
8 Alexander Wendt, "Constructing International Politics," *International Security* Vol. 20, No. 1, (1995): 73.
9 Alexander Wendt, "Constructing International Politics."
10 Peter Katzenstein, ed., *The Culture of National Security: Norms and Identity in World Politics*, (New York: Columbia University Press, 1996), p. 4.
11 Ibid., p. 6.
12 Peter Katzenstein, Robert Keohane, Stephen Krasner, "International Organization and the Study of World Africa," *International Organizations*, Vol. 52, No. 4, (1998): p. 676.
13 John G. Ruggie, *Multilateralism Matters: the Theory and Praxis of an Institutional Form*, (New York: Columbia University Press, 1993), p. 168.
14 Barry Buzan and Lene Hansen, *The Evolution of International Security Studies*, (Cambridge: Cambridge University Press, 2009).
15 Walker *Inside/Outside*, p. 164.
16 R. B. J. Walker, "International Relations and the Concept of the Political," in *International Relations Today*, ed. by Ken Booth and Steve Smith, (Pennsylvania: The Pennsylvania University Press, 1995), p. 321.
17 Walker, *Inside/Outside*, p. 164.
18 Walker, "International Relations," p. 318.
19 Stéphane Dufoix, *Diasporas*, (Berkeley: University of California Press, 2008), p. 23.
20 Clifford, "Diasporas," 311.
21 The British parliament made indenture a policy through Act V of 1837, whereby a number of regulations were put in place to provide the legal basis for indenture. These

included procedures for recruitment (that the emigrant had to appear before an officer designated by the Government of India and the emigration agent who provided a written statement of the terms of the contract), the length of service (5-year terms renewable for a further 5 years), end of indenture requirements (ex: payment of return passage), transportation regulations (in terms of space, dietary requirements, medical provisions, etc.), and institutions to oversee the system (the superintendent of police was charged with carrying out the duties under the act).

22 Stuart Hall and David Morley, *Critical Dialogues in Cultural Studies*, (London: Routledge, 1997).
23 See Varadarajan, *The Domestic Abroad*.
24 Paul Gilroy, *The Black Atlantic: Modernity and Double Consciousness*, (Cambridge: Harvard University Press, 1993).
25 W. E. B. Du Bois, *The Souls of Black Folk*, ed. by Henry Louis Gates Jr., and Tern Hume Oliver, (New York: Norton and Company, 1999), p. 11.
26 Gilroy, *Black Atlantic*, pp. 126–127.
27 See Clifford, "Diasporas," p. 316.
28 Gilroy, *Black Atlantic*, p. xi.
29 Tölöyan makes a similar distinction, but with respect to diasporas and ethnic groups in general. See Khachig Tölölyan, "The Contemporary Discourse of Diaspora Studies," *Comparative Studies of South Asia, Africa, and the Middle* East, Vol. 27, No. 3, (2007), pp. 647–655, on p. 652.
30 See Edward Shils, "Primordial, Personal, Sacred and Civil Ties: Some Particular Observations on the Relationships of Sociological Research and Theory," *British Journal of Sociology*, Vol. 8, No. 2, (1957), pp. 130–145.
31 See Pierre L. Van Den Berghe, *The Ethnic Phenomenon*, (New York: Elsevier North-Holland, 1979), "Ethnicity and the Sociological Debate," in *Theories of Race and Ethnic Relations*, ed. by John Rex and David Mason, (Cambridge: Cambridge University Press, 1988).
32 Clifford Geertz, "The Integrative Revolution," in *Old Societies and New States*, ed. by Clifford Geertz, (New York: Free Press, 1963).
33 Steven Grosby, "The Verdict of History: The Inexpungible Tie of Primordiality – A Response to Elle and Coughlan," in *Ethnic and Racial Studies*, Vol. 17, No. 1, (1994), pp. 164–171.
34 See Jack Eller and Reed Coughlan, "The Poverty of Primordialism: The Demystification of Ethnic Attachments," *Ethnic and Racial Studies*, Vol. 16, No. 1, (1993), pp. 183–202.
35 Nelson Kasfir, "Explaining Ethnic Political Participation," *World Politics*, Vol. 31, No. 3, (1979), pp. 365–388.
36 David Laitin adds that in situations where there is incomplete hegemony and no culture is dominant, elites make choices based on the lines of cleavages they can exploit most advantageously. *Hegemony and Culture. Politics and Religious Change Among the Yoruba*, (Chicago: University of Chicago Press, 1986).
37 See Milton J. Esman, "Diasporas and International Relations," in *Modern Diasporas in International Politics*, ed. by Gabriel Sheffer, (New York: St. Martins. 1986), and *Diasporas in the Contemporary World*, (Ithaca: Cornell University Press, 2009).
38 Walker Connor, "The Impact of Homelands upon Diasporas," in *Modern Diasporas in International Relations*, ed. by Gabriel Sheffer, (London: Croom Helm, 1986): p. 20.
39 Ibid. 20.
40 Virindar Kalra, Raminder Kaur and John Hutnyk, *Diaspora and Hybridity. Theory, Culture and Society*, (UK: Sage Publications Ltd., 2005), 17.
41 William Safran, "Diasporas in Modern Societies: Myths of Homeland and Return," *Diaspora*, Vol. 1, No. 1, (Spring 1991), pp. 83–99.
42 William Safran and Jean A. Laponce, *Language, Ethnic Identity, and the State*, (Philadelphia: Cass, Taylor & Francis Group, 2004), p. 23.
43 Sudesh Misra, *Diaspora Criticism*, (Edinburgh: Edinburgh University Press, 2006).

44 Robin Cohen, *Global Diasporas*, p. 26.
45 Sudesh Misra, *Diaspora Criticism*, p. 48.
46 Patrick Williams, "What Shall We do Without Exile?: The Contradiction of 'Return' in the Palestinian Diaspora," in eds. M. Keown, D. Murphy, and J. Procter, *Comparing Postcolonial Diasporas*, (Palgrave Macmillan, 2009), p. 84.
47 Peter Van der Veer, *Nations and Migration: The Politics of Space in the South Asian Diaspora*, (Philadelphia: University of Philadelphia, 1995), p. 4.
48 See R.B.J. Walker, "International Relations and the Concept of the Political," p. 320.
49 See Linda Basch, Nina Glick Schiller and Blanc Cristina Szanton. *Nations Unbound: Transnational Projects, Postcolonial Predicaments, and Deterritorialized Nation-states.* (London: Routledge, 1994), p. 36.
50 See Thomas J. Biersteker and Cynthia Weber, *State Sovereignty as a Social Construct*, (Cambridge: Cambridge University Press, 1996).
51 Barry Buzan and Lene Hansen, *The Evolution of International Security*.
52 See Walker Connor, *Ethnonationalism: The Quest for Understanding*, (Princeton: Princeton University Press, 1994).
53 Benedict Anderson, *Imagined Communities: Reflections on the Origins and Spread of Nationalism*, (London: Verso, 1991), p. 6.
54 Sheila Croucher, "Perpetual Imagining: Nationhood in a Global Era," *International Studies Review*, Vol. 5, No. 1, (2003), p. 6.
55 Arjun Appadurai, *Modernity at Large. Cultural Dimensions of Globalization*, (Minneapolis: University of Minnesota, 1996), p. 161.
56 Ibid., 169.
57 Yasemin Soysal, *Limits of Citizenship: Migrants and Postnational Membership in Europe*, (Chicago: University of Chicago, 1994), p. 3.
58 Peter van der Veer, *Nations and Migration*, p. 6.
59 Pnina Werbner and Tariq Modood, *Debating Cultural Hybridity: Multi-cultural Identities and the Politics of Anti-racism*. (London: Zed, 1997), 104.
60 Ulf Hannerz, *Transnational Connections: Culture, People, Places*, (London and New York: Routledge, 1996), p. 88. Also see Jana Evans Braziel and Anita Mannur, *Theorizing Diaspora: A Reader*, (Malden: Blackwell Publishing Ltd., 2003).
61 Roxanne Doty, "Sovereignty and the Nation: Constructing the Boundaries of National Identity," in *State Sovereignty as Social Construct*, ed. by Thomas J. Biersteker and Cynthia Weber, (Cambridge: Cambridge University Press, 1996), p. 121.
62 Homi Bhabha, *The Location of Culture*, (London: Routledge, 1994), p. 145.
63 Hall et al., *Critical Dialogues*.
64 Kalra et al., *Diasporas and Hybridity*.
65 Ibid., p. 90.
66 Gilroy, *The Black Atlantic*, p. 217.
67 Kalra, *Diasporas and Hybridity*, p. 92.
68 Ibid.
69 See Avtar Brah and Annie E. Coombes, *Hybridity and Its Discontents: Politics, Science, Culture*, (London: Routledge, 2000).
70 Sandhya Shukla, "Locations for South Asian Diasporas," *Annual Review for Anthropology*, Vol. 30, (2001), p. 554.
71 Hannerz, *Transnational Connections*, p. 6.
72 Appadurai, *Modernity at Large*, p. 19.
73 Ibid., p. 39.
74 See Walker Connor, "Nation-Building or Nation-Destroying," *World Politics*, Vol. 23, no. 3 (1972), pp. 319–355.
75 See Susan Strange, "Political Economy and International Relations," in *International Relations Theory Today*, ed. by Ken Booth and Steve Smith, (Pennsylvania: The Pennsylvania State University Press, 1995), pp. 154–174.

76 See Saskia Sassen, *Territory, Authority, Rights: From Medieval to Global Assemblages*, (New Jersey: Princeton University Press, 2006).
77 See Ronald Robertson, *Globalization: Social Theory and Global Culture*, (London: Sage Publications, 1992); John F. Stack, "Ethnicity and Transnational Relations: An Introduction," in *Ethnic Identities in a Transnational World*, ed. by John F. Stack, (Westport, Connecticut: Greenwood Press, 1981); Jana Evans Braziel, *Diaspora: An Introduction*, (Wiley-Blackwell, 2008).
78 See Stuart Hall and David Morley, *Cultural Dialogues in Cultural Studies;* Anthony Giddens, *Modernity and Self-Identity*, (Cambridge: Polity, 1991).
79 Like Ronald Robertson, *Globalization*.
80 See Linda Basch et al., *Nations Unbound*; Steven Vertovec, *The Hindu Diaspora. Comparative Patterns*, (London and New York: Routledge, 2000).
81 Peter Manderville, *Transnational Muslim Politics: Reimagining the Umma*, (New York: Routledge, 2001), p. 26.
82 Urf Hannerz, *Transnational Connections*, p. 7.
83 Charles Tilly and Lesley J. Wood, *Social Movements, 1768–2012*, 3rd Edition, (Boulder and London: Paradigm Publishers, 2013), pp. 7–8.
84 Alain Touraine, *Return of the Actor: Social Theory in Postindustrial Society*, transl. M. Godzich, (Minneapolis: University of Minnesota Press, 1988); *Can We Live Together? Equality and Difference*, (Stanford: Stanford University Press, 2000).
85 Alberto Melucci, ed. by John Keane and Paul Mier, *Nomads of the Present: Social Movements and Individual Needs in Contemporary Society*, (Philadelphia: Temple University Press, 1989), 63.
86 Marc Edelman, "Social Movements: Changing Paradigms and Forms or Politics." *Annual Review of Anthropology*, Vol. 30, (2001), p. 289.
87 See for example David Plotke, "Representation is Democracy," *Constellations*, Vol. 4, No. 1, (1997), pp. 19–34; Claus Offe, "New Social Movements: Challenging the Boundaries of Institutional Politics," *Social Research*, Vol. 52, No. 4, (1985) pp. 817–867.
88 Steven M. Buechler, "New Social Movement Theories," *The Sociological Quarterly*, Vol. 36, No. 3, (1995), p. 449.
89 John D. McCarthy and Mayer N. Zald, "Resource Mobilization and Social Movements: A Partial Theory," *American Journal of Sociology*, Vol. 82, No. 5, (1977), pp. 1212–1241.
90 Sidney Tarrow, *Power in Movement*, (Cambridge: Cambridge University Press, 1994), p. 23.
91 Edward Shorter and Charles Tilly, *Strikes in France, 1830–1968*, (Cambridge: Cambridge University Press, 1974), Sidney Tarrow, *Democracy and Disorder: Protest and Politics in Italy, 1965–1975*, (USA: Oxford University Press, 1989).
92 Abdulhadi 1998, Donatella della Porta and Mario Diani, *Social Movements. An Introduction*, (UK: Blackwell, 1999); William A Gamson and David Meyer, "Framing Political Opportunity" in eds. Doug McAdam, John McCarthy, and Mayer Zald, Comparative Perspectives on Social Movements, (New York: Cambridge University Press, 1996). An example where the model fails to offer an adequate explanation for the case studies at hand, see Joel Beinin and Frederic Vairel, *Social Movements, Mobilization, and Contestation in the Middle East and North Africa*, (Stanford: Stanford University Press, 2011).
93 Charles Tilly, *The Contentious French*, p. 10.
94 See also Mark Traugott, "Recurrent Patterns of Collective Action," in *Repertoires and Cycles of Collective Action*, ed. by Mark Traugott, (Durham: Duke University Press, 1995), Ann Swidler, "Culture in Action: Symbols and Strategies," *American Sociological Review*, Vol. 51, No. 2, (1986).
95 Sidney Tarrow, *Power in Movement*, 19.
96 Doug McAdams, "Tactical Innovation and the Pace of Insurgency," *American Sociological Review*, Vol. 48, No. 6, (1983), pp. 735–754; *Freedom Summer*, (Oxford and New York: Oxford University Press, 1988).

97 Maurice Agulhon, *The Republic in the Village. The People of the Var from the French Revolution to the Second Republic*, transl. by Janet Lloyd, (Cambridge: Cambridge University Press, 1982), and Ted Margadant, *French Peasants in Revolt. The Insurrection of 1851*, (Princeton: Princeton University Press, 1979). Both cited in Tarrow, *Power in Movement*.

98 Bruce Fireman, and Steven Rytina, *Encounters with Unjust Authority*, (Homewood. Ill.: Dorsey Press, 1982); Robyn M. Dawes, Anthony J. C. Van de Kragt, and John M. Orbell, "Not Me or Thee But We: The Importance of Group Identity in Eliciting Cooperation in Dilemma Situations; Experimental Manipulations," *Acta Psychologica*, Vol. 68, (1989), pp. 83–97.

99 Bert Klandermans, Hanspeter Kriesi, and Sidney Tarrow, *From Structure to Action: Comparing Social Movement Research Across Cultures, International Social Movement Research, Vol. 1*, (Greenwich, Conn: JAI, 1988); Aldon Morris and Carol McClurg Mueller, eds., *Frontiers of Social Movement Research*, (New Haven and London: Yale University Press, 1992).

100 Jeff Goodwin and James M. Jasper, "Caught in a Winding, Snarling Vine: The Structural Bias of Political Process Theory," *Sociological Forum*, Vol. 14, No. 1, (1999), pp. 27–54.

101 Ibid., pp. 36–39. Other critics included William Gamson et al., "Framing Political Opportunities", 275; Sidney Tarrow, *Power in Movements: Social Movements and Contentious Politics*, (Cambridge: Cambridge University Press, 1998), p. 430.

102 Doug McAdam, Sidney Tarrow, and Charles Tilly, *Dynamics of Contention*, (New York: Cambridge University Press, 2001).

103 See for example Ruud Koopmans, "A Failed Revolution, But a Worthy Cause," *Mobilization*, Vol. 8, (2003), pp. 116–119.

104 Marc Edelman, "Social Movements," p. 292

105 See George. Collier with Elizabeth Lowery Quaratiello, *Basta! Land and the Zapatista Rebellion in Chiapas*, (Oakland: Food & Development Policy, 1994), Neil Harvey, *The Chiapas Rebellion: The Struggle for Land and Democracy*, (Durham: Duke University Press, 1988), John Womack Jr. *Rebellion in Chiapas: An Historical Reader*, (New York: The New Press, 1999), June Nash, "The Fiesta of the World: The Zapatista Uprising and Radical Democracy in Mexico," *American Anthropology*, Vol. 99, No. 2, (1997), pp. 261–274, Manuel Castells, *The Information Age: Economy, Society and Culture, Vol. 2, The Power of Identity*, (Oxford UK: Blackwell, 1977).

106 See Edelman, "Social Movements," 294.

107 Joe Foweraker, *Theorizing Social Movements*, (London: Pluto, 1995).

108 Joel Beinin and Frédéric Vairel, eds., *Social Movements, Mobilization, and Contestation in the Middle East and North Africa*, (Stanford: Stanford University Press, 2011).

109 Resource Mobilization Theory was proposed by many including Doug McAdam, "Recruitment to High-Risk Activism: The Case of Freedom Summer," *American Journal of Sociology*, Vol. 92, No. 1, (1986), pp. 64–90.

110 David A. Snow, Louis A. Zurcher Jr., and Sheldon Ekland-Olson, "Social Networks and Social Movements: A Microstructural Approach to Differential Recruitment," *American Sociological Review*, Vol. 45, No. 5, (1980), pp. 787–801; Steven M. Buechler, *Women's Movements in the United States: Woman Suffrage, Equal Rights, and Beyond*, (New Brunswick, NJ: Rutgers University Press, 1990); Verta Tylor and Nancy E. Whittier, "Collective Identity in Social Movement Communities: Lesbian Feminist Mobilization," in *Frontiers in Social Movement Theory*, ed. Aldon D. Morris and Carol McClurg Mueller, (New Haven: Yale University Press, 1992).

111 See James Scott, *Weapons of the Weak: Everyday Forms of Peasant Resistance*, (New Haven: Yale University Press, 1985).

112 Beinin et al., *Social Movements*, 22.

113 Ibid.

114 Ibid., p. 12.

115 Misagh Parsa, *Social Origins of the Iranian Revolution*, (New Brunswick: Rutgers University Press, 1989).

116 Charles Kurzman, "Structural Opportunity and Perceived Opportunity in Social Movement Theory: The Iranian Revolution of 1979," *American Sociological Review* 61 (1997), pp.153–70.

117 Mansoor Moaddel, " Ideology as Episodic Discourse: The Case of the Iranian Revolution," *American Sociological Review*, Vol. 57, (1992), pp. 353–79.

118 See Richard Ballard et al., "Globalization, Marginalization and Contemporary Social Movements in South Africa," *African Affairs*, Vol. 104, No. 417, (2005), pp. 615–634.

119 Richard Falk, "The Making of Global Citizenship," in *Global Visions: Beyond the New World Order*, ed. by J.B. Childs et al., (Boston: South End, 1993).

120 Barry D. Adam, *The Rise of a Gay and Lesbian Movement*, (New York: Twayne Publishers, 1995); Jeremy Brecher, Tim Costello, and Brendan Smith, *Globalization from Below: The Power of* Solidarity, (Boston: South End, 2000), James I. Charlton, *Nothing About Us Without Us: Disability Oppression and Empowerment*, (Berkeley: University of California Press, 1998).

121 Thomas Risse-Kappen, ed., *Bringing Transnational Relations Back In: Non-State Actors, Domestic Structures and International Institutions*, (Cambridge: Cambridge University Press, 1995).

122 Jackie Smith, Charles Chatfield, Ron Pagnucco, *Transnational Social Movements and Global Politics: Solidarity Beyond the State*, (Syracuse: Syracuse University Press, 1997).

123 Peter Waterman, *Globalization, Social Movements and the New Internationalisms*, (Routledge, 2004).

124 Margaret E. Keck and Kathryn Sikkink, *Activists Beyond Borders. Advocacy Networks in International Politcs*, (Ithaca: Cornell University Press, 1998).

125 Edelman, "Social Movement," p. 305.

126 J A Fox, *Assessing Binational Civil Society Coalition: Lessons from the Mexico-US Experience. Working Paper, No. 26*, (Santa Cruz: Chicano/Latino Res. Cent., University of California, 2000).

127 See Fox, *Assessing Binational*, Keck and Sikkink, *Activists Beyond Borders*.

128 See Arjun Appadurai, "Grassroots Globalization and the Research Imagination," *Public Culture*, Vol. 12, No. 1, (2005), pp. 1–19; Marc Edelman, "Social Movements," Jonathan D. Fox and David L. Brown, *The Struggle for Accountability: The World Back, NGOs, and Grassroots Movements*, (Cambridge: MIT Press, 1998), Akhil Gupta, *Postcolonial Developments: Agriculture in the Making of Modern India*, (Durham: Duke University Press, 1998).

129 See Jeffrey M. Ayres, *Defying Conventional Wisdom: Political Movements and Popular Contention Against North American Free Trade*, (Toronto: University of Toronto Press, 1998); M. Ritchie, "Cross-Border Organizing," in *The Case Against the Global Economy and for a Turn toward the Local*, ed. Jerry Mander and Edward Goldsmith, (San Francisco: Sierra Club, 1997); Marc Edelman, *Peasants Against Globalization: Rural Social Movements in Costa Rica*, (Stanford: Stanford University Press, 1999).

130 Sidney Tarrow, *The New Transnational Activism*, (Cambridge: Cambridge University Press, 2005), p. 3.

131 Sidney Tarrow, *The New Transnational Activism*, p. 25.

132 Ibid.

133 Ibid., p. 29.

3   Challenging democracy

Ethnicity in post-colonial Fiji
and Trinidad

Figure 3.1 Suva, Fiji

Fiji and Trinidad are similar in terms of their colonial and post-colonial historical experiences, yet their political outcomes are different. The argument put forth is that constitutional reforms that were adopted by Fiji were unsuccessful because of systemic conditions specific to the country. Sustained by structural features such as land rights and chiefly jurisdiction, and more intangible factors such as cultural identity and nationalism, ethnic identity is the lens through which most public discourse occurs. By contrast, Trinidad does not have these corresponding institutional structures, and the existence of public spaces for the contestation of ethnic identities together with the construction of hybrid identities at the local and national levels, have contributed towards political stability.

Introduction

Fiji and Trinidad are similar in terms of their colonial and post-colonial historical experiences, yet their political outcomes have been different. On 5 December 2006, Commodore Josaia Voreqe (Frank) Bainimarama of the Republic of Fiji Military Forces staged a bloodless coup and assumed executive control of the Republic of the Fiji Islands. This was the fourth coup since the island became independent in 1970.[1] In contrast, Trinidad and Tobago held its eleventh post-independent elections in May 2010 with the first woman, Kamla Persad-Bissessar, becoming Prime Minister. Her coalition party, the People's Partnership, won twenty-nine of forty-one parliamentary seats and took 59.8 per cent of the vote.[2]

This chapter seeks to investigate what has led to relative political stability in Trinidad and instability in Fiji. Both countries have Westminster political systems that were adapted for local conditions; constitutional modifications were intrinsic to the process leading up to independence and thereafter. In Fiji, the constitution was changed dramatically in 1997 in an effort to establish stronger coalition governments with greater inter-ethnic political cooperation. Despite the fact that political tensions have on occasion threatened to destabilize Trinidad, it hasn't actually occurred, but tensions have led to the suspension of democratic processes in Fiji. Given these outcomes, an abiding question remains: can constitutional and electoral engineering ever overcome the problems faced by Fiji? I argue that it is unlikely because of systemic conditions distinctive to Fiji. These include the following: indigenous Fijians have a generational claim on land and identity giving them a prior stake in the region, and positioning Indo-Fijians as outsiders or recent immigrants whose homeland is always India. In contrast, both Afro-Trinidadians and Indo-Trinidadians are immigrants and this has, to some extent, ensured that ethnic claims have to be bargained for. Further in Fiji, the institution of chiefs contributes to indigenous Fijian identity representing generational connections and a stronger sense of community, and there is no such parallel set of institutions in Trinidad. Adding to this sense of community are land rights that favor indigenous Fijians who jointly own and control Fijian land, placing Indians in the position of being perpetual renters dependent on their hosts. In Trinidad in addition to the historical precedent whereby land was initially given to Indian indentured laborers in lieu of a return passage to India, land continues to be available for purchase by all citizens. In terms of the economy, even though ethnic economic divisions are prevalent in both countries, occupational ethnic divisions are to some degree less prevalent in Trinidad.

Significantly, ethnic political leaders in Fiji have been reticent to fully embrace cross-ethnic coalition building. Even though alliances have governed the country since independence, the leaders in power after the advent of the constitutional amendments, designed to address the lack of solid cross-ethnic governance structures, were slow to move towards moderation. In Trinidad too, ethnic-based parties have dominated politics, but the existence of numerous smaller political parties has demanded coalition arrangements. Finally, a hybrid and distinctive Trinidadian culture and nationalism has evolved – in music, carnival, language, food, inter-marriage, and racial mixing – that to some extent mitigates prolonged ethnic tensions. There are very visible public spaces for the contestation of identity; during carnival and in soca and chutney musical genres, there is constant sparing over ethnic stereotypes. There are no equivalent spaces in Fiji and even though there is evidence of cultural and social overlap, there is less evidence of novel ethnically hybrid identities. Television media and newspapers are largely separated into vernaculars, though all share English.

It must be noted that both Trinidad and Fiji have state nationalisms that to some extent prioritize Afro-Trinidadians and indigenous Fijians, respectively. But even though ethnic identities play a significant role during elections in both countries, inter-ethnic relations are relatively harmonious between election cycles. For this chapter, an important fact is that Trinidad has had eleven democratic elections and neither violent ethnic conflict nor undemocratic changes in government has followed. In contrast, democracy has been derailed on a number of occasions in Fiji, and, though ethnic tensions have not led to sustained violent conflict, these bouts of instability have increased inter-ethnic suspicions.

In sum, constitutional and electoral reforms designed to encourage ethnic political cooperation will not be successful if systemic conditions undermine the trust and commitment required for sustained coalition building. With this in mind, this chapter sets out to highlight these conditions in Fiji, using Trinidad as a comparative framework. Given the ongoing debates around Lijphart's consociational model for ethnically divided societies, and Horowitz's alternative vote option for multi-ethnic societies, this comparative endeavor seeks to show that neither choice has a chance of success if the groundwork for mutual trust and commitment to broader (cross-ethnic) objectives are not well established. This comparison makes visible the notion that the post-colonial modified Westminster system has in fact been quite malleable and conducive to multi-ethnic societies (even if it is sometimes fraught with ethnic tensions), and hence the reasons for continued instability might need to be sought elsewhere. In this case, it includes institutional structures, as well as more intangible factors pertaining to nationalism, citizenship, and identity.

The chapter is framed around a few key comparative variables: intangible factors such as culture and citizenship, structural features including the economy, land, and chiefs, the army, and post-colonial politics. In both countries, culture and identities of the major ethnic groups have evolved to suit local conditions. It will be shown that in Trinidad there is more evidence of cultural hybridity. In terms of institutional structures, besides comparing the economy, which have some similarities, the land policies in Fiji and the role of chiefs are highlighted as distinctively Fijian. Other variables that will be compared are the role of post-independent leaders in defining both societies, the impact of trade unions and other opposition movements (like the Black Power Movement in Trinidad), and the role of the military and post-constitutional reforms in Fiji. Lastly, democratic transitions and the transfer of power in both countries will be compared.

Why Fiji and Trinidad?

Both Trinidad and Fiji were British colonies integrated into the imperial economy through the production of cash crops. Trinidad was colonized in 1797 and joined by Tobago in 1888. Ruled directly until 1925, it became independent in 1962. Fiji came under British rule via a Deed of Cession signed by leading ethnic Fijian chiefs in 1874 and became independent in 1970. About half of the population of each country is Indian, indentured during colonialism to replace emancipated slave labor in Trinidad, and to provide a new source of labor in Fiji. In Trinidad, 134,183 Indians were indentured from 1845 to 1917. By 1946 Indians accounted for about 35 per cent of the population.[3] In Fiji 60,000 Indians were indentured between 1879 and 1916, and by 1945 they outnumbered Fijians. Both countries are islands and roughly the same size in population – Fiji has 837,271 people (2007 Census), while Trinidad has 1,175,523 (2000 Census).

An important difference is that the other large ethnic group in Trinidad is of African descent. When the British took control of Trinidad from the Spanish in 1797, they relied on the trans-Atlantic slave trade for labor. Though British slavery officially ended in 1807, it continued in Trinidad until 1834, with the period of apprenticeship ending in 1838. By then there were 20,657 former slaves in the region, most leaving the plantations for peasant farming and work in towns and cities.[4] The British tried to recruit free Africans from the West Indies, but over a period of 30 years, only 36,000 entered Trinidad. Plantation owners were unwilling to change their exploitative labor practices or to pay higher salaries to free workers, their preference was to maintain previous profit margins that were based on slave labor. With the apprenticeship period still underway, they looked to India for a new source of cheap labor. Indians contributed to the success of the colonial economy but also cheapened labor, making it even more difficult for freed slaves to make a living. This placed them in opposition to Afro-Trinidadians.

Another difference between the two countries is the way in which the British administered Fiji. The first governor, Sir Arthur Hamilton Gordon, ruled Fiji in a way that protected indigenous Fijian interests and culture. Policies like the system of land rights placed land under the control of indigenous Fijians, making it inalienable and immutable. The indenture of Indian laborers to work on the colonial enterprises protected the traditional livelihoods of indigenous Fijians, yet created the conditions that potentially kept the two main ethnic groups apart. Furthering this separation, indigenous Fijians were governed indirectly through their chiefs and a codified system of "customary law", while Indians were ruled directly by the Agent-General of Immigration. There were also some instances when Fijians were instructed by the British not to shelter any runaway indentured Indian laborers; and, where indigenous Fijian labor was used, they were housed separately from Indians and under different contracts.[5] Paradoxically, indentured Indians helped to sustain indigenous Fijian lifestyles, but also perpetuated an economy that inextricably linked Fiji to global capitalist markets.

Democracy in plural societies

The debate over whether democracy is possible in ethnically divided societies is ongoing. Broadly speaking, the pessimistic views espoused by Mills and others propose that democracy in such societies will always be flawed and, in some cases, is not possible.[6] Rabushka and Shepsle conclude that democracy, as it is practiced in the West, cannot be sustained in plural societies.[7]

Opposing these views is M. G. Smith, who argues that democracy in plural societies is possible but requires control and dominance by one group.[8] Van den

Berghe calls this "despotic minority rule,"[9] and Milne suggests that a "stable hegemony of one group over the other" will endure in bipolar ethnic societies.[10] Kuper further cautions that domination by one group always carries the threat of violence towards the other, which can undermine the stability of the democracy.[11] There are numerous situations where this has been the case as in Rwanda, Burundi, Iraq, and Sri Lanka.

Lijphart and Horowitz have taken these theoretical propositions a step further – they offer practical solutions based on the assumption that in ethnically divided societies, it is expedient to incorporate and institutionalize ethnic diversity into the political system. Both their proposals are pertinent to this study because they became the basis for constitutional reforms in Fiji in 1997 and electoral reform in 1999. Lijphart proposed the consociational model based on four key principles: grand elite coalitions (among ethnic leaders representing all segments of society), mutual veto (or concurrent majority rule to protect minority interests), proportionality (proportional representation (PR) as the electoral system), and segmented autonomy (high degree of autonomy for each segment to run their own internal affairs).[12] These arrangements are designed to encourage elite ethnic cooperation, or as Lijphart explains, "government by elite cartel designed to turn a democracy with a fragmented political culture into a stable democracy."[13] Plural societies, he says, "may enjoy stable democratic government if the political leaders engage in coalescent rather than adversarial decision-making."[14] He viewed consociational democracy as the reason why stability existed in Switzerland, Scandinavia, and the Low Countries, all of which were segmented and divided. Indeed, according to him, plural societies face two choices: consociational engineering or no democracy at all.[15]

In an early review essay, Daalder recognized several research tasks that the consociational model had to address in order to be successful: the effects of political culture on consociational systems, the differences between democratic and non-democratic consociationalism, and the capacity for elite cartels to absorb demands for greater popular participation.[16] Even though Lijphart responded to many of his critics, he failed to adequately address some of these factors. Of significance for this chapter are the effects of the Fijian political culture on consociational arrangements, which have tended to undermine the success of shared ethnic leadership. Barry aptly suggested that in ethnically divided societies, there is the possibility of leaders becoming embroiled in battles with rivals within their segments creating the "potential for civil war or of civil war averted by effective oppression by one group of the other."[17] In Fiji, tensions between indigenous Fijian civilian leaders and the military have led to several coups.

Fraenkel draws our attention to the 1994 interim constitution in South Africa that was based on a consociational model. Nelson Mandela and F.W. de Klerk agreed to a power-sharing arrangement to usher in a new majority government.[18] This was however an interim solution, and as Laitin observed earlier, the consociational model was not an option in South Africa where Black majority violence and active political engagement made an elite cartel-like arrangement improbable.[19] In retrospect, Fraenkel says that from the available cases where the consociational model is used, it appears that multiparty cabinets representing a host of minority communities are preferable, and that power-sharing governments need to clearly show accomplishments. Importantly, visionary leaders are required and so is a shift from the oppositional arrangement of the Westminster system. All these criticisms remain relevant to the Fijian experience.

Another innovation in Fijian politics was the adoption of the alternative vote (AV) electoral system, which emphasizes moderation and compromise. Unlike proportional representation, which is based on a single vote made by eligible voters, AV asks the voter to rank candidates on a ballot in order of preference, either their own or based on the recommendations of party leaders. It requires 50 per cent of the vote plus one for victory. Where no candidate receives the required 50 per cent of voters' first preferences, the candidate with the fewest first-preference votes is eliminated and that candidate's second-preference votes are redistributed as if they were first preferences. This process is repeated until a candidate wins. A basic assumption is that parties "assess opportunities afforded by the electoral system to enhance their success at the polls by making vote-pooling arrangements across ethnic line," this leads to greater moderation and compromise.[20] According to Horowitz, AV is more effective in divided societies than proportional representation: "Proportionality is generally indifferent to moderation, and moderation is indifferent to proportionality."[21]

The alternative vote was used in Fiji in 1999 for national parliamentary elections. Fraenkel and Grofman have been critical of the outcomes of AV, and they argue that it hasn't led to moderation; in fact bipolar divisions were exaggerated.[22] Others have also questioned the reasoning behind such voting arrangements, which tend to focus on stability rather than equality. O'Flynn correctly suggests that attention should shift from attempts to regulate conflict between ethnic groups, to developing theories and practices that best match specific societies.[23]

In terms of these theories, it would seem that M. G. Smith's proposition that democracy is possible in plural societies if one group is dominant at state level, rings true for both Trinidad and Fiji in the period following independence until 1986 and 1987, respectively. However, in Fiji it is also possible to argue as Kuper does, that this situation had within it the threat of conflict with the other major ethnic group. Early indigenous Fijian hegemony succeeded in maintaining stability for a period until the coups of 1987 and 2000 when Indians made in-roads into state power. Trinidad challenges the theories of Mills and others in that democracy has been sustained, even though analysts like Meighoo have made convincing arguments that democratic institutions still haven't matured.[24] Fiji adds further evidence for the theoretical propositions that see democracy as unsustainable in plural societies. It also offers an example to critique the propositions of Lijphart and Horowitz illustrating that constitutional engineering and voting arrangements can only be successful (in terms of sustaining democracy through each election period) if other conditions in society have also changed.

Intangible factors: culture and citizenship

In this section, it will be shown that while ethnic groups in both countries have undergone changes over time, in Trinidad there is a greater blurring of boundaries, more noticeable movement towards hybrid and multi-cultural identities, and more indications that a nationalist Trinidadian identity is slowly being constructed. This process is certainly not without challenges and counter-movements. Munasinghe highlights a key problem when she observes that: "Despite the ample empirical evidence that pointed to East Indians mixing with other groups, what is significant . . . is the absence of *social* recognition of such mixing."[25] In both countries ethnic group divisions are pervasive, but there appears to be more instances of inter-ethnic mixing in Trinidad than in Fiji.

In the 1947 Census, indigenous Fijians were 45.5 per cent of the population, and Indians were in the majority at 46.4 per cent. These ratios changed after the various coups, which precipitated an increase in Indian emigration to Australia, New Zealand, Canada, and the United States. In the 2007 Census, indigenous Fijians were 56.8 per cent and Indians 37.5 per cent with predictions that by 2030, the percentages will be 68.3 and 25.9, respectively.[26] Fijian emigration, estimated at 91,000 between 1987 and 2004, is dominated by Indo-Fijians (88–89 per cent) and by skilled professionals.[27] The decreasing numbers of Indians in Fiji suggests that in the long run, it will be strategic for them to rely on multi-ethnic political platforms.

Most indigenous Fijians are Christian, and the Methodist Church is dominant. Hierarchical identity is primarily constructed within the domestic group, and beyond that, it is premised on relations of rank (chiefly or commoner clans), seniority (relative age), and gender.[28] The group identity of indigenous Fijians is challenged from a number of sides. There are ongoing disputes over land use and land distribution.[29] Indigenous Fijians are divided by class, status, regional and sub-cultural differences, and these tensions will continue to impinge on political allegiances and voting patterns in the future.

Religion divides Indo-Fijians into Hindus, Muslims, and Sikhs. Hindus are further divided between those who trace their ancestors to North or South India, and between Gujaratis (from Gujarat) and Punjabis (from Punjab or other parts of India). Early indentured Indians known as "coolies" by the British but calling themselves *girmitiyas* (from the Hindi word *girmit* for the agreement made in the indenture contract), were also divided along the lines of religion, language, caste, and culture. The Indian caste system largely disintegrated with indenture, and what has remained is caste as a constraint on inter-marriage, a source of social esteem, and in some cases, social and cultural avoidances.[30] Various religions organizations have developed, each representing different regional and religious groups.[31] They provide a forum for cultural and political discourses. The result is that Indians have not always voted as a bloc, instead supporting different political parties at different historical junctures. As is true for many in the Indian diaspora, a localized language flourished, and in the case of Fiji it is "Fiji Hindi" – a derivative of Hindi that includes other Indian dialects and Fijian English words.

In Trinidad, according to the 2000 Census, Africans or Afro-Creoles and Indians or East Indians make up 37.5 and 40.0 per cent of the population, respectfully. Afro-Creoles have a diverse heritage that includes former-slaves and their descendants. Part of this group is also of mixed race or Mulattos, mainly of European and African ancestry, who define themselves as distinct from other

Afro-Creoles. There is also a growing Dougla population (racial mixing of Africans and Indians), the exact number is impossible to estimate given that most
individuals in this group choose one of the ethnic groups to identify with.

In terms of religion, Catholics are the largest group (30 per cent), followed by
Hindus (24 per cent), with smaller numbers for other sects.[32] The Presbyterian
Church, following the strong legacy of the Canadian Presbyterian mission (which
entered the region in 1865) in supporting schools and education among Indians,
claimed 50 per cent of Indian professionals in the early 1970's.[33] Bhojpuri, which
is the Hindu dialect of eastern Bihar, is the *lingua franca* of Indians in Trinidad,
who also speak Creole and English.[34] Caste differentiation largely disappeared
and religious practices were standardized over time in favor of a "Sanatan Dharm
style of Hinduism."[35]

An ethnic pattern of marriage tends to exist in both Trinidad and Fiji, although
there is a greater level of mixing in the former. In a study based on San Fernando
in Trinidad in 1971, Clarke found that there was "considerable racial and religious
integration."[36] More recently in her work on the Douglas in Trinidad, Munasinghe
observed that the mixing of the two races (Indian and African), both considered 'inferior' by colonial administrators, demarcated this group as illegitimate and polluted, as
opposed to the assertion of pride associated with Creoles.[37] Moreover, Dougla is not a
collective identity, but an individual one that disappears within the first generation.[38]
Nevertheless, the presence of Douglas illustrates the fact that ethnic groups in Trinidad are not isolated from one another, and social boundaries are more permeable.

Though relations between indigenous Fijians and Indians are amiable, communal attachments are strong. Intermarriage is rare. As Jayawardena puts it: "The
cultures are recognized and co-existent, equal, different."[39] Based on more recent
fieldwork, Trnka claims that there is little contact between the two main groups,
and social interactions are further constrained by Indian concerns over eating
"polluted" food, or food from Fijians or Muslims that might have been contaminated by contact with beef.[40] Although there are a few cases of intermarriage,
"many people in Fiji claim never to have heard of such a thing, much less to
contemplate such a possibility for themselves or for their children"[41] Both major
ethnic groups in Fiji are family oriented, but indigenous Fijians value a communal
lifestyle, while Indians are more individualistic.

In both countries, Indian culture has changed over time. In Fiji for example,
Hindus have shifted from celebrating Holi (a public celebration), to Diwali that
is more family- and community-oriented. Kelly sees this as representing a shift
from a celebratory expression of the destruction of evil, to a more sedate, private
celebration with capitalist "prosperity on hand as God enters Fiji through the pure
hearts of dutiful devotees."[42] Mishra makes a similar observation in his study of
"tazia", which is a Shia festival lamenting the martyrdom of Imam Husain.[43] Initially practiced by Indians in Fiji, it is now slowly disappearing. He suggests that
the practice of tazia "dramatized the potential for an alternative social arrangement" and its decline reflects the "triumph" of bourgeois modernity."[44] Indians
have also adopted some Fijian customs and terminology. For example, Indians
use the Fijian word "talanoa," which means "general conversation" in Fijian,

but connotes "idle chatter" like gossip, when used by Indians.[45] They also drink *yaqona* or grog sitting with friends and kinsmen, but don't practice the Fijian rituals and social norms associated with it. The indigenization of Indian culture has not necessarily led to greater collaboration and mixing with Fijians.

In Trinidad the language and communication used by Indian youth has been 'Creolized' reflecting a localized national identity.[46] Munasinghe shows how conservative Indian leaders and community members have struggled to propagate the notion of Indian 'purity' amidst the reality of an increasingly Creolized Indian culture.[47] A distinctive festival in Trinidad is the annual Carnival, which over the years has reflected increasing Indian Creolization, underplayed by both Afro-Trinidadians and Indians.[48] The heart of the festival is calypso, a predominantly African musical genre that is a force of personal, social, and political commentary and includes attacks on all social groups and political leaders.[49] In recent years, soca (soul-calypso) has become as popular, representing a fusion of African, Indian, and Latin musical forms. Indians have invented chutney-soca, an "Indo-Creolized" version of calypso and carnival culture. Drawing from "Indian folk traditions, devotional songs and film music, as well as from calypso, soca and rap," chutney music is much like its namesake – a crushed mix of fruit, vegetables, and spices.[50] "Pitchakaree" is another Indian cultural invention starting in 1989 as a smaller version of carnival. It serves as a platform for commentaries on Indian life, as well as a forum for songs that respond to the calypso criticisms leveled at Indians. The practice of carnival and other festivals, and the concomitant music and culture, offer public spaces for the contestation of ethnic identity, a place to spar over ethnic stereotypes in a non-violent, highly visible way. Fiji does not have similar spaces, and the political arena, especially during elections, has become the space for ethnic confrontations.

Ravuvu sees the relationship between indigenous Fijians and Indians in terms of *taukei* (indigenous or owner) and *vulagi* (visitor or foreigner), or host and guest, whereby the "host is generally in command, and the guest must comply with the host's requirements if he is to be accepted and accommodated."[51] Trnka further suggests that the historical emphasis by the British of "Fijian paramountcy" has over time been used to "support the claim that indigenous Fijians have a unique, moral right to rule Fiji."[52] The Fijian cultural situation resembles the plural society that Furnivall, Mills, and others have written about, separate ethnic groups that only meet in the marketplace.

Both Indians and Afro-Trinidadians have a Creolized identity and the outer margins of group identities are permeable.[53] In Trinidad, the nation is broadly defined as Creole, but neither Afro-Creoles nor Indians recognize the category of Indo-Creole. In Fiji, indigenous Fijians tend to define the nation, which celebrates indigeneity and underplays the presence of Indians.

Structural features: the economy

Trinidad has maintained a strong economic position in the Caribbean with overall economic growth of over 8 per cent as compared with the regional average of 3.7

per cent.[54] By 1943, oil production accounted for 80 per cent of all exports, and by 2007 it was responsible for 40 per cent of the GDP.[55] The strong economy has provided a source of upward mobility for the main ethnic groups. The lucrative energy sector is dominated by Afro-Creoles, while Indians tend to dominate the private business sector and agriculture. By the 1980s, both groups were level in income[56] Employment and jobs still tend to be divided along ethnic lines. The small European, Chinese, and Syrian communities are mainly in trading, construction, and business. Indian representation is low in public service, although they are highly represented in certain specialized areas like medicine, accounting (40 per cent of all accountants), and engineering (43.7 per cent).[57] As in Fiji, Indians are under-represented in the armed forces constituting 9.84 per cent of army posts and16 per cent of the Coast Guard.[58] Even though some degree of ethnic divisions in the economic arena exist in Trinidad, these divisions do not correlate to class divisions, nor are they replicated in residential areas.[59] Occupation-by-ethnicity is not rigid, and Yelvington noted in his study in the early 1990s, it is being replaced by a "common but permutating class structure . . . produc(ing) cultural practices which are more and more held in common across ethnic boundaries."[60]

In Fiji the economy is racially and ethnically divided. Whites dominate commerce, and foreign companies control the major industries except for sugar, which was nationalized in 1973.[61] In 1966, 45 per cent of indigenous Fijians were still engaged in subsistence agriculture.[62] In the 2007 Census, while 32 per cent of indigenous Fijians and 16 per cent of Indians were living in rural areas, the percentage of indigenous Fijians relying on subsistence only had dropped to 5.9 per cent of the total economically active population and another 5.4 per cent relied on money income as well as subsistence. Amongst Indians, the Gujaratis who arrived as free immigrants from India came to dominate shop-keeping and small businesses. Between 1924 and 1945 they made up 298 of the 557 Indian businesses in Fiji.[63] Over time, Indians monopolized land transport, construction, and wholesale and retail trades. They were also disproportionately employed in professions and professional services like medicine, law, accounting, and banking.[64]

The indigenous Fijian elites are mainly in the public sector; some are part owners of resorts and other enterprises, and others own small-scale agricultural cooperatives. The bulk of the indigenous Fijian population owns relatively little.[65] They are well represented in the government bureaucracy, constituting 62 per cent of all civil service jobs and 85 per cent of top civil service posts.[66] They also make up over 90 per cent of the armed forces; in the 2007 Census, 3517 indigenous Fijians were in the armed forces, and only 23 Indians.[67] Indigenous Fijians have resisted commodity forms and the market economy, even though this situation is changing constantly. Rutz shows that from colonial occupation onwards, there was constant tension between the moral economy and the market economy. The former is based on reciprocity, obligatory communal behavior, and moral sanction, while the later is more individualistic and emphasizes personal consumption and wealth accumulation.[68] Poverty levels in Fiji have been estimated at 45 per cent, up from 2007 when the census reported it as 32 per cent.[69] In Trinidad in 2007, 17 per cent of the population lived below the poverty line.[70] With increasing movement to the urban areas of both indigenous Fijians, who are finding it difficult to sustain a subsistence economy, and Indians, many of whom have lost their land leases, there have been considerable changes in the country's demographics. Rural stagnation, deprivation, inadequate infrastructure, lack of safe water, and few good health services or schools have also precipitated movement to the urban areas.

The economy in both countries is to some extent ethnically divided. In Fiji these divisions are compounded by the land policies that pose a challenge for Indian tenants, and Indian ownership of small businesses creates further tensions in urban areas. Ethnic economic divisions are breaking down in Trinidad, and the country's relative affluence has contributed to greater economic stability.

Structural features: land and chiefs

The ownership and distribution of land in Trinidad and Fiji have contributed to the capacity for stable democratic institutions to survive. In Trinidad, in lieu of a return passage to India after the end of an indenture contract (1869–1879), free Indians were offered 10 and later 5 acres of land. Some 2614 Indians accepted the offer, and 356 Indians purchased crown land. Furthermore, 89,222 acres were sold or granted to Indians between 1885 and 1912, leading to the creation of many free Indian villages.[71] The result was that Indians made the transition from indentured labor to peasant farming, some becoming successful agricultural business owners and others joining the market economy as free laborers.

In contrast, in Fiji about 83 per cent of the total land area is held in inalienable right by indigenous Fijians. In 1918 the Native Lands Commission designated the *mataqali* (roughly equivalent to a clan or lineage) as the unit that owned and controlled this land.[72] By the 1930s, Indians constituted 51 per cent of the population but owned only 2 per cent of the land, while Fijians who were 43 per cent of the population owned 84 per cent of the land.[73] Indians relied mainly on leasing arrangements, and by the 1980s they made up 80 per cent of sugar cane farmers producing 90 per cent of Fiji's sugar.[74] By then, sugar accounted for 15 per cent of the GDP, 60 per cent of exports, and 25 per cent of jobs. Conflict over land management and leasing arrangements (to Indians) has added to ethnic tensions. Indigenous Fijian landowners lease land to tenants through the Native Lands Trust Board (NLTB), and rent is set at a certain percentage of the unimproved land value, with leasing periods for 30 years. The leasing system is structured in a way that gives 20 per cent of rents received to the NLTB, 30 per cent to the chiefs, and 50 per cent is distributed between the remaining clan members. The small payments received by most members of owning clans, and the lack of information provided to them regarding this allocation system, has added to misguided perceptions about their lessees. Some feel that Indians are paying too little, but they make disproportionately more. Many leases were not renewed after they expired, resulting in lower levels of sugar production, increasing poverty in both ethnic groups, greater movement away from rural areas, and increasing emigration.

Fijian chiefs constitute a distinct institution; their power is more symbolic and advisory, but their elevated status has helped some to make economic gains in the capitalist economy. Chiefs represent a diverse array of cultural variations, and they are all represented in the Bose Levu Vakaturaga (BLV or Great Council of Chiefs). Under the previous constitutions, they had a strong role in dealing with issues pertaining to land and indigenous Fijian customs. They were also influential in the Department of Fijian Affairs and had the authority to remove the president of Fiji. After the last coup, the Great Council was suspended, as was the constitution, and chiefs have been marginalized by the new leaders. Through the years the number of chiefs in national politics has been declining, but as Tuimaleali'ifano argues, this is not due to diminishing Fijian support for their chiefs, but rather because of "intense competition among rival candidates for chiefly titles."[75] Even though chiefly authority endures in Fiji, education, worldly experience, and church involvement, have become important in political leadership battles.

The chiefly system has on occasion provided the basis for political mobilization. For example, the Conservative Alliance – Matanitu Vanua (or CAMV) that included leaders from the three confederacies to which all Fijian chiefs belong – merged with the Soqosoqo Duavata ni Lewenivanua Party (SDL or United Fiji Party) of the incumbent Prime Minister Laisenia Qarase, to win the elections of 2006 (80 per cent of indigenous Fijians voted for this alliance). Their joint political platform included affirmative action for indigenous Fijians, perceived as a means to address systemic disadvantages that kept indigenous Fijians in an economically backward position.[76] Fijian chiefs have symbolic power that sustains communal cultural lifestyles and indigenous identity, even though these are changing consistently.

Post-colonial democratic systems

Trinidad gained independence from Britain in 1962, and Fiji in 1970. Both countries adopted variations of the Westminster systems. A distinctive feature of the post-colonial system in Trinidad was the role played by the first Prime Minister, Eric Williams. He created the People's National Movement (PNM) and mobilized a majority behind its agenda. Williams strongly opposed communal representation advocated by Indian leaders, instead insisting on a common voters roll. Even though he often talked about the need for a united Trinidadian nation, he was pro Afro-Trinidadian and Indian leaders mobilized for greater representation throughout his tenure. A charismatic and pragmatic leader, Williams was also an authoritarian. It can however be argued that the centralized structure and Trinidadian nationalism that he mobilized steered the country towards greater stability.[77] The PNM dominated politics until 1986 and maintained a two-thirds majority until Williams' death in 1981. Throughout this period, the party faced a weak and fragmented opposition.

The Alliance Party led by Ratu Sir Kamisese Mara dominated the post-independence period in Fiji. In power from 1966 to 1987 (except for a brief period of 4 days in April 1977), Ratu Mara led a government that was largely pro-indigenous Fijian. By the 1987 elections, the rise of the Indian-dominated Fiji Labour Party (FLP) presented a challenge. Forming a coalition with the National

Federation Party, it won majority seats in the House of Representatives and Dr. Timoci Bavadra became Prime Minister of a multi-ethnic parliament. He held office for a month before he was ousted by a coup.

The strong labor movement in Trinidad contributed to elevating class over race and ethnicity. As early as 1919 for example, workers from both ethnic groups engaged in spontaneous strike action in part mobilized by the Trinidad Working-men's Association. By 1934 it had a membership of 130,000.[78] The trade union movement in Fiji was formally recognized in 1942 when the Department of Labor was created, and the number of unions rapidly increased from three the previous year to fifteen by 1949.[79] With fewer possibilities for political participation, Indian leaders used the union movement as a source of political mobilization. The Fijian labor movement led to the formation of several political parties, but the divisions along ethnic lines continued to undermine class as an organization tool.

Early post-independent Trinidad also experienced resistance from a Black Power movement, albeit a relatively short-lived oppositional front. For a brief period starting in late 1969 and ending in May 1970, the National Joint Action Committee (NJAC) organized across ethnicities to oppose the Williams government.[80] Opposition to Williams' authoritarian rule and the subsequent call for constitutional reform was undertaken by many social and political movements, some of the most powerful being the United Labor Front, the Democratic Action Congress, and the Tapia House Movement. Even though opposition was fractured, opposition movements were robust and consistent, and contributed towards a sustained critique of the ruling party.

The role played by Ratu Mara (especially between 1966 and 1987) cemented indigenous Fijian hegemony, as did Eric Williams (between 1970 and 1986) for Afro-Trinidadians in Trinidad. Yet the period following their rule was different in each. In Trinidad, the presence of a strong trade union movement and other oppositional groups (even within the Afro-Trinidadian community) challenged the power of Williams and the PNM, and created the precedent for strong civil opposition. In contrast, several systemic features supported Ratu Mara's administration, but there was less opposition from within the indigenous Fijian community.

Recent politics and the sustainability of democracy

In Trinidad, political power shifted from the PNM in 1986 when 67 per cent of the electorate voted for the multi-ethnic National Alliance for Reconstruction (NAR). The NAR was an alliance of progressive organizations that hoped to address some of the negative consequences of sustained PNM rule. In 1995 Basdeo Panday, an Indian and head of the United National Congress (UNC), became the fifth Prime Minister of Trinidad, and the UNC won a second term in 2000. In 2007 the multi-ethnic Congress of the People (COP) challenged the bi-party system by winning 22.64 per cent of the votes. And in 2010 the People's Partnership won the elections.

These political transitions bode well for democracy in Trinidad, yet challenges remain. For example, under the Westminster system the party that wins also gets the most number of seats in the bicameral Parliament, even if the margin of victory was small. Furthermore, a third party that makes substantial gains is left unrepresented in the government, as was the case in 2007. The first-past-the-post electoral system and the constitutional primacy given to the Prime Minister, favors the ethnic party in power and marginalizes the other ethnic group. One of the weaknesses of the political system in Trinidad is the dearth of disciplined and durable national political parties.[81] The current political coalition includes COP, NJAC, the Tobago Organization of the People (TOP), and the Movement for Social Justice (MSJ). The way in which the coalition is managed will surely be a test for the longevity of the government.

While political mobilization in Trinidad is largely ethnically based, it is "not for ethnic ends."[82] Meighoo for example sees the real danger in Trinidad as "malaise, dysfunction, apathy, and anomie."[83] Violent conflict has not occurred, but there has been an increase in crime, suicide, and divorce. Overall the impact of intangible factors mentioned earlier, have had a positive effect on national politics. Leaders are cognizant of the changing nature of ethnic identities, and have been more willing to compromise and appeal to cross-ethnic constituencies, as was the case with the victory of Kamla Persad-Bissessar in 2010.

Fijian politics has been rocked by instability ever since the elections of 1987 when the multi-racial coalition government was formed. In many of the coups that followed, the military played a pivotal role. An underlying reality of Fijian history has been the professionalization and increasing power and prestige of the Republic of Fiji Military Forces (RFMF). First fighting on behalf of the British, and thereafter actively participating in United Nations peacekeeping initiatives, the RFMF has become a formidable force. By 1987 it consisted of "2,600 men, three infantry battalions, several small supporting units and a 100-man navy."[84] The military acts as a third force – the "arbiter of government and guardian of the constitution."[85]Ratuva argues that the military has moved between two positions: its professional duty to protect the "civic and national spirit," and its ideological leanings to act as the guardian of indigenous Fijian interests.[86] The Fiji military is part of the elite power structure, and their role in the various coups in Fiji reflects this strategic position.

Another significant development during this period was the appointment of a Constitutional Review Commission in 1995, leading to the adoption of the Constitution Bill on 3 July 1997 by the House of Representatives. To promote a multi-ethnic government, and recognizing the history of ethnic divisions in Fiji, the committee proposed a combination of two political science perspectives – the "Horowitz approach to electoral system design meshed together with the Lijphartian recommendation of top-level power-sharing among elite."[87] The new constitution included a 71-seat House of Representatives, with 23 seats reserved for candidates elected by indigenous Fijians, 19 elected by Indians, 1 by Rotumans and 3 from smaller racial and ethnic groups. In other words, a communal system prevailed. However, 25 seats were elected from all communities registered on the open electoral roll. This system encouraged leaders to engage in coalition building. The 32-member Senate, appointed by the president, was loaded towards indigenous Fijian representation.

The elections of May 1999 were the first to be held under the new constitution, and resulted in victory for the "People's Coalition" made up of the FLP, the Party of National Unity (PANU), and the Fijian Association Party (FAP). Labor won 37 of 71 seats in the House of Representatives and an Indian, Mahendra Pal Chaudhry was appointed Prime Minister. These results affirmed the fact that both constitutional engineering and the alternative vote had enabled elite power sharing. Yet a year later on 19 May 2000, George Speight, a disaffected businessman, took the Prime Minister and his cabinet hostage for 56 days. Speight was eventually arrested and imprisoned, and in 2001 the Court of Appeal restored the 1997 constitution. This coup does not disprove the success of constitutional changes; it does highlight weaknesses in the Fijian socio-political system that enabled a civilian, albeit one with ties to conservative political groups, to brazenly execute a plan to take the government hostage This led to military intervention on 29 May 2000 under Commodore Bainimarama, who declared martial law but did not reinstate Chaudhry. Instead, he appointed an "obscure senator and banker from Lau, Laisenia Qarase" as interim Prime Minister, who went onto win the elections held in 2001.[88]

The elections of 2006 led to a narrow SDL (Soqosoqo ni Duavata ni Lewenivanua Party) victory and the creation of a government that included the FLP in a multi-party cabinet. Even though this parliament resembled a consociational model, it also reflected the lack of will among the leaders to embrace consociational arrangements. Prior to the 2006 elections, the SDL introduced the controversial Promotion of Reconciliation, Tolerance, and Unity Bill, which included a clause that would allow former coup leaders to apply for amnesty. Although the bill was shelved just before the elections, it further polarized the electorate. In the immediate aftermath of the electoral victory of the SDL, Qarase asked the leader of the Labor Party to join him in a coalition government in line with the 1997 constitution. Even though nine Labor Party members were given cabinet positions, Chaudhry refused to take an official position instead pushing to be the parliamentary opposition leader. Qarase, still cognizant of the demands made by his conservative allied partners, refused to take an unequivocal conciliatory stance. There was also increasing tension between the army and the administration.

The December coup of 2006 clearly exposed the growing power struggles among indigenous Fijians, between army and civilian leaders. Bainimarama pledged to clean up and root out corruption, and to investigate alleged fraudulent practices in the Native Land Trust Board and the Fiji National Provident Fund. By implementing this coup he had effectively acted against the majority of indigenous Fijians who voted for the SDL – in the May 2006 election, four out of every five Fijians had voted SDL.[89] He was also opposed by many of the labor unions, most of the leading chiefs of the Great Council of Chiefs, and the Methodist Church.

Conclusion

Constitutional engineering, communal representation, and the alternative vote electoral system, has not led to greater political stability in Fiji. Yet in Trinidad, where there have been fewer changes to the electoral process and common representation is the norm, relative political stability prevails. This paper has argued that the reasons for political instability in Fiji lie in systemic conditions that include structural and more intangible forces. Land Rights and the chiefly system, together with economic and cultural distinctions, have encouraged political leaders to rely on ethnic mobilization and to display a reticence to embrace cross-ethnic coalitions.

In Trinidad, while the PNM had been in power for most of the time following independence, a coalition government with strong Indian support led the country in 1986. In 1995 and 2010, Indians became Prime Ministers. Furthermore in 2007 the Congress of the People, a splinter group from the predominant Indian United National Congress, mobilized on a multi-ethnic political platform and won nearly a third of the votes, and in 2010 a multi-ethnic coalition government won the majority vote. The Westminster bi-cameral system has problems and ethnic divisions prevail, but it is clear that intangible factors like increasing cultural hybridity has made rigid ethnic categorization fuzzy and ethnic political mobilization more challenging.

In both countries, the policies pursued by British colonialists determined the political framework of these nascent states. In Fiji the policy to maintain the coherence of Fijian communities gave way to land and cultural policies that over time kept many indigenous Fijians isolated from the market economy and capitalist competition. Indentured Indians took the lead in economic and professional achievement, despite the prohibition from purchasing land. The coups have also exposed tensions among indigenous Fijians – especially between the military and the traditional leaders. Even though indigenous Fijians have been in power for most of the post-independent period, the country has not been stable.

Indian leaders have not been above the fray, and they have shown a general lack of will to engage in real collaboration. Few speak Fijian; there seems to be a superficial understanding of indigenous Fijian cultural practices, and the personal ambitions of leaders have clearly been detrimental to long-term compromises. Indigenous Fijian leaders too have played on xenophobic fears. This comparison also suggests that a reformed Westminster system can work in multi-ethnic societies, if the social and economic fabric of civil society makes shifts towards greater collaboration and ethnically hybrid identities. Furthermore, systemic features must be more malleable to encourage and allow for greater inter-ethnic collaboration and change.

Notes

1 For the purposes of the paper, the December 1987 coup or "palace coup" is not counted as the removal of an elected government.
2 Henceforth called Trinidad. Tobago is smaller than Trinidad, and joined it in 1888 forming a single Crown Colony. Tobago is populated mainly with people of African descent and this paper is based on the study of interactions between the main ethnic groups.
3 Bridget Brereton, *Race Relations in Colonial Trinidad, 1870–1900* (Cambridge: Cambridge University Press, 1979), p. 9.

4 Hugh Tinker, *A New System of Slavery. The Export of Indian Labour Oversees, 1830–1920* (London: University of Oxford Press, 1974), p. 15.
5 See John D. Kelly, "Threats to Difference in Colonial Fiji, Cultural Anthropology," Vol. 10, No. 1 (1995), pp. 64–84.
6 John Stuart Mills, *Considerations on Representative Government* (New York: Liberal Arts Press, 1958), p. 230.
7 Alvin Rabushka and Kenneth A. Shepsle, *Politics in Plural Societies: A Theory of Democratic Instability* (Columbus: Charles E. Merrill Publishing Company, 1972), p. 92.
8 See Leo Kuper and M.G. Smith, eds., *Pluralism in Africa* (Berkeley: University of California Press, 1969).
9 Pierre Van den Berghe, "Pluralism and the Polity: A Theoretical Exploration," in *Pluralism in Africa*, p. 79.
10 Robert Stephen Milne, *Politics in Ethnically Bipolar States: A Comparative Exploration* (New Haven: Yale University Press, 1977), pp. 17–18.
11 Leo Kuper, "Some Aspects of Violent and Nonviolent Political Change in Plural Societies", in *Pluralism in Africa*.
12 Arend Lijphart, "Consociation and Federation: Conceptual and Empirical Links," *Canadian Journal of Political Science*, Vol. 12, No. 3 (1979), pp. 499–515.
13 Arend Lijphart, "Consociational Democracy," *World Politics*, Vol. 21. No. 2 (1969): p. 216.
14 Arend Lijphart, *Democracies in Plural Societies: Comparative Exploration* (New Haven: Yale University Press, 1977), p. 99.
15 Lijphart, *Democracies in Plural Societies*, p. 238.
16 Hans Daalder, "The Consociational Democracy Theme," *World Politics*, Vol. 26, No. 4 (1974). For a good overview of the debate, see Ian S. Lustick, "Lijphart, Lakatos, and Consociationalism," *World Politics*, Vol. 50, No. 1, (2007), Fiftieth Anniversary Special Issue.
17 Brian Barry, "Political Accommodation and Consociational Democracy," *British Journal of Political Science*, Vol. 5, No. 4, (1975): 504–505.
18 Jon Fraenkel, "Multiparty Cabinet and Power-Sharing: Lessons from Elsewhere," in Jon Fraenkel and Stewart Firth, eds., *From Election to Coup in Fiji: The 2006 Campaign and its Aftermath*, (Canberra:ANU Press, 2007).
19 David Laitin, "South Africa: Violence, Myth, and Democratic Reform," *World Politics* Vol. 39. No. 2, (1987).
20 Donald L. Horowitz, "Where have all the parties gone? Fraenkel and Grofman on the alternative vote – yet again," *Public Choice*, Vol. 133, No. 13 (2007): 16.
21 Donald L. Horowitz, "Electoral Systems: A Primer for Decision Makers," *Journal of Democracy*, Vol. 14, No. 4 (2003): p. 123.
22 See Jon Fraenkel and Bernard Grofman, "The Failure of the Alternative Vote as a Tool for Ethnic Moderation in Fiji: A Rejoinder to Horowitz," *Comparative Political Studies*, Vol. 39, (2006); Jon Fraenkel and Bernard Grofman, "Does the Alternative Vote Foster Moderation in Ethnically Divided Societies?" *Comparative Political Studies*, Vol. 39 (2006); Jon Fraenkel and Bernard Grofman, "The Merits of Neo-Downsian Modeling of the Alternative Vote: A reply to Horowitz," *Public Choice*, Vol. 133, No. 1–2 (2007).
23 See Ian O'Flynn, "Review Article: Divided Societies and Deliberative Democracy," *British Journal of Political Science*, Vol. 37 (2007).
24 See Kirk Meighoo, *Politics in a Half Made Society. Trinidad and Tobago 1925–2001*, (Oxford: James Currey Publishers, 2003).
25 Viranjini Munasinghe, "Nationalism in Hybrid Spaces: The Production of Impurity out of Purity," *American Ethnologist*, Vol. 29, No. 3 (2002): 679.
26 Fiji Islands Bureau of Statistics, Statistical News, No. 45, (15 October 2008), accessed on 26 January, 2011, www.spc.int/prism/country/fj/stats/

27 See Brij V. Lal, "Migration Information Source – Fiji Island: From Immigration to Emigration, 2003," accessed on January 20, 2011, www.migrationinformation.org/Profiles/display.cfm?ID=110

28 Lynda Newland, "The Role of the Assembly of Christian Churches in Fiji in the 2006 elections," in Fraenkel and Firth, eds., *From Election to Coup*, on p. 302. Also see Cristina Toren, "Making the Present, Revealing the Past: The Mutability and Continuity of Tradition as Process," *Man, New Series*, Vol. 23, No. 4, (1988).

29 Stephanie Lawson, "The Myth of Cultural Homogeneity and Its Implications for Chiefly Power in Fiji," *Comparative Studies in Society and History*, Vol. 32, No. 4, (1990), pp. 818–819.

30 Chandra Jayawardena, "Culture and Ethnicity in Guyana and Fiji," *Man, New Series* Vol. 15, No. 3, (1980): 436.

31 See Jonathan Prasad, "The Role of Hindu and Muslim Organizations During the 2006 Election," Fraenkel and Firth, *From Election to Coup*.

32 Ibid., p. 27.

33 See Yogendra K. Malik, "Socio-Political Perceptions and Attitudes of East Indian Elites in Trinidad," *The Western Political Quarterly*, Vol. 23, No. 3, (1970).

34 Steven Vertovec, *Hindu Trinidad. Religion, Ethnicity and Socio-Economic Change*, (London: Macmillan Education, 1992), p. 94.

35 Ibid., 111.

36 Colin G. Clarke, "Residential Segregation and Intermarriage in San Fernando, Trinidad," *Geographical Review*, Vol. 61, No. 2, (1971): 210.

37 See Viranjini Munasinghe, "DOUGLA LOGICS. East Indians, Miscegenation, and the National Imaginary," in Susan Koshy and R. Radhakrishnan, eds., *Transnational South Asians. The Making of a Neo-Diaspora*, (Oxford: Oxford University Press, 2008).

38 See Ibid. and Viranjini Munasinghe, *Callaloo or Tossed Salad? East Indians and the Cultural Politics of Identity in Trinidad*, (Ithaca: Cornell University Press, 2001).

39 Jayawardena, "Culture and Ethnicity," p. 442.

40 See Susanna Trnka, *State of Suffering. Political Violence and Community Survival in Fiji*, (Ithaca: Cornell University Press, 2008).

41 Ibid., p. 33.

42 John D. Kelly, "From Holi to Diwali: An Essay on Ritual and History," *Man, New Series*, Vol. 23, No. 1, (1988): 49.

43 See Sudesh Mishra, "TAZIA FIJI! The place of Potentiality," in Koshy and Radhakrishnan, *Transnational South Asians*, pp. 71–94.

44 Ibid., p. 77.

45 See Donald Brenneis, "Grog and Gossip in Bhatgaon: Style and Substance in Fijian Indian Conversation," *American Ethnologist*, Vol. 11, No. 3, (1984).

46 See Aisha Khan, "What is 'a Spanish'? Ambiguity and 'mixed' ethnicity in Trinidad," in Kevin A. Yelvington (ed), *Trinidad Ethnicity*, (Knoxville: The University of Tennessee Press, 1993).

47 See Munasinghe, *Callaloo or Tossed Salad?*.

48 See Munasinghe, "Nationalism in Hybrid Spaces;" and "Theorizing World Culture through the New World: East Indians and Creolization," *American Ethnologist*, Vol. 33, No. 4, (2006).

49 See Gordon Rohlehr, *Calypso and Society in Pre-Independent Trinidad*, (Port of Spain: Trinidad, 1990).

50 Tina K. Ramnarine, ""Indian" Music in the Diaspora: Case Studies of "Chutney" in Trinidad and London," *British Journal of Ethnomusicology* 5 (1996).

51 Asesela Ravuvu, *The Façade for Democracy: Fijian Struggles for Political Control*, (Suva: Reader Publishing House, 1991), pp. 59–60.

52 Trnka, *State of Suffering*, p. 52.

53 See Munasinghe, " Nationalism in Hybrid Spaces."

54 https://www.cia.gov/library/publications/the-world-factbook/geos/td.html, accessed January 20, 2011.
55 https://www.cia.gov/library/publications/the-world-factbook/geos/fj.html, accessed January 20, 2011.
56 See Ralph R. Premdas, "Ethnic Conflict, Inequality and Public Sector Governance in Trinidad and Tobago," in Bangura, *Ethnic Inequalities*. Also see Kevin A. Yelvington, "Ethnicity at Work in Trinidad," in Ralph R. Premdas, *The Enigma of ETHNICITY: An Analysis of Race in the Caribbean and the World*, (Trinidad and Tobago: University of West Indies, 1993); and Jack Harewood and Ralph Henry, *Inequality in a Post-Colonial Society: Trinidad*, (Trinidad: Institute of Economic and Social Research, University of West Indies, 1985).
57 Premdas, "Ethnic Conflict, Inequality and Public Sector Governance," p. 103.
58 Ibid., p. 106.
59 See Clarke, "Residential Segregation."
60 Yelvington, "Ethnicity at Work in Trinidad," p. 100.
61 Robert Norton, *Race and Ethnic Politics in Fiji*, (New York: St. Martin's Press, 1977), p. 16.
62 Ibid., p. 11.
63 John D. Kelly, "Fiji Indians and "Commoditization of Labor,"" *American Ethnologist*, Vol. 19, No. 1, (2002), p. 100.
64 See Ibid.
65 See Ibid.
66 Fraenkel, "Regulating Bipolar Divisions," p. 82.
67 See Yusuf Bangura, "Introduction: Ethnic Inequalities and Public Sector Governance," in Bangura, *Ethnicity*, p. 10.
68 See Henry J. Rutz, "Capitalizing on Culture: Moral Ironies in Urban Fiji," *Comparative Studies in Society and History*, Vol. 29, No. 3, (1987).
69 Fiji Times, April 21, 2010.
70 www.nationmaster.com/country/td-trinidad-and-tobago/eco-economy, accessed January 20, 2011.
71 See Munasinghe, *Callaloo or Tossed Salad?*, p. 90.
72 See Stephanie Lawson, *The Failure of Democratic Politics*, (Oxford: Clarendon Press, 1991).
73 Ibid., p. 539.
74 Brij V. Lal, *Islands of Turmoil. Elections and Politics in Fiji*, (Canberra: Australian National University Press, 2006), p. 28.
75 Morgan Tuimaleali'ifano, "Indigenous Title Disputes: What it Meant in the 2006 Election," in Fraenkel and Firth, *From Election to Coup*, 264.
76 See Alumita Durutalo, "Defending the Inheritance: The SDL and the 2006 Elections," in Fraenkel and Firth, *From Election to Coup*, pp. 78–88.
77 See Kirk Meighoo and Peter Jamadar, *Democracy and Constitutional Reform in Trinidad and Tobago*, (Kingston: Ian Randle Publishers, 2008).
78 See Selwyn Ryan, *Race and Nationalism in Trinidad and Tobago. A study of Decolonization in a Multicultural Society*, (Toronto, Buffalo: University of Toronto Press, 1972).
79 Lawson, *Failure of Democratic Politics*, p. 159.
80 See Ivar Oxaal, *Race and Revolutionary Consciousness. A Documentary Interpretation of the 1970 Black Power Revolt in Trinidad*, (Cambridge, Massachusetts: Schenkman Publishing Company, 1971).
81 Ibid.
82 Meighoo and Jamadar, *Democracy and Constitutional Reform*, p. 148.
83 Meighoo, *Politics in a Half Made Society*, p. 272
84 Andrew Scobell, "Politics, Professionalism, and Peacekeeping: An Analysis of the 1987 Military Coup in Fiji," *Comparative Politics*, Vol. 26, No. 2, (1994): 190.

85 Ibid., p. 195.
86 Steven Ratuva, "The Pre-Election "Cold War,"" in Fraenkel and Firth, *From Election to Coup*, p. 30.
87 Robert Norton, "Understanding Fiji's Political Paradox," in Fraenkel and Firth, *From Election to Coup*, p. 441.
88 Michael Field, "The Media and the Specter of the 2000 Coup," in Fraenkel and Firth, *From Election to Coup*, p. 179.
89 Jon Fraenkel, "Melanesia in Review: Issues and Events, 2007: Fiji," *The Contemporary Pacific*, Vol. 20, No. 2, (2008), p. 454.

4 Mauritius and the Indian diaspora

The main argument in this book revolves around the implications of location on the national identities of indentured Indians. As a diaspora that was created through indenture, Indians experience a distancing and marginalization from both their motherland (India) and homeland (former British colonies), this displacement from both states situates them in a *transnational locality*. It if from this placement that Indians construct their identities reacting to their status as perpetual outsiders, ethnic others, non-indigenous and un-assimilated residents. Given that Indo-Mauritians are a majority, constituting 68 per cent of the population, do these propositions regarding displacement still hold – it other words, are Indo-Mauritians affected by diaspora identities that define them as perpetual ethnic outsiders? The position taken in this chapter is that like indentured Indians throughout the diaspora, Indo-Mauritians have ambiguous relationships, in terms of identity, with India and Mauritius. Here it is argued that Indo-Mauritian identity is as much about the minority Creole peoples as it is about diaspora connections with India; the strengthening of relations with India are employed to bolster Mauritian-Hindu hegemony in the state, but the desire to claim purity, authenticity and ancestral heritage represents an effort to substantiate their position in the nation, where identity contestations are most intense. The legacies of slavery and indenture under three European powers (Dutch, French, and English) left behind structural and institutional memories of racism, Whiteness, social and cultural hierarchies, and social divisions of difference variously defined in terms of race, ethnicity, religion, language, gender, generation, and class. These histories continue to define the Mauritian state and conceptions of nation and citizenship. Colonial administrations in tandem with global capitalism created institutional structures that met their needs for labor; these new centralized administrations were unchallenged by pre-colonial structures (of which there were none) or by aboriginal social systems. The ancestors of the current peoples in Mauritius were slaves, indentured laborers, and immigrants.

A noticeable difference between Indians as a minority (as in South Africa) and as a large majority (as in Mauritius) is that in the former a concerted effort is made to express indigenized-Indian identities and weak ties with India, whereas in the latter connections and continuities with India are emphasized. Indo-Mauritians underplay evidence of their indigenous/Creolized/hybridized identities even though the majority among them speak Mauritian-Creole, and about a quarter of the population speaks Mauritian-Bhojpuri. Indo-Mauritians have ensured that the "ancestral languages" of Hindi, Tamil, Telegu, Urdu, Marathi, and Arabic, which are rarely spoken among them, are taught in schools. Furthermore Indo-Mauritians claim to have deeper historical and cultural roots by associating with India, they claim authenticity that elevates and sets them apart from Creoles. Ultimately both Indians and Creoles are diaspora communities, as in Trinidad, the majority of Indians arrived as indentured laborers on the Island between 1834 and 1919 and Africans entered as slaves under the Dutch in 1638, during French rule from 1715 and under British colonialism from 1810 until the mid to late 1920s. Slavery was abolished in 1835. By this time the Afro-Mauritians population (including minority Creole or colony-born) were in the majority, constituting two-thirds of the population. Within 36 years (by 1871) indentured Indians became the majority making up two-thirds of the population.[1]

In Trinidad, Creoles claim indigeneity and hence hegemony, whereas in Mauritius they are politically and socially marginalized. The Mauritian-Hindu-dominated state is democratic with protections and rights for citizens, but it also subjects the majority of Creoles, who constitute about one-third of the population,[2] to the borders of society where poverty, low wages, and under-employment define them as a "social disease," locally referred to as "*le malaise Créole.*"[3] Using the distinction that Chatterjee makes between civil society (citizens with rights and who mobilize through civic organizations) and political society (those who are not rights-bearing citizens in the former sense), Creoles can best be understood as being part of political society. They operate through 'illegal' and extra-parliamentary spaces that are frowned upon by the state – they engage in squatting, spontaneous protest, overt and covert resistance to the norms of society, "unruly" behavior like consuming an excess of alcohol and indulging in *sega* music and dancing, and speaking Mauritian Kreol.[4] Despite having roots in Africa (mainly Mozambique, East Africa, and Madagascar) Creoles have maintained separateness and distance from the Africa, there has been little concerted political organization among them, and they are structurally in weak economic and political positions.

Mauritius brings to the fore some of the most significant differences between slavery and indenture. As articulated in Chapters One and Two, the violence of slavery resulted in a rupture, disjuncture, and displacement that defined a diaspora identity severed from the African mainland. In every location across the world the African diaspora was defined by displacement and subjugation; yet for a sizable portion of the African slaves in Mauritius, who were from Madagascar, the close proximity and intercommunication between the two islands made the transition less distant, but equally alienating. Malagasy was widely spoken, and communities retained cultural customs even though the overarching framework of slavery violently severed them from their motherland.[5] The institutionalization of Kreol by the Catholic Church and the French administrations, together with the individualism and insularity perpetuated by these oppressive political and social institutions, undermined Malagasy and connections with the motherland. After abolition, indentured Indians replaced freed men and women, and while this kind of bonded labor shared similar institutions to slavery, it also included checks and balances that made it markedly different. Bonded labor in the form of indenture had regulations for recruitment, transportation, and labor contracts in the colonies. Like slavery it was premised on racism, on notions of Western modernity, on the elevation of Christianity over all other religions, and on sentiments of superiority associated with the Enlightenment and Whiteness. People of color were relegated to the position of the uncivilized, 'traditional' or 'pre-modern,' enabling their exploitation and violent subjugation. However the legacy of slavery eviscerated selfhood and undermined a united sense of community; even though indenture also destroyed individual relations to family, friends, neighbors, and fellow citizens in India, it nevertheless allowed for a sense of belonging (however distant and weak) to the motherland. To some extent the relative success of Indians throughout the diaspora can be traced to this imagined or real relationship. This is also a relationship that was propagated by host-nations, by demarcating Indians as ethnic others they presume a lasting identification with India.

Indians in Mauritius have defined their identities in terms of authenticity, purity, and high culture in opposition to Creole hybridity/mixed race or ethnicity, and indigenized cultures that celebrate local and national versions of dance, language, and music. By institutionalizing closer connections to India, Mauritian-Indians distance themselves from Creoles despite being "Creolized" themselves. Indians speak Mauritian-Creole or Mauritian Bhojpuri; both languages are 'mixed' and indigenous to Mauritius. While it can be argued that successful globalization has reified class divisions and hence pushed more Indians into the middle classes and more Creoles into the poorer classes, the situation is more complex. At some level racial suspicions still haunt this country – Indians who were also once subjugated in indentured servitude are now rulers of the country. The political and cultural institutions of colonialism have not been eradicated but rather continue to exist, albeit in different forms. Racial divisions between Franco-Mauritians (White), Indo-Mauritians, and Creoles are replicated within the various groups where divisions along the lines of religion, language, ethnicity, and class prevail.

In South Africa Indians were defined as outsiders under colonialism, in the settler colonial state, under apartheid, and in the current democratic system – always associated with India and outsiders in Africa. In Mauritius the majority Indo-Mauritians have chosen to define themselves in terms of India and have distanced themselves from Africa, the continent to which they belong. From the time of indenture Indians were positioned as outsiders replacing freed slaves in the sugar plantations – scab labor that undercut wages and undermined local efforts to establish independent economies, and to survive outside the hegemonic colonial system. Colonial administrators and estate managers deliberately used Indian labor to maintain low production costs, and to undercut the bargaining position of freed Africans and Creoles. Indians in turn survived by using this forced insularity to develop strong community attachments and to recreate and reinstitute cultural 'traditions' and customs that they had practiced back in India, albeit in conditions where concepts of caste, class, region, religion, and language, that were located in India, were either contaminated, undermined, adulterated, and/or destroyed. From the time of the passage from India, caste and religiously related rituals and taboos were undermined as individual indentured laborers from various parts of India travelled to work in the plantations of Mauritius. It is no wonder that Mauritian-Bhojpuri and Mauritian-Creole became the new mother tongue; over the generations these traditions, customs, and taboos were recreated in the new homelands. Even though the claim is one of purity with respect to an Indian heritage, the resulting rituals, observances, and ethnic differences are indigenous, hybrid, and mixed, strongly influenced by the diversity of Indo-Mauritians, Creoles, Franco-Mauritians, Sino-Mauritians, and others. The Indo-Mauritian diaspora culture is mixed and indigenous to Mauritius but is represented as 'pure' and authentic. These notions of purity are exemplified by the agendas of several Indo-Mauritian groups to push for the teaching of ancestral languages in schools, and it has also positioned the state in an advantageous position to make the most of the rising global economic presence of India, and to some extent, China.

Mauritius is economically successful having smoothly made the shift from the reliance on a monocultural economy (sugar was the main export) to a multi-pronged and global-oriented economy that positions Mauritius as follows: an export oriented manufacturing producer, a cyber (IT) hub, an offshore banking haven, an export processing zone (EPZ), and a tourist mecca. Following through with the structural adjustment conditions set by the International Monetary Fund (IMF) and the World Bank, Mauritius has nevertheless continued to support a moderate welfare and interventionist state. This rapid and tighter integration with the global economy has resulted in the Indo-Mauritian majority making a stronger effort to institute ancestral languages in the education system and to support closer cultural ties with India. The Hindu elite amongst them has also made a concerted effort to equate Mauritian-Bhojpuri (spoken by a small percentage of Hindus) with Hindi, which is an ancestral language that Mauritians rarely speak.[6] Many Indian nationalists fear that Indo-Mauritian cultural values are being slowly eroded by Westernization and the usage of Mauritian-Kreol in everyday communication.

There are some trends in Mauritius that militate against ethnic conflict and intra-ethnic unity: a democratic political system that demands coalitions and alliances, a welfare system that redistributes resources and provides a safety net, and a strong economy that has made the transition to greater global integration with success. But heavy reliance on skilled and educated labor, and tighter connections with Indian corporations, the Indian government, and Indian cultural enterprises, tends to further marginalize Creoles.

It is significant that much of the scholarship on Mauritius focuses on Indo-Mauritians and language policies with far less research on Creole identity and Mauritian-Kreol. Slaves were multilingual and multicultural and the Malagasy language served as the contact language along with French Creole into the mid-nineteenth century. However cultural histories have emphasized the Creolization or nascent Creole society formation and underplayed the continuing impact of African languages and cultures. This erasure is due to the structure of colonial archives, the prioritization of French (language, literature, and culture), the cultural dominance of Indo-Mauritians, and Creole politics.[7]

This chapter focuses on one aspect of Mauritian society: how diaspora connections affect identity, nationalism, and participation in social movements among Indo-Mauritians. Though there is wide variation in the idea of diaspora, a common trait is the acknowledgement of a homeland and this real or imagined place influences language, religion, and custom. As Cohen observes:

> all diasporic communities settled outside their natal (or imagined natal) territories, knowledge that 'the old country' – a notion often buried deep in language, religion, custom, or folklore – always has some claim on their loyalty and emotions. . . demonstrated by an acceptance of an inescapable link with their past migration history and a sense of co-ethnicity with others of a similar background.[8]

Following the abolition of British slavery in 1833 Indians were indentured to colonies throughout the empire, under contract and assigned to Estate owners to replace emancipated slave labor, or to provide a new source of labor where indigenous peoples refused to or were protected from, entering the labor market. In the case of Mauritius 453,063 Indians were indentured between 1834 and 1912. By 1980 the number of Indians in Mauritius was 632,000 and by 2006 they constituted 68 per cent of the total population of about 1.3 million. Indo-Mauritians are not a homogenous community; constituting 68 per cent of the population, 48.5 percent are Hindu (those who are Hindu, Tamil, Marathi, and Telugu), and 17.3 percent are Muslim, with smaller percentages of Christians and others. Creoles, who are 27 per cent of the population, are primarily descendants of Afro-Malagasy and African slaves; some are mixed African with Chinese, Indian, and/or White. Chinese make up about 3 per cent of the population, and Whites (Franco-Mauritians) 2 per cent.

As a majority Indo-Mauritians do not act as a coherent bloc but rather as discreet groups divided along the lines of religion, language, and regional origin from India. The focal issue for many of the social movements among them has been status and support for ancestral languages. Given the rapidly transforming economic landscape and increasing social distance between Indo-Mauritians and Creoles, there have been moves towards ensuring that customs are maintained as, what they believe to be, the markers of 'purity' and authenticity.

History of indenture

The French occupied Mauritius from 1721 to 1810 and Governor Mahé de Labourdonnais (1734–1746) was the first to bring Indian laborers to the island.[9] Some of them were imported as 'free' artisans but others were bought as slaves from the French ports in India such as Cochin, Goa, and Malabar. Africans were introduced as slaves under the Dutch from 1638, and the system continued under the French. By 1797 the population in Mauritius had risen to 60,000, of these 50,000 were slaves mainly from Madagascar and Mozambique.[10] Under the governorship of Decaen (1803–1810) a second generation of Indians entered Mauritius, many of whom later adopted Christianity and merged with the mixed populations. Indians who arrived under French rule were called "Bengali" (from North India) or "Malabars" (from Kerala, but including Tamils from South India); by 1800 there were some 6000 Indian slaves in Mauritius.[11] When the British captured Mauritius in 1810 there were about 75,000 inhabitants, a thriving city of Port Louis, and at least two Indians owned large sugar plantations.[12]

The Slavery Abolition Act passed by the House of Commons in 1833 conferred freedom to all slave children in the plantation colonies who were not over 6 years of age, and all those children born after the passage of the Act. All those over 6 years of age became free but were required to work for their former owners as "apprentices" for a limited period – 4 years for domestics and 6 years for those in agriculture. Estate owners were compensated with £20 million. The apprenticeship system in Mauritius started on 1 February 1835 and ended in 1839; at the time of abolition there were 61,045 apprentices.[13] A year later, an agent of the Mauritian planters, Mr. Arbuthnot, recruited 36 laborers from India and by 1850 this number had increased rapidly to 48,112.[14] Indians were under indentured contracts for 5 years and were entitled to free return passage to India at the end of service. They received 5 Rupees as wages each month as well as daily rations of 2 pounds rice, ½ pound dhal, and small quantities of salt, ghee, oil, and mustard. They were also supplied with one "dhoti" (loincloth), one blanket, one sheet, and two caps. Like elsewhere in the colonies they were subjected to the double cut whereby two days wages were deducted for every day of absence, and pass laws mandated that an identification document was carried at all times. There were further rules and regulations imposed on the various estates. A high death rate due to cholera, plague, and small pox epidemics, as well as infant mortality, led to relatively slow population growth. Many Indians also opted to return to India after the termination of their indentured contracts; by 1910 of the 450,000 Indians who had arrived 160,000 had returned to India.[15]

In 1851 the right to free return passage to India was abolished, and Indians were granted citizenship in Mauritius. Around the 1830s they began to move from indentured servants to small planters via a process called "morcellement." They purchased small pieces of land on long-term agreements, some began to cultivate sugarcane and when they sent the cane to the mill, the proceeds went towards repayment of the loan. By 1935 Indian small holders came to own 40 per cent of sugarcane land in Mauritius.[16] In the late 1990s more than 50 per cent of the sugar industry was owned by a handful of Franco-Mauritian families, while 33,000 small planters of Indian origin owned the rest.[17]

Diasporas and transnationalism

In terms of definitions King correctly notes: "there is no 'nationally grounded' theoretical paradigm which can adequately handle the epistemological situation."[18] If we focus on diaspora we are essentially talking about "dispersion," which has multiple connotations. As Shukla explains "within the very topic of diaspora there is an immanent tension between the specific and the general that may be variously rendered as the local and the global, the particular and the universal, or the national and the regional."[19] The term diaspora captures movement from a homeland to other states (the hostlands), but there remains definitional fuzziness associated with the relationship between the homeland and the host-land versus relationships, if any, between the various dispersed communities that share the same homeland. The position of Indo-Mauritians is caught in this definitional maze – while maintaining ties with India reinforces their position in the Mauritian state and nation, ties and relations with the wider Indian diaspora (in South Africa, Fiji, Trinidad for example) are virtually non-existent. In referring to Mauritian Indians as a diaspora community then, the writer needs to specify that here the meaning of diaspora reflects historical ties with India only, and if the term is used to identify the South Asian diaspora in general, it is more of an intellectual category rather than one that is derived from the relationships between its members.

Furthermore diasporas are not created only by displacement but also depend on the continued construction of a relationship with the homeland, however imagined.[20] To some extent diasporas are a subjective category that gains import if and when the relationship with the homeland is deployed. There is also an equally compelling debate about hybrid identities and transnational migrations. This is the notion that diasporas are dispersions that "compress time and space such that it enables the experiences of many places at what would appear to be one moment."[21] Diasporas have hybrid identities because they experience several places at one time, a "deterritorialization" of cultural practices that are experienced as "temporal simultaneity in experiencing a diversity of place-bound cultural tradition."[22] A diaspora identity is not necessarily a hybrid one but is "shaped by the ways transnational cultural flows are deployed in relation to the experience of spatio-temporal displacement."[23] The distance between the homeland and the host-land, in terms of physical and psychological space, is mediated by constructions of identity that can emphasize language, religion, culture, and purity associated with the imagined homeland. In Mauritius Indians celebrate ancestral languages and religious traditions as a way of maintaining links to India (as it is constructed in a given time and space), and emphasizing difference with respect to Creoles.

Several theorists have argued that the state is being seriously challenged by globalization, especially in terms of sovereignty and jurisdiction over its citizens. ". . . The world is being organized vertically by nation-states and regions, but horizontally by an overlapping, permeable, multiple system of interaction," says Cohen.[24] Appadurai maintains that he is convinced "that the nation-state, as a complex modern political form, is on its last legs."[25] Hall contends that while the state is losing ground to globalization, the reaction has been "a regression to a defensive and highly dangerous form of national identity. . . driven by an aggressive form of racism."[26] Wallerstein adds that even though the state is the "most powerful cultural force in the modern world," it is the "most schizophrenic."[27] However despite the long history of globalization, states have not disappeared. On the contrary, as Sassen argues, the state has denationalized what has been constructed as national by enabling global trends and influences or reconfiguring what is considered national.[28] If we see the state as a set of institutions that organizes political identity and authority in a particular way,[29] then globalization and the formation of diaspora communities can be seen as operating above or below this state, nevertheless recognizing its salience. While many theorists have predicted the demise of the state, few tell us why nations persist.[30] A possible place to begin is to distinguish nation from state; nations are difficult to define as they are intangible, reflecting a psychological and subconscious bond, while states include institutions that constitute the political, economic, and socio-ideological systems of a society.[31]

Indians, specifically the Hindu majority, dominate the state in Mauritius. While the hegemonic discourses of the nation are associated with connections to the Indian diaspora via ancestral languages and cultural practices, it is a contested terrain with Creoles (the largest minority) and Franco-Mauritians (a small minority with significant cultural and economic capital). Mauritian democracy can best be understood as a state in a plural society as defined by Furnivall:

> Each group holds by its own religion, its own culture and language, its own religion, its own ideas and ways. As individuals they meet, but only in the market-place, in buying and selling. There is a plural society, with different sections of the community living side by side, but separately, within the same political unit.[32]

The society is based on discreet divisions that compartmentalize the economic, political, and social systems. Each group coverts certain occupations, and upward and outward mobility is dependent on membership in a particular group. The political system that was adopted ensures that minorities are represented; this model has been successful, and the Mauritian state is stable and celebrated as a standard of success. The nation is however contested; abiding tensions associated with the plural society contribute to this contestation. Here too Furnivall's observations are accurate; he recognizes that in a plural society racial or ethnic groups, while participating in the political system as groups, are made up of an "aggregate of individuals" and not an organic whole.[33] Broadly defined groups are internally divided and members engage with the society as individuals – in Mauritius this is particularly pertinent as all its habitants entered the island as owners or laborers of capitalist enterprises. From its very inception Mauritius was built on notions of commodification, production, profit, consumerism, and monetary value. Unlike the situation in South Africa or Fiji where an aboriginal population determined and demarcated race and ethnic relations, in Mauritius the system that evolved was one that was based on individuals as each created and contributed to the development of a competitive extractive capitalist structure. The kinds of social movements that developed and the weaknesses of many of them, especially in comparison with the robustness of such movements in South Africa and Fiji, allude to the specific character of Mauritian and to some extent Trinidadian society. Many of the organizations among Mauritians are geared towards ensuring that cultural elements are supported and sustained by the state, less attention is paid to mobilizing for more rights, a higher standard of living, and other material rights that all people should enjoy. The inability of Creoles to form united organizations and to distance themselves from the African continent is symptomatic of a plural society. As are the low-level battles among various sectors of Indo-Mauritians to ensure their place in the competitive cultural, political, and economic landscape.

Creoles and Indians: identity and citizenship

Hindu Mauritians offer validity to their prominent position in the nation by constructing diaspora ancestral cultures.[34] This notion of cultural citizenship has privileged origins in India over indigenous subjecthood. Hence, Indian ancestral languages have come to determine strong belonging to Mauritius displacing those linguistic traditions that claim indigenous authenticity.[35] The maintenance of ancestral languages became a sign of Hindu hegemony in Mauritius. Eriksen proposes that the spread of Mauritian Creole throughout the land shows that Mauritius has become "culturally homogenized."[36] Boswell instead says that Creoles primordialise their identity because "Mauritian society consists of hegemonies where *fictions* of cultural and ethnic homogeneity are imperative to the maintenance of hierarchy."[37] Given the relative stability of Mauritius in economic, political, and social terms, the key question to ask is why stability and harmony have prevailed despite ethnic/racial divisions.

In Mauritius Creole identity is considered a non-identity – from 1972 they were officially categorized as the "General Population" or the Catholic religious group, Creoles were made invisible. With the emphasis placed on ancestral languages, Creoles are further marginalized by not claiming an ancestral language even though a sizable proportion of slaves in colonial Mauritius spoke Malagasy. The lack of an ancestral language, weak notions of an African homeland, and weak connections to Africa, exemplify the Creole non-identity. These non-identifying elements have served to act as a backdrop for the construction of Indian identity, which emphasizes homeland, ancestral language, and historical connections to religious traditions and culture. The presence of the Creole other in Mauritius has served to construct the Indian, mainly Hindu, self. As Boswell rightly points out, Creole identity is hybrid and furthermore, *le malaise Créole* has "become a construct used and usable by both dominant groups in Mauritius and to a certain extent, by Creoles themselves, to create a homogenised past and present identity for Creoles."[38] Significantly, Creole hybridity is not celebrated, it is instead "trapped in the culture "grids" created by the state," which have come to appear as normal.[39] Going back to Gilroy's proposition regarding the African slave diaspora, the identity of Creoles in Mauritius can best be understood as a *changing same*, defined in a discursive space of indigeneity/hybridity *and* the sameness of displacement, temporality, suffering, and the violent severing of self from the homeland. Some have reacted to this marginalization by attempting to recreate primordial cultural identities around heritage sites, dance, music, and language. Yet Creoles have been reluctant to identify with Madagascar, their closest neighbor and from whence many can claim ancestry.

Leading up to independence in 1968 Creoles mobilized under *Muvman Morisyen Kreol Afrikain*/Movement for Black Mauritian Creoles, *Mouvement Pour*

Le Progrés/Movement for Progress, *Rassemblement Organization Creoles*/Union of Creole Organizations, and *Organisation Fratenal*. Hindu-Creole clashes and rioting occurred in 1964–65, and Creole-Muslim riots occurred 6 weeks before independence in 1968. In the early days of independence a multi-ethnic revolutionary socialist party emerged, *Mouvement Militant Mauricien* (MMM), that denounced communalism and supported labor in rural and urban institutions. Their successful mobilization among the youth and women around political and cultural activities led to the imposition of a State of Emergency between 1972 and 1975. MMM members were detained and elections were deferred; the MMM entered the government in 1982 when its founder Paul Bérenger became the minister of finance. He was instrumental in implementing the neoliberal reforms that had been negotiated by the previous government.

In February 1999 the death in police custody of popular Creole musician, Kaya, sparked an outbreak of mass violence. Kaya had been arrested for smoking marijuana at a demonstration about the legalization of the drug. Rioting, looting, and some retaliation from Hindus in several Hindu-dominated villages left five dead, hundreds injured, and dozens of the homes of Creoles were burned. The spontaneous reaction of Creoles and the unrest that ensued was used as evidence of the "social disease" that permeated the island.[40]

Mauritius has no indigenous population, and Africans first arrived on the island in 1638 as slaves to the first Dutch settlement. In the 1720s the French took control and more Africans entered the island as slaves mainly from Mozambique (40–45 per cent) and Madagascar (30–35 per cent).[41] Under British rule from 1814 slavery continued until abolition in 1835, which was followed with a 4-year apprenticeship period. By this time some 135,000 slaves in Mauritius and Bourbon were from Madagascar, and Malagasy was the most prevalent tongue.[42] Larson shows that during this period neither the native-born majority (French Creole) nor the emerging Kreol language eliminated Malagasy, which was widely spoken. Many spoke Malagasy and French or Kreol. The undermining of Malagasy and the elevation of Kreol was the result of its institutionalization in churches, labor relations, hospitals, the judiciary, and other administrative institutions. Kreol was best suited to the French overlords, and it was the language through which all slaves, and later indentured laborers, communicated with their owners/employers and the colonial administration. Weekly catechism inculcated enslaved children with church doctrines, they were also taught the language of their masters and their individuality was emphasized (they engaged with the church as individuals), thus building a Creole community that spoke Kreol and was severed from Africa. When Mauritius was ceded to the British, the 1814 Treaty of Paris reinforced the understanding that the French language would be officially preserved, and the Act of Capitulation in 1910 guaranteed that inhabitants could retain their religion, culture, and property. The exception was the judiciary; in 1845 the British decreed that English would be the language of the higher courts. These administrative structures contributed to the erasure of other African languages and instilled the primacy of Kreol as the official language of slaves and former slaves. Indentured Indians also spoke Kreol, and it remained the *lingua franca* of the large majority of Mauritians.

By the 1860's Indians outnumbered Creoles, making up two-thirds of the population by 1871.[43] But as Miles correctly states, "Numerical outnumbering does not in and of itself account for the marginalization of the Mauritian Creole masses."[44] In Trinidad for example, where Creoles and Indians are almost equal in number and both groups were brought to the island (as slaves or as indentured laborers), Creole claims of indigeneity are employed to legitimize their hegemony in the nation and political system. Indo-Trinidadians are viewed as outsiders with permanent ties to India while severance from Africa has given Creoles a claim to authenticity, indigenous culture, and stronger roots in Trinidad. Being Creole does not automatically lead to marginalization. Furthermore, the political system in Mauritius has many checks and balances against an ethnic majority oppressing or systematically marginalizing an ethnic minority. Mauritian democracy is based on the "best-loser" system that demands governing coalitions and ethnic representation; it also includes a system of consulting all groups on policy initiatives, thereby managing ethnic tensions. The reasons for the position of Creoles in Mauritius have to be sought elsewhere, it has historical roots in the socio-economic legacy of slavery and Creole group identity.

By piecing together important bits of data Allen shows that during the apprenticeship period as well as immediately after, free Africans were economically competitive, or relatively self-sufficient on the island.[45] By 1930 the free population controlled about one-fifth of the island's agricultural wealth.[46] Yet by 1871 only 683 of 8196 gardeners were non-Indian, and in 1881 the latter accounted for only 2 per cent of the island's 10,222 gardeners.[47] The competitiveness of Creoles was undermined by cheap Indian labor and weak access to financial resources. In contrast by relying on wage labor, family and communal assistance, between 1864 and 1900 Indian's accounted for one-third of the value of all property changing hands.[48] Allen contends that historians have been reticent to question why one community of smallholders failed to consolidate its position while another did so successfully. He sees the failure to investigate this as contributing to the conclusions that "ignorance, indolence, and insubordination" are typical of the Creole population.[49] Instead, he points to the underdeveloped credit institutions that existed during this early period; while Creole's had the capacity to buy land, they didn't have the fiscal resources to cultivate it. Weak access to capital and the sheer magnitude of Indian indenture worked to undermine the ability of Creoles to effectively compete in the changing economy.

Another equally debilitating structural experience for Creole's was the 'apprenticeship' period following abolition. In 1833 the British Parliament passed a bill that outlawed slavery throughout the empire, those over 6 year of age who became free were required to work for their former owners as apprentices for a limited period. The apprenticeship system in Mauritius started in 1835 and ended in 1839; it was a violent exploitative system instituted to protect estate owners from having to negotiate with and meet the demands of newly freed workers. Some former slaves reacted by submitting and suffering silently in light of impending abolition, others engaged in more militant resistance. "Their chief instruments were stealing, "drunkenness," insubordination, mutilation of farm animals, lateness

for work and, above all, marooning."[50] The plantation managers employed puni-
tive measure to punish these protestors and special magistrates imposed penal
sanctions. Former slaves came to be seen as "disobedient, insolent, and robbers,
driven to commit these vices by idleness, malignant will, indolence, and habitual
drunkenness."[51] When the system was terminated in 1839 the mass-withdrawal of
former slaves left the estates all but devoid of labor. After leaving the plantations
Creoles became laborers, peasant cultivators on purchased or leased land, and
squatters in remote areas. Thousands succumbed to illnesses like smallpox and
cholera. Most never wanted to participate in plantation labor again – the system
was abhorrent and forever associated with slavery.

Indian indenture resumed in 1842; in 1834 there were forty Indian laborers
working in Mauritian plantations, but within 4 years this number increased to
24,000.[52] With the massive input of Indian labor, sugar production soared reach-
ing over one billion pounds by 1842.[53] Indians were exploited as cheap labor for
the sugar industry, a highly competitive global trade cheapened through the use
of bonded labor and minimal production costs (the use of rudimentary technology, labor-intensive production, and exploitative labor practices). Former slaves
were placed in a structurally weak position even though they were 'free.' They
had to contend with the pernicious and debilitating apprenticeship system, the
use of indentured labor from India to replace slave labor, and the absence of
strong and available credit lending institutions that might have facilitated greater
upward mobility. The changing demographics in the country made them a minority within a few years after abolition, and this status was to also adversely affect
their chances of competing in the robust global capitalist system.

Mauritius: "tiger in paradise"

Mauritius has successfully made the transformation from reliance on sugar cul-
tivation to agricultural diversification, it has constructed itself as an export processing and offshore business and banking center, offering an investment-friendly
environment, and it has become a cyber-hub of sophisticated computer networks
and high-end computer literate employers. Together with robust tourism, Mauritius is a model of economic success – a state in the developing world that has
astutely managed globalization, structural adjustment, and significant international and national transformations.

When the European Union stopped preferences for cane sugar from former colonies, Mauritius took measures to reduce the number of sugar mills, to improve
productivity and reduce the workforce through voluntary retirement, and from
2005 to restructure production towards energy generation.[54] Launched in 1971 the
exporting processing zone (EPZ), which expanded in 1982 to include the entire
island, was actively supported by the Mauritian government and offered direct
investment for foreign companies. The EPZ provided a conduit for direct investment in francophone West Africa and Anglophone East Africa; it also provided
a labor market for women and foreign migrants from India, China, Sri Lanka,
and Bangladesh. In 1979 and 1985 Mauritius took loans from the International

Monetary Fund (IMF) and the World Bank and began a program of structural adjustment with devaluation, cuts in state subsidies, reduction in government spending and taxes for foreign investors. In other words, Mauritius embarked on a path of neoliberalism which Harvey succinctly defines as: "a theory of political economic practices that proposes that human well-being can best be advanced by liberating individual entrepreneurial freedoms and skills within an institutional framework characterized by strong private property rights, free markets, and free trade."[55] The function of the state is to facilitate and provide optimum conditions for the operation of the free-market; this demands less government intervention and a smaller leaner state that generates robust market engagement in all aspects of society. Mauritius has prevented some of the more problematic side-effects of neoliberalism by continuing to maintain some degree of state intervention like import controls, job security provisions, price controls, and export taxes. A welfare system has also been retained featuring free health services, free education, public housing, and public pensions. It has been labeled a "developmentalist state" or state-led development model in that it is able to make decisions free from the capitalist class, and to selectively engage with market forces.[56] However given the strident demands of the neoliberal economic framework, some of the implications of the reduced role of the state have negatively affected the Creole minority. In line with the neoliberal demand that values the market exchange relationship over all else, and in tandem with the notion of ethnic pluralism, relations between ethnic groups in Mauritius are commercialized whereby contractual relationships in the marketplace are prioritized. Individuals meet each other in the marketplace and their identities as fellow Mauritians are forged through these relationships.

Starting with the Lomé Convention in 1975, Mauritius used its diaspora ties to Britain and France to negotiate the largest sugar quota in the European Union at a guaranteed price that was about 90 per cent above market price. This allowed them to tax the largest plantation owners and protect small Indian land holdings while financing the welfare needs of the state. This tax was abolished in 1994. The creation of the EPZ in 1970 with incentives for foreign capital investment led to significant growth in the export-oriented clothing industry, accounting for 15 per cent of employment and about a quarter of the GDP by 2005.[57] By 1990 about 600 firms in the textiles and garment industry employed over 90,000 workers (about one-third the total workforce).[58] In the early 1990s the country also developed economic policies and infrastructure for offshore banking activities. With the double taxation avoidance with India, many foreign investors in India are routed through the island, and in 2000 Mauritius became the largest source of direct foreign investment in India.[59] Finally, with strong economic support from India, Mauritius is transforming itself into a cyber-hub for software development.

These changes have made Mauritius an economic success, yet all these innovations have served to further marginalize Creoles and reinforce the strong position of Indians in the economy – especially as demands increase for employees who are skilled in computer technology, management techniques, and proficient in English and French. Moreover, as the island has effectively employed its diaspora connections to enhance its economic standing, the ethnic divide between Indians and Creoles has widened, as have class divisions. The government continues to address some of these disparities, for example large buses containing computers travel the island offering classes in basic computing, and the purchase of one computer per household is subsidized.

Economic success in Mauritius is contingent on different ethnic groups occupying certain sectors of the economy. Hindus predominate in public service, some professions, and agriculture. Muslims are disproportionately represented in urban commerce. Creoles are at the bottom of the socioeconomic ladder and work in urban factories, white-collar jobs, as domestics, and in fishing. A small minority among them, many of who are lighter-skinned and mixed with Whites, form an educated and prosperous elite. The Chinese minority is influential as entrepreneurs and shopkeepers, while Franco-Mauritians are in manufacturing in the EPZ, tourism, and financial services.

Mauritian modernity epitomized by the slogan "A Tiger in Paradise" is modeled ambiguously between the notion of paradise – a Western description emoting bucolic places untouched by the vicissitudes of modernization but nevertheless catering to the modern desires of Westerners – and an Asian Tiger, ferocious but in a benign and user-friendly way.[60] Much like the so-called Asian Tigers of Singapore, Hong Kong, Taiwan, and South Korea, Mauritius draws on a state-led development model actively pursuing global economic investment while ensuring a high level of state intervention to facilitate the free-market and to support the population through welfare. In these endeavors Mauritius has benefited from three powerful diasporas: Indian, Chinese, and French. The Hindu majority has forged close connections with India, further separating Mauritius from Africa and from the Creole minority. Mauritius is of tactical importance to India in its pursuit to enhance its presence in the Indian Ocean, where China has made strategic inroads. India is the largest trading partner of Mauritius and its largest exporter of goods and services since 2007; India's exports are mainly petroleum products and several Indian Public Enterprises function in Mauritius, including the Bank of Baroda, Life Insurance Corporation (Mauritius) Offshore Ltd., Indian Oil (Mauritius) Ltd., Mahanagar Telephone, and the State Bank of India. Other India-assisted projects include the Jawaharlal Nehru Hospital, the Cyber Tower at Ebene, and the Swami Vivekananda International Conference Center. There are numerous cultural investment programs like the Indira Gandhi Center for Indian Culture (IGCIC) that promotes Indian cultural activities in Mauritius; about 100 ICCR scholarships are awarded annually for higher education in India. Furthermore, over 200 students enroll annually in Indian universities.[61] In addition to direct investment and banking arrangements, India has gained a foothold in the country by negotiating to upgrade sea and air links on the remote Agalega islands, which is located northeast of Madagascar and south of the Seychelles, and has a majority Creole population of about 200.[62]

Mauritius provides India with a location for offshore banking and a conduit for direct investment in India – with the double taxation avoidance agreement, Mauritius is a possible site for money laundering.[63] In the process corruption has also increased as India gains more status as a global economic power. Close and lucrative relations with India have raised the status of Indo-Mauritians in the state and global economy; at the national level, greater ties with India privileges Indian culture, ideals, and institutes a "governability which strongly advocates censorship and other oppressive policies."[64] In the construction of a nation Indo-Mauritians have attempted to assert authority but are challenged by counter-hegemonies such as that of Creoles and other minorities. Tighter socio-economic connections with India have positive and negative implications.

Language, education, and Creole marginalization

With the island economy largely based on employees who are highly educated and/or skilled, Creole's are in a disadvantaged position. The education system, while robust and very competitive, tends to marginalize Creole pupils through its national examination system and the gateways to better schools, entrance to universities, and positions in government and business. It is in schools that have a predominantly Creole student body that "the highest educational failures are recorded."[65]

As an ethnic group, Creoles have a distinctive indigenized culture removed from Africa; in 1977 Tinker observed that "Very few feel even the vaguest affinity with Africa. To them, Africa is barbarous; and this aversion extends to the Malagasy people with whom they have the closest contacts."[66] By the late 1990s anti-Africanist attitudes were commonplace,[67] but there is growing evidence that a movement towards primordialising Creole identity is developing.[68] While ancestral roots, religion, and language have provided the basis for group cohesion among Mauritians of Hindu, French, Chinese, and Muslim origin, Creoles have avoided looking to their cultural and linguistic African heritage. The small islands of Rodrigues and Agalega, which are part of the Republic of Mauritius, are exclusively inhabited by Creoles and in both the low level of economic development and dependence on the main island has put them in a kind of neocolonial relationship. The commemoration of February 1st as the day slavery was abolished in 1835 is now a metaphor for social deprivation and exclusion.[69] There are two significant ways in which the Indo-Mauritian majority has attempted to elevate and cement their position in the state and nation: through language policy and in the education system.

Indo-Maritians are officially divided into "Hindi-speaking" (about 41 per cent of the population), "Tamil-speaking" (6 per cent), "Telugu-speaking" (3 per cent), and "Marathi-speaking" (2 per cent). Hindi is the ancestral language claimed by Hindus of north Indian backgrounds, and they have dominated politics in Mauritius since 1968. If there is a hegemonic discourse in Mauritian nationalism, it is the discourse that surrounds the place and status of the Hindi language and culture. Three of the four prime ministers have been from this group and a concerted effort has been made to support this identity.

The language spoken by the vast majority of Mauritians is Kreol, a hybrid and indigenized language that includes among others French and Malagasy. However Kreol is denigrated as "broken French" and is neither recognized as an official language nor taught in the school system. Kreol is the everyday language of communication that is maligned as impure, mixed, hybrid, lacking ancestral roots, and historical and cultural authenticity. As was discussed earlier, under French colonialism estate owners, administrators, and Catholic priests favored Kreol. This was the language perpetuated under British colonialism even though the official administration and judicial system employed English. Moreover severance from Africa was concretized through slavery, the system assiduously treated slaves as labor, individualized and commoditized. It undermined Malagasy and other African languages making Kreol the only language through which capitalist labor relations were conducted. It can be argued that because of the close proximity to Madagascar and the East Coast of Africa, Creoles were acted upon in this way to produce servile and efficient labor. Indians were allowed to maintain connections to India as they were assumed to be temporary residents who would one day be repatriated to India. The apprenticeship system placed Creoles in a structural position that was defined by marginality – from competitive capitalist production, from the Indian indentured majority, and from the Mauritian state.

The economic system that has developed in Mauritius places a heightened premium on education. The education system is rigorous and has several crucial gateways that work against Creoles but in favor of Indian higher achievement. There are three major national exams: the Certificate of Primary Education (CPE) for entrance into the best or five star institutions in the country, the Secondary Certificate (SC), and the Higher Secondary Certificate (HSC). About 30,000 students sit for the CPE exams taken after 6 years of primary school education, less than two-thirds pass. Only 2000 students are admitted to the Star Colleges (secondary schools); these are the prestigious and exclusive institutions in which most political leaders and managerial elite were educated. Success in these exams requires extensive private extra-curricular tutoring and strong family support – Creoles are less likely to be able to access these pathways to success. The situation is made worse by the impoverished schools in Creole-dominated areas with poor facilities, unmotivated and poorly prepared teachers, and uncompetitive learning environments that lacks the nurturing and focus that others schools have.

Of all the subjects tested in the CPE exams, only English, French, mathematics, and environmental sciences count for ranking and entrance to Star Colleges. However students can also take one of seven ancestral Asian languages: Hindi, Urdu, Tamil, Telegu, Marathi, Mandarin, and Arabic. Besides Kreol the *lingua franca* of all Mauritians, Bhojpuri is the *only* Indian language commonly spoken roughly by one-quarter of the population.[70] Indentured Indians from present-day Bihar and eastern Uttar Pradesh in Northern India spoke a variety of Bhojpuri, in Mauritius they created a composite kind of Bhojpuri that is spoken by Mauritians of South Indian origin as well. Mauritian Bhojpuri became the language of communication for indentured Indians from various linguistic backgrounds; this is much like Fiji-Hindi and Trini-Hindi spoken among Indo-Fijians and Indo-Trinidadians, respectively. Bhojpuri is known locally as *motiya* or the 'course one' and *kalkattiya*, referring to the Indian port of departure of most of its speakers. Mauritian Bhojpuri is considered a rustic, unsophisticated language used by indentured laborers in the rural cane fields, nevertheless it also references India as the motherland – it is looked upon with a degree of disdain *and* pride. More recently there has been a push from some Hindus to make Bhojpuri the recognized language of Hindus in Mauritius, but retaining Hindi as the assumed "ancestral language" that is barely spoken. It must be noted that in India Bhojpuri is considered a dialect with a limited literary tradition and has low prestige; Hindi is considered superior and is spoken by many. The new emphasis to place Mauritian Bhojpuri within the framework of Hindi reflects the desire to "stop a shift toward French-lexicon Mauritian Creole," and the need to prevent the perceived implications of rampant globalization.[71] This is a contentious proposition given that the teaching and learning of Hindi is regarded as "purifying" in a culturally "Creolized" environment. Several Hindu nationalist groups such as the Aryan Samaj, the Rashtriya Svayamsevak Sangh (RSS), and the Vishnu Hindu Parishad (VHP) have supported the inclusion of ancestral languages as a subject in schools. However Mauritian Bhojpuri is seeping into the media in an attempt to ensure that it remains relevant in a culturally diverse environment. Many Hindu organizations perceive globalization as the driving force behind increasing crime, the disintegration of families, drug abuse, sexual relations before marriage, and so on – Hindus aim to indigenize Hindi in the form of its local dialect Mauritian Bhojpuri to claim purity, connectedness to India, and separateness from Kreol and Creole hybridity. The notion of Hindi being an ancestral language is clearly fabricated as the vast majority of indentured immigrant "ancestors of present-day Hindus in Mauritius were illiterate Bhojpuri speakers."[72] Moreover sanskritized Hindi only became more widely used in India at the end of the nineteenth century, so it couldn't have been the language of the ancestors. Indians claim purity through language in contrast to Creole 'impurity' and mixed linage.

While Kreol is the *lingua* franca, Bhojpuri is spoken exclusively at home by a small proportion of people,[73] a smaller group speaks French, and English is retained as the language of politics, state and legal administrations, and the medium of instruction in schools. French dominates the private sector economy and the media – 93 per cent of all Mauritians watch television news in French.[74] Ancestral languages are supported by the state through the media (Mauritian Broadcasting Corporation television), and through state subsidies of religious organizations and other institutions that propagate these languages.

Eisenlohr observes that the states' support for Hindi rather than Mauritian Kreol, "is a way of legitimizing an ethnic perspective on political power sharing in a Mauritius where Hindus dominate."[75] It can be added that state support for ancestral languages over the home-grown languages of Mauritian Kreol and Bhojpuri is due in part to the small size and isolated nature of the island – the Mauritian state goes to considerable lengths to ensure that its people are competitive in the global markets, and they seek to maintain strong diaspora connections. The political, judicial, and education systems reflect this decision.

For the first time in the 1962 census Indians were listed as Hindus and Muslims. Fifty-two per cent of the Mauritian population is middle class and Hindus make up 41 per cent of the group dominating state institutions.[76] Muslims constitute 17 per cent of the population and they too have come to rely on ancestral cultures and diaspora connections. Some Muslims were indentured and others came as free traders; these earlier groups (Kutchi Memon caste) became the new elite establishing madrassas and maintaining links with Sunnis in India. Their status was challenged in the 1950s when Muslims from indentured backgrounds, who had become more educated and wealthier, began to make closer connections with transnational Islamic groups. This intra-ethnic tension played out in the choice of ancestral language choses – Urdu (favored by Memons) and Arabic (hegemonic in the diaspora). To a considerable extent, the elite status of Muslims in Mauritius has enabled them to make demands at the state level despite the fact that they are a smaller minority then Creoles.

Social movements and organization

Mauritian Creoles are a diverse ethnic group – social movements have not been strong among them. In addition to the political organizations that have been mentioned as a group, Creoles have been slow to engage in united sustained action. Poverty and marginalization have further splintered the group. Creole's haven't as yet been able to assert hybridity as a counter-concept to the cultural hegemony of purity and ancestral connections.[77] While Indo-Mauritian, Muslims, and Sino-Mauritians have defined their group identities by asserting diaspora connections despite having hybrid and mixed cultural heritage, Creoles have been marginalized because of their mixed identities. They also occupy the lowest rung of society in positions that are poorly paid, and many are unemployed even though the Mauritian economy is robust. When the MMM party tried to implement Kreol in the media and schools, it was met with resistance from Indo- and Franco-Mauritians and Creoles. Besides seeing it as a pidgin language, its official usage was deemed to further isolate Mauritius and it was still associated with Creoles as an ethnic group.[78] Creoles continue to be viewed as having no fixed members and "Creoledom means impurity, openness, and individualism."[79] Furthermore, Mauritian Creoles are defined with an essentialist identity of weak international organizations and "a chronic problem of leadership, lack of a myth of origin . . . external stereotyping as been morally and culturally opportunistic."[80] Hindus in contrast make every effort to perpetuate a unified identity, as is the specific goal of the Vishnu Hindu Parishad (World Hindu Council).[81]

The debates that followed the 1995 proposal from Prime Minister Anerood Jugnauth for "Oriental Languages" to be included in the CPE rankings illustrates the intensity of the discourses surrounding definitions of the nation. Jugnauth headed a coalition government of the Militant Socialist Movement (MSM), the MMM, the Democratic Labor Movement (MTD), and the Organization of the Rodriguan People (OPR). Jugnauth had been Prime Minister since 1982 when he led the MMM, which spilt in 1983 to form the MSM. At the time the reasons given for the split was the insistence of the MMM and its leader, Paul Bérenger, to elevate Mauritian Kreol as a national language to be used in the national anthem (specifically during the independence day celebrations in March 1983) and news media. By the 1995 elections Jugnauth had been in power for 13 years and, given the general apathy that surrounded his reelection, he saw upgrading Indian languages as a possible way to win the support of the Indian majority. He seriously miscalculated the depth of emotions that surrounded the issue of language, misjudging the level of distrust that existed in furthering Indian hegemony.

The new rules that were to be implemented in late 1995 were that students who studied an Oriental language would take five subjects instead of the four taken by others. The lowest score on French, environmental studies, and the Oriental language would be dropped and then the rankings would be computed. As soon as the ruling was made public the Common Front for Justice on the CPE was formed, and the organization took the government to court. Opposition included members of the general population, the classification of Creoles and Franco-Mauritians, as well as those Indians whose children did not learn an ancestral language. On 27 October 1995 the Supreme Court declared that the CPE policy was "unfair and arbitrary and offended the principle of equality before the law and equal protection of the law embodied in Article 26 of the International Covenant on Civil and Political Rights enshrined" in the country's constitution.[82] The court further said that inclusion in the rankings of an Oriental language discriminated against non-Indians and handicapped a large number of students. The Privy Council in London overturned this decision in 1998.

While Hindu cultural organizations and the Hindu Teachers Union supported the new ruling, the Common Front for Justice on the CPE expanded to include the General Workers Federation, the Association of Mauritian Jurists, and the bishop of Port Louis. Furthermore, on 15 November 1995 the amendment was rejected by parliament (the governing coalition could not get the two-third's majority required to amend the constitution), and Jugnauth dissolved parliament and called new elections for 20 December 1995. He was defeated by the Labour Party-MMM coalition in a 60–0 vote, the new Prime Minister was Navin Ramgoolam (the son of the first Prime Minister Seewosagur Ramgoolam) and the deputy Prime Minister was Paul Bérenger. They continued with the interim language policy that Jugnauth had instituted – reserving a small number of places in the best schools for those who excelled on the Oriental languages CPE test and whose CPE rankings were above a high threshold.

It is well known that the language issue was not the main reason for Jugnauth's failure. His long stint as head of government had created dissatisfaction and a desire for change among voters. His language proposal did however draw attention to the general feeling that he had become more ethnocentric. Some see the 1995 CPE crisis as revealing that "politicians can not automatically count on ethnic languages in mobilizing local political support . . . Ethnicity is being rivaled (if not supplanted) by other forces, processes and institutions, notably industrialization, migration, and tourism."[83] However, in 2004 the decision was taken to count ancestral languages in the CPE ranking system reinforcing differences between Creoles and Indo-Mauritians.

The Mauritian state has been keen to homogenize the narrative of the culture of Creoles and to downplay the diversity and divisions that exist among them. One of the mechanisms used has been the protection of heritage sites commemorating slavery and indenture, but there is relative silence on the contributions of former slaves to Mauritian success. Some Catholic priests have pushed to create a Black position; social movements that push for rights at the state level. However other Creoles have chosen to resist by retracting from the competitive capitalist system, actively pursuing Rastafarianism and other independent forms of subsistence like hunting, fishing, brewing beer, and cooking using local resources. By forming strong and resilient communities in remote areas, they have also elevated music and dance as cultural legacies. The state has attempted to appropriate these spaces by framing them as being marginal and dangerous. The village of Chamarel for example, has been portrayed as underdeveloped, pre-modern, natural, promoting the perspective that associates Creoles as "primitive and unprogressive."[84] The state has attempted to package Chamarel as an eco-tourist attraction with local crafts and pristine environments. Maroon slaves who were newly freed created Chamarel as a site of liberation and freedom. In Le Morne Village, which shares a similar history, five hotels have already been constructed and tourist packages conceal the black Creole presence.

Despite their majority, Hindus and others influential sectors in the society have not been able to claim dominance in the construction of the nation. By eventually ensuring the ancestral languages became part of the schooling and examination system, Hindus gained a major foothold in defining the nation. But the Creole presence, their success in creating a parallel economy, and their persistence in the national imaginings of the nation, present challenges. Numerical dominance has not led to national hegemony.

The politics of accommodation

Mauritius is divided into twenty 3-seat constituencies (for a total of 60 seats) and the island of Rodrigues has one 2-seat position. In addition there is also the "best loser" system that allocates 8 additional seats in a complex formula to balance ethnic representation. An Electoral Supervisory Commission makes this selection on the basis of the four recognized ethnic groups: Hindus, Muslims, Sino-Mauritians, and the "General Population," which includes Creoles and Franco-Mauritians. This system aims to provide balance for ethnic minorities but has been criticized for essentializing ethnic categorization and reinforcing communal divisions.[85] With the wide array of political parties, party discipline is weak and defections are common, making coalition governments the norm. In the 2000 elections for example, there were 536 candidates and 43 political parties. Yet as Srebrnik recognizes, "Hindus have a guaranteed majority of seats in the National Assembly and their dominance in the legislature has remained the bottom line ever since independence."[86] Even though Indians are in the majority they always need to compromise in order to form a coalition government. In 1991 the political system shifted to include both a President and Prime Minister, which also helped to balance ethnicity, and in 2003 Paul Bérenger became the first French Prime Minister of the country.

The political history since independence clearly reflects the bargaining and compromise that ensues as each government is formed. In the first elections the Mauritian Labour Party (LP) headed by Sir. Seewoosagur Ramgoolam formed a coalition with the Hindu Independent Forward Bloc and the Comité d'Action Muselman (CAM) to win the elections. As soon as Ramgoolam took power he brought the Creole Parti Mauricien Social-Démocrate (PMSD) into his coalition. This was the party that had opposed independence and instead wanted Britain to retain control of security and defense. In the 1982 elections when the LP-PMSD alliance lost, Hindus moved to the Parti Socialiste Mauricien (PSM) (a left-wing break-away from the LP), which formed a government with the more radical MMM. Even though the Franco-Mauritian Paul Bérenger was the leader of the MMM, it was an Indian, Anerood Jugnauth, who became Prime Minister. Tensions within the coalition led to its collapse and new elections occurred in 1983. Once again a coalition government was formed with Jugnauth's new party (Mouvement Socialist Mauricien MSM), and the LP, PMSDF, and CAM. This represented an ethnic alliance between Indians, middle-class Creoles, and Franco-Mauritians. In the 1991 elections Jugnauth made a pact with the MMM and won a resounding victory, but the alliance fell apart in 1993. Jugnauth tried 2 years later to attract Indian votes by proposing the inclusion of ancestral languages in the CPE rankings and failed miserably. The new coalition that was victorious was the LP-MMM alliance. Bräutigam rightly says: "The extraordinary ability of Mauritian political parties and ethnic groups to forge a consensus and build coalition governments has its roots in necessity."[87] Except for one instance (when the MMM secured a majority seats, but had to form a coalition because it had applied to the electoral commission in advance to do so), all parties have had to form a coalition government and consensus has been necessary.

The coalition partners in the governing body have forced the Mauritian state to follow "Fabian socialism" – a socialist democracy instituted through reform. Policies include subsidies for basic food staples, old age social security benefits,[88] subsidized housing loans for low-income households, a well-established free public school system, comprehensive state-supported medical care, and equitable wage levels (the after-tax earnings of the highest levels in the public service are kept at a maximum of 6.5 times the lowest salary levels.)[89] Apart from numerous other institutions, the 'civic network', which is a consultative tool started in 1979, is a process whereby finance ministers consult (via public meetings) with major interests (NGO's, trade unions, business associations) before big budget decisions are made.[90] In the political realm, state institutions are designed to ensure that minority representation and coalition governments is the norm. This provides the basis for Creole and other minority rights. But these institutional checks do not undermine the Mauritian-Hindu dominance in state structures and governing bodies. While the nation is an arena of contestation, the state is in the control of the Indo-Mauritian majority.

Conclusion

This chapter has argued that Indo-Mauritian identity is produced and reproduced over time by creating a hegemonic discourse of the nation by maintaining cultural and ideological connections with an imagined homeland to reinforce local identities and power. The political system however demands that Indians form coalitions with parties across the ideological spectrum in order to constitute the government. This ensures that Creoles, the second largest ethnic group, while marginalized, cannot be ignored.

The Hindu majority has ensured that the Hindi language and economic and social ties with India have been strongly supported by the state. By designating Hindi and other Asian languages as ancestral, and hence including them in the national examinations for admissions to secondary and tertiary educational institutions, Hindus have marginalized Creoles. While the majority of the population speaks Mauritian Kreol, it is not considered an ancestral language and hence is not taught in schools nor is it supported by cultural and social institutions. The competitive education system that requires after-school tutoring, tends to disadvantage Creole pupils who are generally poorer. Finally, while Mauritius is known for its successful economy, this success is largely based on transforming the island into an industrial base that is dependent on skilled and educated employees. Here too, Creoles have been marginalized and struggle to compete in the labor market.

The political system that demands coalition governments together with the "best loser" system ensures that Creole demands are not ignored. Instead, the state has sought to increase welfare benefits throughout the post-Colonial period, and Creoles have also benefited. Recognizing that their hegemony is contested, Hindus have constructed a nation that highlights the diasporic connection with India and have emphasized ancestral languages, religion, and culture, to highlight their difference with respect to Creoles. Indo-Mauritian identity is more about its relations with Creoles than it is about being "authentic" enough for India. The identity of the indentured Indian diaspora is national, local, and employs India to reinforce and reproduce its hegemony in the Mauritian state and to increase its bargaining position with respect to the nation.

Notes

1 William F. Miles, "The Creole Malaise in Mauritius," *African Affairs* Vol. 98, No. 391, (1999): pp. 214–215.

2 At end of 2014 the population of the Republic of Mauritius was 1,262,721. Statistics Mauritius, accessed on May 5, 2015, http://statsmauritius.govmu.org/English/Pages/default.aspx. Ethnic breakdown of the population: Indo-Mauritians 68 per cent, Creole 26.3 per cent, Sino-Mauritians 3 per cent, Franco-Mauritians 2 per cent. Religion: Hindu 48.5 per cent, Roman Catholic 26.3 per cent, Muslims 17.3 per cent, other Christian 6.4 per cent, other 0.6 per cent, non 0.7 per cent, unspecified 0.1 per cent (2011 estimates). Creole 86.5 per cent, Bhojpuri 5.3 per cent, French 4.1 per cent, two languages 1.4 per cent other 2.6 per cent (includes English, the official language, spoken by less than 1 per cent of the population), unspecified 0.1 per cent (2011 est.), accessed on May 5, 2015, Index Mundi, www.indexmundi.com/mauritius/demographics_profile.html.

3 Miles, "The Creole Malaise in Mauritius," 211.
4 Pratha Chatterjee, *The Politics of the Governed. Reflections on Popular Politics in Most of the World*, (New York: Columbia University Press, 2004).
5 Piers M. Larson, "Enslaved Malagasy and "Le Travail De La Parole" in the Pre-Revolutionary Mascarenes," *The Journal of African History* Vol. 48 No. 3, (2007). pp. 457–479.
6 Patrick Eisenlohr, "Register Levels of Ethno-National Purity: The Ethnicization of Language and Community in Mauritius," *Language in Society* Vol. 33, No. 1 (Feb, 2004), pp. 59–80.
7 See Larson, "Enslaved Malagasy."
8 Robin Cohen, *Global Diasporas: An Introduction*, (Seattle: University of Washington Press, 1997), ix.
9 K. Hazareesingh, "The Religion and Culture of Indian Immigrants in Mauritius and the Effect of Social Change," *Comparative Studies in Society and History*, 8, no. 2 (1966).
10 S. Chandrasekhar, *The Population of Mauritius. Fact, Problem and Policy*, (New Delhi: Indus Publishing, 1990), 49.
11 Hugh Tinker, "Between Africa, Asia and Europe: Mauritius: Cultural Marginalisation and Political Control." *African Affairs* 76. no. 304, (1997): 324.
12 W.E. Frere and V.A. Williamson, *Report of the Royal Commissioner Appointed to Enquire into the Treatment of Immigrants in Mauritius*, (London, William Clorves & Sons, 1875), pp. 15–16. Quoted in Hazareesingh, "The Religion and Culture," 242.
13 Moses D.E. Nwulia, "The "Apprenticeship" System in Mauritius: Its Character and Its Impact on Race Relations in the Immediate Post-Emancipation Period, 1839–1879." *African Studies Review*, Vol. 21, No. 1 (Apr, 1978), p. 91.
14 Hazareesingh, "The Religion and Culture," 244.
15 Chandrasekhar, The Population of Mauritius, 53.
16 Ibid., 61.
17 Monique Dinan, Vidula Nababsing, and Hansraj Mathur. "Mauritius: Cultural Accommodation in a Diverse Island Polity." In The Accommodation of Cultural Diversity: Case Studies, ed. by Crawford Young, (New York: St. Martin's Press, 1999), 76.
18 Anthony D. King, Ed. Culture, Globalization and World-System. Contemporary Conditions for the Representation of Identity, (Minneapolis: University of Minnesota Press, 1977), x.
19 Sandhya Shukla, "Locations for South Asian Diasporas." Annual Review of Anthropology, 30 (2001): 551.
20 Patrick Eisenlohr, Patrick. *Little India, Diaspora, Time, and Ethnolinguistic Belonging in Hindu Mauritius*, (Berkeley, University of California Press, 2006), 8.
21 Shukla, "Location for the South Asian Diaspora," 551.
22 See Arjun Appadurai, *Modernity at Large: Cultural Dimensions of Globalization*, (Minneapolis: University of Minnesota Press, 1996).
23 Eisenlohr, *Little India*, 12.
24 Robin Cohen, "Diasporas and the Nation-State: From Victim to Challengers." *International Affairs* 72, no. 3 (1996): 517.
25 Appadurai, Modernity at Large, 19.
26 Hall, Stuart. *Culture, Globalization and World System. Contemporary Conditions for the Representation of Identity*, (Minneapolis: University of Minnesota Press, 1977), p. 26.
27 Immanuel Wallerstein, "The National and the Universal: Can There Be Such a Thing as World Culture?" In Culture, Globalization and World-System: Contemporary Conditions for the Representation of Identity, ed. by Anthony D. King, (Minneapolis: University of Minnesota Press, 1977), 99.
28 Saskia Sassen, *Territory, Authority, Rights: From Medieval to Global Assemblages*, (Princeton: University of Princeton Press, 2006).
29 Walker, R.B.J. "International Relations and the Concept of the Political. In International Relations Theory Today," ed. by Ken Booth and Steve Smith, (Pennsylvania: The Pennsylvania State University Press, 1995).

30 Sheila L. Croucher, "Perpetual Imagining: Nationhood in a Global Era." *International Studies Review* 5. no. 1 (2003).

31 Walker Connor, *Ethnonationalism: The Quest for Understanding*, (Princeton NJ: Princeton University Press, 1994).

32 J. S. Furnivall, *Colonial Policy and Practice. A Comparative Study of Burma and Netherlands India*, (Cambridge: University of Cambridge Press, 1948), p. 304.

33 Ibid., 306.

34 Eisenlohr, *Little India,* 5.

35 Ibid., 7.

36 Thomas Hylland Eriksen, *Common Denominations: Ethnicity, Nation Building and Compromise in Mauritius*, (Oxford, UK: Berg, 1998), 19.

37 Rosabelle. Boswell, *Le Malaise Créole: Ethnic Identity in Mauritius*. (New York: Berghahn Books, 2006), xviii.

38 Ibid., 14.

39 Ibid., 206.

40 William F. S. Miles, "The Creole Malaise in Mauritius." *African Affairs* 98 (1999): 211.

41 Miles "The Creole Malaise," 213.

42 Larson, "Enslaved Malagasy Population," p. 463.

43 Miles, "The Creole Malaise," 215.

44 Ibid., p. 216.

45 Richard Allen, *Slaves, Freedmen, and Indentured Laborers in Colonial Mauritius*, (Cambridge: Cambridge University Press, 1999).

46 Ibid., p. 104.

47 Ibid., p. 148.

48 Ibid., p. 180.

49 Ibid., p. 180.

50 Ibid., p. 94.

51 Nwulia, "The 'Apprenticeship' System," pp. 96–97

52 Ibid., p. 99

53 Ibid., p. 100

54 David Lincoln, "Beyond the Plantation: Mauritius in the Global Division of Labor," *The Journal of Modern African Studies* Vol. 44 No. 1, (2006).

55 David Harvey, *A Brief History of Neoliberalism*, (New York: Oxford University Press, 2007), p. 2.

56 Richard Sandbrook and David Romano, "Globalization, Extremism and Violence in Poor Countries," *Third World Quarterly* Vol. 25 No. 6, (2004).

57 Richard Sandbrook, "Origins of the Democratic Developmental State: Interrogating Mauritius." *Canadian Journal of African Studies* 39, no. 3 (2005): 565.

58 Thomas Meisenhelder, "The Developmental State in Mauritius." *The Journal of Modern African Studies* 35, no. 2 (1997): 290.

59 Sandbrook, "Origins of the Democratic," 567.

60 See N. L. Aumeerally, ""Tiger in Paradise": Reading Global Mauritius in Shifting Time and Space," *Journal of African Cultural Studies* Vol. 17 No. 2, (2005).

61 "India-Mauritius Relations," High Commission of India, Port Louis, Mauritius, accessed on May 18, 2015, www.indiahighcom-mauritius.org/pages.php?id=33

62 In a United States memorandum leaked by Wikileaks, Mauritius denied that they planned on ceding Agalega islands to India for strategic purposes, possibly establishing a military or naval base or an eavesdropping station, or for oil exploration. Accessed on May 18, 2015, https://wikileaks.org/plusd/cables/06PORTLOUIS752_a.html

63 "Mauritius assures help to India in black money probe," *The Hindu*, April 11, 2014, accessed on May 18, 2015, www.thehindu.com/news/national/mauritius-assures-help-to-india-in-black-money-probe/article6561191.ece

64 Aumeerally, "Tiger in Paradise," p. 172

65 Miles, "The Creole Malaise," 217.
66 Hugh Tinker, "Mauritius: Culture and Political Control." *African Affairs,* 76 no. 304 (1997): 335.
67 See Miles, "The Creole Malaise," 225.
68 Boswell, "Le Malaise Creole."
69 Miles, "The Creole Malaise."
70 Patrick Eisenlohr, "Register Levels of Ethno-National Purity: The Ethnicization of Language and Community in Mauritius," *Language in Society,* Vol. 33 No. 1, (2004): p. 64.
71 Ibid., 59.
72 Ibid., p. 71.
73 The Central Statistics Office of Mauritius that conducts the national census had not collected data on ethnicity since 1983. Any statistics that are reported after this period are estimates.
74 Miles, William F. S. Miles, "The Politics of Language Equilibrium in a Multilingual Society: Mauritius." *Comparative Politics* 32, no. 2 (2000): 218.
75 Eisenlohr, *Little India,* 33.
76 Partick Eisenlohr, "The Politics of Diaspora and the Morality of Secularism: Muslim Identities and Islamic Authority in Mauritius," *The Journal of the Royal Anthropological Institute,* Vol. 12 No. 2, (2006).
77 See Rosabelle Boswell, "Unraveling Le Malaise Créole: Hybridity and Marginalization in Mauritius," *Identities: Global Studies in Culture and Power,* Vol. 12 No. 2, (2005).
78 Thomas Hylland Erikson, "Creolization in Anthropological Theory and in Mauritius," in *History, Ethnography, Theory,* ed. by Charles Stewart, (Walnut Creek: Left Coast Press, 2006).
79 Ibid., p. 163
80 Ibid.
81 Lynn M. Hempel, " Power, Wealth and Common Identity: Access to Resources and Ethnic Identification in a Plural Society," *Ethnic and Racial Studies* Vol. 32 No. 3, (2009).
82 Miles 2000, p. 223.
83 Miles 2000, p. 227.
84 Rosabelle Boswell, "Heritage Tourism and Identity in the Mauritian Villages of Chamarel and Le Morne," *Journal of Southern African Studies,* Vol. 31 No. 2, (2005): p. 289.
85 See Nave, Ari. "The Institutionalisation of Communalism: The Best Loser System." In Consolidating the Rainbow: Independent Mauritius, 1968–1998, ed. by Marina Carter, (Port Louis, Mauritius: Center for Research on Indian Ocean Studies, 1998).
86 Henry Srebrnik, " 'Full of Sound and Fury': Three Decades of Parliamentary Politics in Mauritius," *Journal of Southern African Studies* 28. no. 2 (2002): 289.
87 Deborah Bräutigam, "Institutions, Economic Reform, and Democratic Consolidation in Mauritius." *Comparative Politics* 30, no. 1 (1999): 53.
88 A universal Basic Retirement Pension (BRP) at 60 years of age, includes pensions for widows, invalids, and orphans. See Sandbrook, "Origins of the Democratic."
89 Bräutigam, "Institutions, Economic Reform," 56.
90 Sandbrook , "Origins of the Democratic," 562–563.

5 Indians in South Africa

Figure 5.1 Houtbay, Cape Town

In post-apartheid South Africa the ruling tripartite alliance of the African National Congress (ANC), the Congress of South African Trade Unions (COSATU) and the South African Communist Party (SACP), chose not to re-classify Indians as African or Afro-Indian or Indo-African, but to keep their classification as Indian. Although Indians have been living in the country for over 150 years, they continue to be categorized in terms of a diaspora identity that is associated with India and correlates with the category of outsiders. They are *ethnically* seen as "Coolie"(named as such during indenture and used pejoratively), Asiatic (another colonial category that included Indians, Arabs, Malays, and Chinese), and Indian (a colonial, apartheid, and post-apartheid category). The rest of South Africa is classified in terms of race: Black African, White, Coloured. This chapter is centered on the reasons for the adoption of apartheid era racial and ethnic categories by the post-apartheid state and its implications for Indians.

The constitution of the post-apartheid state is rightly celebrated as a progressive document that recognizes and protects people who were previously marginalized – women, children, the disabled, sick, and elderly. Despite these constitutional protections, the plight of the poor, the majority of all people of color, remains dire. The structural parameters of the state are such that it has struggled to meet the needs of the poor while simultaneously engaging with global economic systems. The result is a state skewed towards the rich, both nationally and internationally, in the pursuit of creating the optimum conditions for neoliberal economics. Nevertheless, it is also a state that has to meet the needs of the vast majority who were, subjugated under colonialism, settler colonialism, and apartheid, and who suffer the consequences of underfunded and weak educational and health care facilities, substantial backlogs and underdevelopment in housing and living conditions, and high unemployment levels. This was the majority that supported the ANC in the last few elections; the party also recognizes the need to publicly commit to programs and policies that address some of these issues. From its adoption in the mid-1990s, the neoliberal economic frame of reference has generally failed to effectively redistribute income to the lower levels of society. The increase in protests and resistance a decade later reflect growing discontent among the poor. Throughout its tenure the state has continued to rely on ethnic and racial divisions that were historically in place, and that continue to divide the majority serving to undermine united resistance. While affirmative action programs ensure that the middle classes grow, ethnic and racial classifications continue to divide the population, maintaining low-level tensions and competition among the various groups. In other words, by keeping the racial classifications of apartheid, the post-apartheid state also kept the narratives of racism that had been propagated under 42 years of apartheid (1948–1990) and 130 years of colonial and settler self-rule (1814–1947).

The implications for Indians are twofold. First, a majority of them are poor due to unemployment, under-employment, low wages, weak social services, inadequate welfare programs, and underfunded education facilities. Second, even though Indians and Coloureds[1] are officially included in affirmative action programs, they are practically excluded. Despite majority rule, state functions are still dependent on racial divisions; voting rosters, access to government programs, affirmative action programs, educational, and other services are facilitated through racial classification. The reasons for the adoption of this kind of state are worth debating, as are the repercussions for the poor majority. Indians have experienced this state from the perspective of a small minority divided along the lines of class and ethnicity (religion and regional origin from India are still relevant). As they are not officially considered African (in terms of South Africa) or Indian (in terms of India), Indians occupy the *transnational locality*, neither wholly belonging to South Africa nor to India. They are designated as the ethnic other, and structurally marginalized from the post-apartheid state. The discourse on race put forth by this system do not interrogate the constructs of race, on the contrary, it has re-emphasized them while at the same time re-instituting new levels of class disparities across all ethnic and racial groups.

This analysis is based on a structural argument; despite the powerful mobilization and action by social movements in the country, the manner and terms of the negotiations leading up to the democratic transition as well as the characteristics of the post-apartheid system, were decided upon by elites far removed from the masses. While the actions of social movements helped to push the country towards the political transition, their role during and after the transition was negligible. Global and local capitalists, national and international government elites, and the exiled, detained, and national leadership of social movements facilitated the transition to a post-apartheid system. The social movements among Indians responded to the various state systems in myriad ways: during colonialism Indians formed many political organizations focused on rights; during apartheid they allied with the broader anti-apartheid movements or joined organizations that concentrated on local demands; in the post-apartheid system Indians have been active in local level social movements dealing with social and political issues. Throughout these periods, religious organizations also gained strength. In sum, Indians were active in social movements from the early periods of indenture, yet have been unable to influence structural shifts at state level. Their ethnicity and diaspora identities have been constantly used to marginalize, subjugate, and separate them from the black majority. Social movement theories shift attention to agency – to the people that actively participate in organizations to increase their rights with respect to the state. In this chapter, I will show that despite the action of Indians over the duration of their settlement in South Africa, the various states have reacted by granting them rights, but ultimately falling back to ethnic definitions to control and marginalize them. By employing this ethnic category, these states have also used Indians to divide the majority and to undermine united action – during colonialism they were seen as scab labor and outsiders whose relative upward mobility came to be resented by the black proletariat; during apartheid they were used as a buffer between Whites and Blacks (both figuratively and in geographical and political segregation), and in post-apartheid they have been sidelined and isolated from mainstream politics and treated as 'outsiders.' It is my contention that an emphasis on structures is the most compelling way of understanding the plight of Indians in South Africa today.

The necessity to articulate with the nation from an ethnic position in a population that is segregated by race and where Black Africans constitute the vast majority, has made the resulting notions of Indianness peculiar to the country, but also very much associated with the diasporic condition. South African Indians are one of the most indigenized of any in the diaspora – they were isolated from a newly independent India after it imposed a cultural boycott on South Africa, and have been ghettoized within the country by segregationist policies and later under apartheid legislation. One of the distinctive features of Indians in South Africa is their insularity from India and the rest of the diaspora; this has led to

Africanization/indigenization that is not recognized by the post-apartheid state, nor by the majority of Indians themselves.

This chapter will engage with the history of Indians under indenture and apartheid to expose the structures that contributed towards the current position of Indians. It will also focus on their agency through social movements that were created to fight for rights within these systems. The limited success that Indians have had in changing their position with respect to the post-apartheid state has roots in these periods, and speaks directly to their objective and subjective status as belonging to a diaspora. The chapter starts with the period of indenture under British segregationist policies when Indians were treated as imperial subjects (although here too they were subjects of the colonial administration), albeit as foreigners or temporary residents in the colony. This is followed by the apartheid era when Indians were ruled and treated as a discrete ethnic group among many others – while Africans were categorized as Black or African, they were further categorized in ethnic terms (Zulu, Xhoza, and so on). To some extent Indians were given more status than their numbers warranted. Under apartheid while Indians were employed as a racial/ethnic barrier between Whites and Blacks, they came to be seen as "insiders" (even though they were distanced and distrusted) by the state, but retained an outsider quality with respect to both Whites and indigenous peoples.

The second part of the chapter focuses on the characteristics of the transition process from apartheid to a post-apartheid system; here attention will be given to the reasons for the kind of state structures that were adopted and its implications for Indians. It will show that despite the strong role played by Indians in anti-apartheid social movements, they, together with other grassroots organizations, failed to make a strong impact on the democratic state. Even though the majority gained the right to vote together with multiple protections guaranteed by the constitution, the core structures of the state were weighted towards providing the conditions for national and international capital investment. Furthermore, affirmative action laws and other policies prioritized African upward mobility while general economic policies have pushed more Indians into the ranks of the poor, polarizing class differences. The implications for contemporary social movements and the position of Indians in the current system will be discussed.

Segregation/racism and white settlers in Natal

Indians were indentured to Natal by the British to provide labor for the enterprises of settler colonialists and British investors. The local African people, numbering a few hundred thousand at the time, were self-sustaining, and the Zulu kingdom was a powerful political force (only defeated in 1879 with the Anglo-Zulu war) that either recruited people to join their Kingdom or forced them to flee. These factors acted to dissuade African people from entering the colonial labor market. The Dutch East India Company had first introduced foreign labor to the region in the seventeenth century; the slaves that they brought to the Cape were ethnically diverse, hailing from Malaysia, the Indian coasts, and Indies archipelago. These diverse origins were reflected in the languages that were first spoken, a mix of

Javanese, Malay, Bengali, and Kannada.[2] Consecutive white regimes categorized descendants from these groups using such terms as Cape Malay, Cape Colored, Other Colored, and Indian, mainly to define them as mixed race or as part of an existing classified racial category. 63,000 slaves entered the Cape between 1652 and 1808.[3] More than half a century later, indentured laborers from various parts of India arrived in Natal.[4]

Indenture was facilitated through the Natal Law 14 of 1859[5] under which a "Coolie Immigration Department" was set up to deal with the financial administration (potential employers paid three-fifths of the cost), registration and allocation of indentured Indians. The contract was for 5 years and was renewable for another 5, wages were to be at least 10 shillings a month and upon expiration of the initial contract Indians became free. After 10 years they were eligible for free passage to India or the Governor could commute the cost of return passage into a grant of Crown land. 154,641 Indians entered Natal between 1860 and 1911. In addition, from the 1870s onwards, "passenger" Indians arrived and by the 1890s they numbered about 5,500.[6] In 1894 Indians surpassed Whites in Natal, they totaled 43,000 and 40,000 respectively.[7] The majority were employed in the sugar industry directly contributing towards transforming it from a backward enterprise to one of the most efficient producers in the world.[8] In the 2011 census there were 1,274,867 Indians in South Africa making them the largest number in this diaspora; they are a small minority in the country constituting 2.5 per cent of the population.[9]

This section will focus on two aspects of colonial politics that set up the structural conditions that defined Indians as perpetual outsiders: first, the settler colonial system that demarcated those who were considered citizens (Whites) with rights, and those who were subjects (African, Indian, Coloured) who had few if any rights. Second, settler colonialists devised racist laws for the growing Indian population who were nevertheless imperial subjects, thus demanding policies that were *within* ordinary law. By ignoring and undermining Indian rights they relied more heavily on exclusion, force, and punishment[10] – factors that became foundational in ruling over and controlling all people of color under apartheid. British settlers were influenced by the segregationist policies implemented throughout the empire.[11]

Settler Colonialism is different to colonialism in significant ways, the most important of which is that settlers immigrated in order to occupy territory and to form a new community, as opposed to immigrating solely to extract labor and resources. Even though capitalist gain was an important motivating factor, settler colonization initially focuses on territorial gain and the formation of a community by dispossessing indigenous communities and establishing a hegemonic economic and cultural presence in a region.[12] Unlike colonialism, that situates indigenous people in a relationship that recognizes their existence but relegates them to a place of permanent subservience, settler colonials attempt to "erase" indigenous peoples (African and "Coloureds") by positioning themselves as pioneers, distinctive from speculators (colonial and global investors) and "newcomers" or more recent settlers (Indians).[13] As Mamdani states, "The notion of "settler" distinguishes conquerors from immigrants."[14] Settlers create structures to ensure their continued hegemony making them "impervious to regime change."[15] In reaction to resistance settler colonialists might institute reforms, but here too the emphasis is on maintaining their hegemony while denying the presence of indigenous and other non-Native subjects. While indigenous African people were the vast majority in the region, the settler colonialist in Natal "erased" them by forcing them to live in areas segregated from white towns and cities, and by controlling their employment. Indians were targeted for legislation designed to subjugate, silence, and relegate them to the periphery of the political, economic and cultural landscape. As Lord Milner succinctly said in 1904, 40 years from the time of indenture: "The Asiatics are strangers, forcing themselves upon a community reluctant to receive them."[16] This community was the settlers who viewed Indians as a potential counter-hegemonic force.

Indians moved out of indenture at a rapid rate; by 1909 only 7,006 of 25,567 indentured workers remained on the cane fields.[17] In market gardening they soon supplanted all other rivals and took over the industry. Street hawkers sold fresh vegetables door-to-door in Durban. Indian farmers successfully cultivated sugar, maize, tobacco, and other vegetables.[18] They were employed as domestic servants or as laborers on the railroads, the Durban Municipality, the coalmines, and other companies. In 1936 in Natal 36.8 per cent were still working in agriculture but by 1970 only 4.8 per cent remained, the vast majority were employed in urban related industries.[19] Indian competitiveness was based on a strong work ethic and the social support and shared financial resources of an extended family.[20] Whites attributed their success to racial inferiority, sub-par social and cultural habits, and a low standard of living, all of which enabled them to live a frugal lifestyle while accumulating capital. This is illustrated well in an editorial of the Johannesburg *Star*:

> . . . . the coolie. . . lowers the standard of comfort, and closes the avenues to prosperity to the European trader. Economically, he is of no advantage to the country he visits – for, be it remembered that he does not settle. He accumulates money by virtue of the wretchedness in which he lives – a wretchedness constituting a terrible danger to the rest of the community – and he takes 80 percent of that money back again to Asia. In Natal we actually have the spectacle of European trade being gradually destroyed by the impossible competition of the coolie. The Asiatic is thus a menace to the European's life, an obstacle to his commercial progress. . . .[21]

The sugar industry in Natal grew substantially after 1887 when Zululand was annexed,[22] attracting investors from throughout the empire.[23] Yet those who supported this industry came to be resented. Swanson talks of the white "sense of alarm and annoyance;"[24] another observer noted:

> It might be recorded that the writer found South Africans in different parts of the Union more ready to assert the gravity of the problems arising out of their quarter-million Indian minority than to face the likely consequences of the growth of nationalism among their numerically dominant eight million Bantu.[25]

As newcomers, Indians were perceived as posing a threat to the settler sense of superiority[26] and status as pioneers who first paved the way for civilization and Westernization.

White settlers devised racist practices to protect their position.[27] Focusing specifically on the spate of laws instituted to undercut the capacity of street hawkers to trade, Vahed shows how a licensing officer conceded that these laws were used as an instrument of segregation.[28] Indians in turn began to cater to the needs of Africans and came to dominant retail networks throughout these areas. Indian traders outperformed African competitors because they had "better access to capital, business expertise, and ready source of supply, while they performed better than whites by providing a personalized service, cheaper prices, and longer hours."[29] Segregationist policies in Natal set the basis for white rule in the country. Indians challenged the identities of settler colonialists and whiteness in general, a construct that was divided along ethnicity (English-speaking and Afrikaans-speaking), class (elite, middle classes, and working poor), generation (South African born and new immigrants), and race (miscegenation, mixed race). But despite consistent resistance throughout this period they continued to be "erased" as an ethnic group. Even though they gained a few rights, their position within the structures of the settler colonial state did not change at all.

Indenture separated Indians from India – both spatially and psychologically they became entrenched in local affairs. Resistance to oppression became part and parcel of permanent settlement and survival. Ranging from social transgressions (suicide, alcoholism, drug abuse, spousal abuse, and sexual assault), to public and private cultural/religious events (large festivals, elaborate wedding ceremonies), and overt resistance (passive resistance, political engagement, radical opposition), Indians resiliently persisted. Over several generations they became more removed from India and the Indian diaspora and more rooted in South Africa.

Through social movements Indians were able to gain some freedoms, these was marginal in comparison to the rights enjoyed by white citizens but slightly more than those for Africans. The first concerted attempts to change the laws governing indenture were organized by Mohandas Karamchand Gandhi in South Africa between 1893 and 1914. Fighting on the side of traders who were mainly Gujarati-speaking and had entered the country as 'passengers', Gandhi drew a distinction between indentured Indians on contracts (hence dependent on the rules imposed by Estate owners and local policies) and trader Indians who relied on "imperial relations" to determine legislation pertaining to immigration.[30] He placed import on the Proclamation of 1858 that recognized Indians as subjects of the British Empire. Although he eventually broadened resistance to include all Indians (in terms of status, class, and religion), he never expanded his movement to include other oppressed races. As Bose says: Gandhi's

> political worldview shows a racialism wholly transplanted from educated Anglophone circles of the nineteenth century, as so many of his efforts stemmed from an anxiety of how laws in colonial South Africa would "degrade the Indian to the position of the Kaffir" and bespeak an extreme

fear of miscegenation and classification alongside the African populations of the region.[31]

The social movements that were influenced by Gandhi initially maintained a distance from other oppressed groups and only later did they become more inclusive organizations.

The 1913 strike was one of the most effective acts of resistance; Swan sees it as marking a crucial moment "in the emergence of the modern South African Indian working class."[32] Living conditions for Indians after the end of their contracts – some 52 per cent stayed mainly in Natal – worsened when an annual £3 tax was levied on all those who entered indenture after 1895. By 1913 nearly 65 per cent of the indentured workforce was under renewed labor contracts.[33] The Natal Indian Congress (NIC) which was created in 1894 represented the interests of traders and was distant from the working classes – it was the new white collar Indian elite that begun to develop ideologies of resistance and rallied workers for support. Numbering about 300 in the census of 1904, they were mainly Natal born, Western-educated, and Tamil. They formed alternate organizations like the Natal Indian Patriotic Union, the Colonial Born Indian Association, and the South African Indian Community, and all organized around the repeal of the £3 annual tax. These activities together with the strong support they received pushed Gandhi and the NIC towards taking up the issue as well. Action against the tax escalated when Gandhi called for strikes in October 1913 and relied on local leaders (from the new elite) and seasoned passive resisters to mobilize support. Starting in northern Natal where 4,000 to 5,000 workers supported it, the strike spread to southern Natal, where over 15,000 came out in support.[34] By the end of the year a commission was appointed and by April 1914 it recommended the abolition of the £3 tax and settlement for the passive-resistance movement. During this period of intense Indian mobilization against the imposition of an annual tax, the state continued to create structures that segregated Africans in a more structured manner. The passage of the Natives Land Act (No. 27 of 1913) pertained to those of an "aboriginal race or tribe" making it legal for them to own land in 7 per cent of the country, later increased to 13.5 per cent. Laws dealing with anti-squatting and scheduled areas (reserves) were later included. During this period structures were created to control and place all people of color in racially and ethnically defined areas, leaving the vast majority of land for white occupation. Resistance had little effect on changing this structure.

Indian leaders with a more radical bent began to take over the main political organizations and the ideology among these leaders soon led them to a closer alliance with the larger black political resistance movement. The Doctors Pact of 1946 exemplifies this liaison when the leaders of the NIC, the Transvaal Indian Congress (TIC) and the African National Congress (ANC) agreed that:

> . . . having fully realized the urgency of co-operation between the non-European peoples and other democratic forces for the attainment of basic human rights and full citizenship for all sections of the South African

peoples, has resolved that a joint declaration of co-operation is imperative for the working out of a practical basis of co-operation between the national organization of the non-European peoples.[35]

The pact called for greater co-operation between Africans and Indians to work towards a full franchise for all South Africans – by this time Indian leaders began to look to rights for all people of color. The well-orchestrated and organized passive resistance campaigns of 1946–47 against the Asiatic Land Tenure and Indian Representation Bill (which later became known as the Ghetto Act)[36] were successful in marshaling political activism among Indians; 1,710 passive resisters were imprisoned.[37]

Two events changed the tenor of resistance during this period. First, the victory of the National Party in 1947 and the steady institutionalization of apartheid (the implications of which will be analyzed below); second, the Durban riots of 1949.[38] The riots of Africans against Indians took place over three days in January 1949 and left 142 dead, 1,087 injured, and the destruction of numerous buildings and properties.[39] Most analysts see the implications of segregationist policies, which continued to be operative in 1949 (apartheid legislation hadn't as yet been implemented), as the source for the riots. Some look to African resentment of Indian upward mobility and the negative attitudes and practices of Indians towards Africans; others have suggested a conspiracy between Whites and Africans against Indians.[40] Given the weak bargaining position of the African proletariat at the time, Edwards et al. explain the spontaneity and ferocity of the riots in terms of Africans sensing "a moment of opportunity to use popular force in challenging the state and its designs, not directly but through communal assault on a vulnerable racially defined target."[41] There is ample evidence to substantiate most of these claims. It is important to note that in 1951 the total Indian population was around 365,000; over 300,000 of lived in Natal and of these about 150,000 lived in Durban.[42] In the city the population was evenly divided among the three main racial groups: 151,000 Africans, 161,000 Indians and 151,000 whites.[43] Woods says that by 1951 the actual Indian population in Durban exceeded whites by 10 per cent.[44]

Segregationist laws were propagated under the Union government established in 1910 when the four British colonies of the Cape Colony, Natal Colony, Transvaal Colony, and Orange River Colony united as a dominion of the British Empire. The political, social, and economic system that was created was based on racism as its working ideology and segregation as its operating principle. These laws had complex implications for relations between the various peoples of color. For example, Indian families in areas like Cato Manor had sub-let their homes to Africans. Between 1939 and 1949 the African squatter population in this area had increased from 2,500 to 50,000.[45] By 1949 the Cato Manor area had been transformed from supporting Indian market gardeners to supporting African shack dwellers renting from Indian property owners.[46] The riots represented the culmination of segregation and heralded the transition to apartheid. A year later the National Party imposed the Group Areas Act and by 1958 Cato Manor was declared a white area – Africans were evicted or forcibly removed to the townships of KwaMarshu and

Umlazi while Indians were moved to Chatsworth. In 1979 Cato Manor was de-proclaimed (as white) and again designated Indian. At the time about 500 Indians families still remained; they had resiliently stayed on despite legislation barring them from the area. Currently a growing African shack settlement has taken root and the post-apartheid government had yet to deal with their need for housing.[47] The riots provided Afrikaner nationalists with an argument for stricter segregation especially with respect to the African population – relocation and control became the basis of new policies.

Apartheid – the national party and racism

The National Party came into power in 1948. What is clear is that the segrega-tionist policies of whites in Natal who were mainly non-Afrikaners had already constructed the framework for apartheid. Even the mayor of Durban in 1957 rec-ognized that apartheid "was the traditional policy of the burgesses of Durban and their urban representatives long before the Nationalists came to power."[48] Some 90 per cent of White voters in the Durban municipality had voted against Indian representation in 1947. But apartheid was distinctive in that legislation no longer needed to be couched under a liberal façade, instead a litany of laws were passed that segregated the various racial groups, controlled and policed their movement and employment, and violently oppressed political opposition and resistance. For the majority of Indians who began to fill the ranks of the urban working classes, the new regime forced them to become more insular in their private lives – to operate in a parallel universe structured around their own communities in segre-gated neighborhoods.

The National Party saw Indians as "temporary sojourners in South Africa" who had to be "repatriated as soon as possible," a conclusion made after Indians had been in the country for nearly 90 years.[49] The attitude towards Indians was clearly articulated in a Party brochure:

> The National Party holds the view that the Indians are a foreign and out-landish element which is inassimilable. They can never become part of the country and must, therefore, be treated as an immigrant community. The party accepts as a basis of its policy the repatriation of as many Indians as possible. . . So long as there are still Indians in the country a definite policy of separation will be applied.[50]

Van den Berghe suggests that Indians "symbolized everything that the Afrikaner Volk" (nation) opposed – they were *uitlanders* (outsiders), city folk, and trading people.[51] While the policies of apartheid were contested among the ruling elite,[52] its outcomes were not – the country was rigidly segregated and every effort was made to regulate the supply of labor with the creation of Bantustans and institutions for the implementation of an internal migrant labor system. In the racial hierarchy Africans were subjected to the harshest and most strictly monitored apartheid leg-islation, and even though Indians and Coloureds were also segregated, they had marginally more freedoms. Of the numerous rules and regulations imposed on Indians, the Group Areas Act of 1950 had the most far-reaching impact. Maasdrop and Pillay note that when the bill was discussed in parliament there was unanimity among all parties (including the opposition United Party and Labour Party) on racial-residential segregation; there was some disagreement on its application.[53] In a government White Paper the bill was devised for two purposes:

> firstly, to bring persons of the same racial origin together for the purposes of ownership and occupation, and so to reduce to a minimum racial points of contact and therefore possible racial friction, and secondly, to permit each racial group to develop along its own lines, according to its language, culture, and religion, and to give members of the Native and Coloured groups an opportunity under proper guidance ultimately to assume responsibility for their own local government.[54]

Spatial and physical segregation was the cornerstone of apartheid – the creation and maintenance of towns and cities, capital and trade, for Whites only, with people of color providing labor and services only when needed.

Eventually in 1961 the National Party decided to grant Indians citizenship (albeit continuing to be subjects and denied the vote) and a separate department of Indian Affairs was created. Instead of seeing Indians as inassimilable they were now contained and controlled on the basis of their ethnicity, in line with the general public rationale of apartheid.[55]

It is estimated that under the Group Areas Act some 80 per cent of Indians were forcibly moved from towns and cities into areas that were further afield, leaving a White central core. In Durban, Indians were moved to the vast townships of Chatsworth and Phoenix, both acting as buffers between white neighborhoods and the African townships of Umlazi and Inanda. Smaller Indian residential areas were scattered around the outskirts of the city each having its own shopping centers, markets, schools, hospitals, cinemas, transport, and other infrastructure.

The transfer of Indian education to the Ministry of Indian Affairs in 1966 and the implementation of compulsory education in 1973 hastened their movement into semi-skilled and skilled employment. Indians with tertiary degrees from universities (including the Indian-only University of Durban-Westville) increased dramatically. In 1985 over 17,000 Indians were enrolled in South African universities and a further 8201 were registered for correspondence degree courses at the University of South Africa (UNISA), a number three times higher than Coloureds, but 40 per cent lower than Whites.[56] Indians had become more entrenched in South Africa and more distant from India – in 1978 it was reported that in Natal 96 per cent of Indians between the ages of 15 and 35 were literate in English, and there was a concomitant decrease in those who spoke Tamil, Telugu, or Hindi.[57]

The reform efforts made by the regime in the mid-1980s included structural changes for Indians and Coloureds in the apartheid representational institutions. Under a new constitution a tricameral parliament was created consisting of a House of Assembly (for Whites), a House of Representatives (for Coloureds), and a House of Delegates (for Indians), with proportional representation of 4:2:1. Africans were not included. Indians and Coloureds were being set up as buffers to African resistance and increasing unrest in the country. Indian leaders, active in anti-apartheid movements for generations, organized a boycott spearheaded by the United Democratic Front (UDF), a broad front that included the Natal Indian Congress and the Transvaal Indian Congress. The boycott was successful; only 20.3 per cent voted nationally (23.7 per cent in the 1989 election). Indians had put themselves firmly in the camp of the UDF, and by extension the African National Congress (ANC).

Under apartheid Indians moved steadily into the working classes, especially in the clothing and textile industries. By 1955 Indians and Coloureds made up 89 per cent of this workforce.[58] Indians also began to move into more skilled jobs that required better education and training. With increasing employment came increasing trade union membership and resistance. Starting with the Falkirk foundry strike in 1937, trade union activity increased again in the apartheid era with massive strikes against the textile mills (Consolidated Textile Mill (Frame's) in 1956/7) and politically motivated stay-aways.

The implications of apartheid were deep and lasting – its impact on identity and community being particularly pertinent for this study. Forced removals and relocations had a devastating impact on Indians, irrespective of class. People were moved from settled and closely knit neighborhoods, many from their family homes, to new townships that were alienating. As a journalist at the time elaborates: forced removals uprooted people "from their hearths, homes, temples, churches, mosques, schools, cultural institutions, and forced into dormitories and sleeping cubicles without the right or the opportunity to choose neighborhoods and neighbors."[59] The new residential areas were inhospitable in terms of the remoteness of their locations, the rudimentary houses that were provided, and the planning templates that prioritized state security over architectural aesthetics and community well-being. Chatsworth, for example, consisted of undulating rows of semi-detached rectangular concrete blockhouses with few internal doors, un-plastered walls, open ceilings, and few if any parks, recreational areas, or community and sporting facilities. Planned for 165,000 people, in 2002 it was estimated that more than 300,000 people lived in the area.[60] This township was home to a sizable proportion of the working classes, many of whom were unemployed, under-employed, and living in poverty. High levels of alcoholism, drug addiction, divorces, child abuse, and gang and criminal activity prevailed.

Despite the difficult circumstances, people in Chatsworth and Phoenix created vibrant neighborhoods with strong communal support from neighbors, families, and friends. They built temples, churches, mosques, and markets. They developed local shebeens (private houses where alcohol was illegally sold and consumed), and informal and formal shopping plazas. The austere rectangular houses were individualized with ornate decorations, colorful paint, elaborate fencing, and other additions that made each house unique.[61] These townships evolved to make Indians more insular and separate from other people of color.

Resistance: Black consciousness and the ANC

Resistance to Apartheid is well documented and the role of Indians is well known. This was a period when a more radical leadership began to initiate political action including boycotts, strikes, and civil disobedience. The South African Indian Congress became closely associated with the African National Congress (ANC) successfully increasing overt resistance against the regime. By the end of 1955 the state banned nineteen Indian leaders and sixty-nine leaders from the ANC and South African Congress of Democrats.[62] Imprisonment and the brutal tactics of the state led to a lull in resistance until it picked up again in the 1970s.

The rise of Black Consciousness, spearheaded by Steve Biko, introduced another level of radicalism in terms of philosophy, mobilization techniques, and ideas about the kind of system that was to replace apartheid. Influenced by revolutionary thinkers, particularly Franz Fanon and the Black Power movement in the United States, Biko's philosophy fused an internal individual psychological struggle with mass organization to overthrow the system. Black consciousness is "immanent in its own eyes," said Fanon of his own consciousness, "I am not a potentiality of something . . . I am wholly what I am."[63] Biko too focuses on the need for liberation from internal fears in order to increase ones consciousness and to overcome the racist identity imposed by Whites – an internal process that required education, struggle and perseverance:

> The first step – is to make the black man come to himself; to pump back life into his empty shell; to infuse him with pride and dignity, to remind him of his complicity in the crime of allowing himself to be misused and therefore letting evil reign supreme in the country of his birth. This is what we mean by an inward-looking process.[64]

Biko saw race as a social construct – a categorization that was created to propagate and perpetuate a hierarchy of power and a mental attitude – Indians and Coloureds who joined the liberation struggle and resisted their oppression were considered Black. He explains:

> We have in our policy manifesto defined blacks as those who are by law or tradition politically, economically and socially discriminated against as a group in the South African society and identifying themselves as a unit in the struggle towards the realization of their aspirations.[65]

Whites were excluded because it was felt that they would undermine black unity. Strini Moodley, who had left the NIC to join the BC movement wrote:

> We have come together on the basis of our common oppression and do not separate on the basis of superficial cultural differences. . . We have the same fears, the same desires and the same experiences. We have to use the same trains, the same buses, the same restaurants.[66]

Many Indians joined the BC movement, some going on to take up leadership positions in other opposition organizations and later in post-apartheid South Africa. BC as a philosophy interrogated notions of Blackness (and Whiteness), it placed race and oppression at the center not only in terms of working and living conditions, but also in terms of the mind and the fear, alienation and acquiescence that goes with it. A popular slogan of students affiliated to the BC-affiliated South African Students' Association (SASO) was, for example: *We are Black students, and not black Students!*[67]

Like Fanon and Antonia Gramci, Biko also focused on the role of intellectuals and activists in the liberation struggle. Fanon was acutely aware of the challenges facing colonial intellectuals who were distant from the masses because of their subject position in the intellectual world of the colonists, a position that demanded that they conformed to colonial bourgeoisie thinking.[68] Biko emphasized self-learning and the pursuit to build individual consciousness before attempting to mobilize the people. Fanon is equally scathing about the way the Black bourgeoisie operates after independence (a harbinger for Black elite leadership in post-apartheid South Africa):

> Because it is lacking in ideas, because it is inward-looking, cut off from the people, sapped by its congenital incapacity to evaluate issue on the basis of the nation as a whole, the national bourgeoisie assumes the role of manager for the companies of the West and turns its country virtually into a bordello of Europe.[69]

Biko called for a complete reorganization of the economy in a non-racial system where the "judicious blending" of private and state enterprises will lead to a "more equitable distribution of wealth." He was skeptical of changes that would merely allow a "few blacks filtering through into the so-called bourgeoisie," while the majority remained poor.[70] The transformation of consciousness would be the "catalyst for mass action."[71] Once the people were conscientized they would ensure that the post-apartheid system was just and that leaders were held accountable. BC activists were encouraged to focus on raising awareness; for example Moodley and Saths Cooper (executive members of the Black Peoples' Convention which was created in 1971 and both former members of the NIC) used theatre to educate people. Other BC activists organized workshops, trade unions, community programs, and cooperatives to increase awareness.

BC was never the mass based movement that the United Democratic Front (ANC driven) was to become; its philosophy was radical and required strong commitments that inadvertently acted against mass mobilization, and it alienated white students and sympathizers who had access to material resources, influential economic and political networks, and international connections. However, it successfully attracted a small group of influential black activists who came to play a significant role in the politics of resistance, and it succeeded in conscientizing a youthful generation who were to be the shock troops of the struggle that starting with the Soweto riots of 1976. BC re-sited the notion of Indianness into the construct of blackness – Indian activists and those who opposed the system were considered Black – a radical departure from the way other organizations defined its participants. The discourses around identity as Black and or Indian are strongly influenced by BC.

The launch of the United Democratic Front (UDF) in 1983 against the tricameral parliament provided a joint political platform for a number of disparate anti-state community, political and trade organizations. The UDF effectively organized against the elections and provided the impetus for concerted and united action from a multi-racial platform. However during this period the role of Inkatha and the Inkatha Freedom Party (IFP) in reinforcing ethnic and racial divisions between Africans (mainly Zulu) and Indians in KwaZulu-Natal cannot be underestimated. Gatsha Buthelezi, the leader of Inkatha, was particularly adept at constructing and mobilizing support around the notion of "Zuluness" – broadly associating it with an ethnic/tribal identity, a warrior tradition (from the time of King Shaka), traditional allegiances (customary rule, rituals, etc.), and indigenous, and therefore "rightfully" resentful of outsiders/Indians.[72] Indian-African tensions have been cited as the reason for the riots of 1949, repeated in 1959–60 in Cato Manor, and again in 1985 in Inanda (a predominantly African township with about 2000 Indians living in the area). In all these instances, racial divisions imposed by segregation and apartheid exacerbated tensions and in some cases, competitive African traders sought to use an ethnic rhetoric to instigate conflict.[73]

While Inkatha was not directly involved in the Inanda attacks, vandalized Indian businesses, homes, and even medical practices reflected the anti-Indian and pro-Zulu ideology of Inkatha leaders in KwaZulu-Natal.[74] These attacks occurred in areas where working class and poor Indians live in close proximity to Africans. In the three elections since the end of apartheid, Indians have not voted as a block, the majority (between 57 and 96 per cent) categorize themselves as independents.[75] What has also become clear is that the upper classes have been more likely to vote for the ANC while the poorer classes have voted for oppositional parties who promise to represent minorities.[76]

Under segregation and apartheid, Indian resistance was consistent. Social movements that organized them ranged from sectarian religious groups (Ramakrishna Vedanta Society, Divine Life Society and so on), to reform-based political organizations (like the House of Delegates), and more radical organizations (the Natal Indian Congress, the South African Indian Congress, the United Democratic Front, and so on). Despite persistent organized resistance for 97 years (1893–1990) Indians were unable to make radical changes to their political, economic, and social position in the country. They too suffered the oppressive implications of segregation and apartheid even though they were marginally better off than the vast majority of Africans. Even when the apartheid regime engaged in reform it was never their intention to give Indians rights that Whites enjoyed. On the contrary it was a move to include Indians into an apartheid system in which they continued to be oppressed, but their subject position was now one that was associated with the agenda of the white regime in its political oppression of Africans. The structures that were created under settler colonialism set the foundation for apartheid. Throughout the period of relentless protests, especially during the 1980s, state structures hardly changed at all. It was only when the high-profile leaders of the apartheid regime, business, the exiled ANC, and national anti-apartheid organizations decided to move into a negotiations process, that the system was transformed. The final transition was not the outcome of people demanding such changes but rather the settlement bargained for and negotiated by the elite. The timing of these negotiations was influenced in part by protests but also by international global capitalist imperatives, the state of the national economy, and the structural tensions the apartheid system had created.

Post-apartheid South Africa

The working poor were the first to experience the negative impacts of a leaner and structurally adjusted post-apartheid state. The replication of government institutions for each racial group was abandoned for centralized administration. Indians became a small relatively voiceless minority in a system that had previously treated them as an independent ethnic group on par with other racial groups in the country. The policies of the ANC government were motivated by two contradictory agendas: the desire to redistribute wealth and social services in order to redress the inequities of apartheid and thereby retain their support base; and the need to reduce the size of the state to remain competitive in the global capitalist arena and hence to maintain local white and international investments. The outcomes were problematic, as recognized by Dennis Brutus, a professor and activist:

> It is pure hypocrisy for this government to parade around as if it is the champion of the anti-racist struggle. It is hypocrisy because its very own economic policies continue to hurt black people, in the most callous fashion . . . they [ANC leadership] make common cause with naked imperialism and oppose policies that could free the South from global apartheid.[77]

After toying with alternative economic models, neoliberalism eventually became the modus operandi in the country; the poor soon experienced its consequences.

Under apartheid South Africa serious structural problems emerged. The country depended on the export of primary products (mainly minerals) and the import of capital, goods, and technology. The fluctuations and drop in the gold price in the 1970s and 1980s contributed towards an economic crisis. With the easing of exchange controls, in part conditioned by an IMF loan in 1982, capital flight increased. The imposition of sanctions added stress to the straining economy that experienced budget deficits, a negative GDP growth rate, and increasing unemployment.[78]

In a comprehensive critique of ANC economic policies Patrick Bond succinctly sums up the challenges as follows:

> . . . we have seen abundant evidence thus far how, as a function of the character of the elite transition, the country's economic and political rulers moved quickly during the 1990s to hoard for themselves the bulk of globalization's

benefits, in the forms of lower tariffs on imported luxury goods and labour-saving machinery; of spoils associated with deregulation, liberalization, out-sourcing and privatization; of rentier profits associated with South Africa's unprecedented high interest rates and share market appreciation; of the inexplicable permission granted by the ANC to move ill-begotten apartheid era savings to offshore banks; and of an extraordinarily anti-redistributive state capacity – via the destruction of the progressive RDP and the imposition of World Bank-friendly social policies – to pass the costs of old and new forms of underdevelopment to the traditional victims.[79]

In 1993 the Macroeconomic Research Group (MERG) chaired by Vella Pillay, a distinguished economist and exiled SACP member, proposed an economic plan of "a low-key welfare state achieved by directing resources, such as pension funds, into such objectives as a large-scale house building" program.[80] These proposals were rejected by the ANC, as its leadership became strongly influenced by international capitalist forces – by February 1992 at the World Economic Forum in Davos, Mandela was convinced that the ANC's promise of nationalization had to be shelved and replaced with neoliberal policies that attracted foreign investment.[81] In his speech he said:

> We visualize a mixed economy in which the private sector would play a central and critical role to ensure the creation of wealth and jobs. Side by side with this, there will be a public sector perhaps no different from such countries as Germany, France and Italy. . . in which the state plays an important role in such areas as education, health and welfare.[82]

The MERG recommendations of "growth through redistribution" was replaced with the Reconstruction and Development Program (RDP) and shortly thereafter with neoliberalism. Harvey defines neoliberalism as "a theory of political economic practices that propose that human well-being can best be advanced by liberating individual entrepreneurial freedoms and skills with an institutional framework characterized by strong private property rights, free markets and free trade."[83] The state facilitates and guarantees the institutional framework for efficient economic activities.

Even before the mid-1980s British businesses tied to South Africa, like Gold-fields, expressed their desire to promote negotiations between the apartheid state and the exiled black organizations.[84] Talks between the ANC, apartheid leaders, and business began after Nelson Mandela was transferred from Robben Island to Pollsmoor prison in 1982; Thabo Mbeki, an ANC member in exile at the time, pursued the same strategy aboard.[85] Freund suggests that inside South Africa future ANC government leaders, who had no interest in socialist transformation, were pushed into "rapid economic training," while the mass of ANC followers in exile were kept in the dark about negotiations or discussions about the post-apartheid system. The lead-up to negotiations was handled by the elites, rank and file ANC, UDF, and COSATU carders were isolated from these processes.

Immediately after coming into power the government adopted the RDP set of policies that were "people-centered" and "people-driven."[86] It proposed development but also recognized the need for a smaller state; it included a redistributive ideology that was more in line with the demands made by social movements during apartheid. But this program was short-lived; 4 years later it was dropped in favor of GEAR – *Growth, Employment and Redistribution*, a neoliberal economic model that imposed less government spending, tax cuts for the rich, tax incentives for foreign investors, the lifting of exchange controls, and the privatization of government holdings. It was a program that prioritized budget cuts, liberalization, deregulation, privatization, and tight monetary policy.[87] Government personnel as well as representatives from the Development Bank of Southern Africa, World Bank, Reserve Bank, and Stellenbosch Bureau of Economic Research devised the model; the outcome was a set of strategies very much in line with the structural adjustment programs touted by the World Bank and International Monetary Fund (IMF). As John Saul observes: "South Africa: running, however ineffectively, with the hares or, as one increasingly suspects to be the case, hunting however guardedly, with the hounds."[88] The poor, unemployed, and unemployable were first to experience the negative impacts of GEAR; a system based on class divisions had replaced one based on racial/ethnic divisions. Freund concludes that GEAR resolved the dual crisis whereby "the deep social and economic problems of the poor have largely remained almost intact but business has got what it wanted and had become absorbed into lucrative globalized patterns."[89]

The housing crises affected people from all races – inadequate housing, poor services, subpar infrastructure, inaccessibility to loans, lack of adequate government subsidization, and so on. RDP had suggested two non-market mechanisms: a "national housing bank, and mechanisms that ensure state expenditures on housing take the form of 'non-speculative' subsidies."[90] To some extent, this model would have continued with the redistributive budget that existed under apartheid, but now designed to include the majority. Instead the new policies were market-centered in favor of banks, private service providers, and private construction companies. The result was increasing unemployment, an increase in the housing backlog, growing numbers of people unable to pay for new and more expensive water and electrical services, and the growth of urban shantytown sprawl. As Bond says: "In a neoliberal, post-apartheid South Africa . . . the mass shanty-towns and squatter towns and squatter villages, the hostels, the decaying inner-city areas, the nooks and crannies where the homeless congregate – are growing, not shrinking."[91]

The post-apartheid constitution was based on substantive equality, which requires a contextual approach, and hence includes affirmative action principles to provide advantages to those who were previously discriminated against.[92] These policies have been color sensitive but class blind, the middle classes continue to gain in strength while the poor get poorer.[93] Klautz adds that "democratization in South Africa has primarily produced incremental policy reforms that, on balance, reaffirms exclusion."[94] Policies like black economic empowerment (BEE) and affirmative action together with economic policies that favor national and international capital has resulted in "globalization triggered by color."[95] Even though the affirmative action policies included Indians and Coloureds, the implementation was mainly for Africans. Alexander makes the point that "the term, affirmative action, can only be meaningful in the context of individuals who are similarly qualified or skilled and where those who 'belong' to one of the 'designated groups' have to be given preference over the others."[96] Hence for affirmative action to work, you need transformational measures to first level the playing field so that at that point the previously disadvantaged can be affirmed. Through these measures and BEE, black (mainly African) entrepreneurs are given concessionary loans, skilled black personnel have become upwardly mobile as the corporate sector has scrambled to meet targets set for blacks in managerial and staffing positions, and black managers and workers have been prioritized in the public sector.[97] Class disparities have increased: 45–55 per cent live in poverty, 10 per cent of African children are malnourished, 25 per cent of children are stunted due to poor nutrition, while the size of the African component with the richest income rose from 9 per cent in 1991 to 22 per cent in 1996.[98] The unemployment rate was officially at 25 per cent in 2011, but in KwaZulu-Natal it was higher at 37.6 per cent.[99] The trickle-down promises of the new model have not shown positive results; in KwaZulu-Natal the Income Dynamic Study found that those with incomes below the poverty line rose from 35 per cent in 1993 to 42 per cent in 1998.[100] Studies have found that more than 60 per cent of households that were poor in 1993 remained poor in 2004, while those households above the poverty line in 1993 maintained their positions and made further headway over time.[101] This data also shows increasing inequality between the middle classes and the poor in terms of income distribution, poverty, and health. The post-apartheid state has had several successes including stable elections, steady improvement in the delivery of basic services, the creation of new jobs and upward mobility for a growing section of the population, a slight increase in state pensions, the introduction of child grants, and other positive changes. But the system has also given rise to corruption (some of which existed under apartheid but has been made more visible by democratic structures) and nepotism. Some claim that many of the beneficiaries of BEE have been "a small elite, many with close links to the ruling party, some of them party officials, plus a few prominent ex-trade unionists. Many became wealthy through board-room deals. . . Self-enrichment rather than empowerment is the order of the day."[102]

Indians were caught in the middle – unemployment rates soared among the poor in general and also among Indians. Unemployment in the country increased from 9.241 per cent in 1980 to 25 per cent in 2011[103] with the highest rate reached in 2003 (29.395 per cent).[104] The unemployment rate for Indians was 10.8 per cent in 2011 (as opposed to 5.6 per cent for whites and 28.9 per cent for black Africans).[105] The real income of those who are employed has also dropped given the high prices for rents, services, and goods. With affirmative action favoring Africans, Indian workers also faced stiffer competition for limited jobs. In Chatsworth, as in other townships, the local council began evicting residents for failing to pay their rents or service bills. This has led to concerted mobilization against the ANC-dominated councils, and in subsequent national elections the electorate in these areas didn't vote or voted for alternate parties. Schulz-Herzenberg shows that even though the ANC has increased its electoral margin from 63 per cent to 69 per cent, the percentage of the voting age population voting for them has not increased. In fact actual support has decreased from 53 to 39 per cent.[106] The municipal elections show the steady increase in support for opposition and independent parties; at end of 1998 50 per cent of African voters, 80 per cent of white voters, and 89 percent of Indian voters saw themselves as independents.[107] In 1994 the Indian vote in KwaZulu-Natal split between the National Party (of the former apartheid regime) and the Minority Front (a predominantly Indian Party headed by Amichand Rajbansi). The ANC received 20 per cent of their votes. By 1999 the Indian vote was still fractured, some voting for the Democratic Party or ANC, some for the Inkatha Freedom Party or Minority Front. Only a few remained loyal to the New National Party. In their appeal to Indians opposition parties claimed that "those that were not white enough under apartheid were not black enough under ANC rule."[108]

Crime has steadily increased throughout the country due to the breakdown of community bonds, weak social control in townships, the impact of political violence, the general level of state-distrust that first developed under apartheid, increasing and visible economic inequalities, and increasing unemployment, especially among the youth.[109] In Chatsworth, with fifteen subunits and eleven informal settlements and a population of 146,000 (in 2004, but this excludes informal squatters and sub-renters who moved in the mid-1990s) within 45 square kilometers, the ratio of police to the population was 1:937.[110] Seventy percent of reported crimes were in Units 7, 9, 11 and Shallcross, all bordering the biggest squatter settlements in the area.[111] According to the police "Chatsworth is a drug Mecca;" drugs include the dagga (marijuana), heroin (usually sold as "sugars" – a mix of heroin and residual cocaine that is cut with anything from rat poison to baby powder), and mandrax (in tablet form with the active ingredient, mataqualone). "Sugars" is most popular and has spread with remarkable rapidity among the youth. It take two hits to be addicted; this potentially lethal drug has had a devastating impact on families, and crime has increased with prostitution, theft, and domestic and sexual abuse rising.[112] The lack of state subsidies for clinics, rehabilitation centers, social services, and anti-drug educational campaigns, has worsened the situation; an inadequate police force has led to corruption. The social challenges faced by the Chatsworth youth are similar to those experienced by youth throughout the country, as observed by Pattundeen:

> As authority structures in families and the community at large have declined in terms of their efficacy, partying, drugs, sexy clothes and a fairly high level of promiscuity are dominant elements in a new, consumerist and decidedly non-political Indian youth culture that shares rather more with African youth culture than most people are willing to admit.[113]

Residents facing eviction in Chatsworth have organized to confront the state – the organizing platform has shifted from focusing on racial oppression under apartheid to class oppression whereby people are evicted or have their utilities cut because they are too poor to make payments. By 2004 at least 10 million people had their water disconnected and 10 million had their electricity disconnected nationwide.[114] The Concerned Citizens Forum (CCF) from Chatsworth was able to make some headway in publicizing and protesting evictions. They clearly artic- ulate their non-racial and inclusive platform in their declaration statement:

> It is supremely ironic, and tragic, that this government's policies continue to barricade the poor into racial ghettoes to fight over neoliberalism's crumbs while a few of the rulers share out the loot. The result, increasingly, is the creation of race hate. Nonetheless, our courage can free us. For example, in this city of Durban where colonial rulers encouraged divisions between Indian, coloured and African people, a sense of non-racialism is defiantly entrenched in the community organizations as we confront our common lot not as separate races, but as "the poors."[115]

Similar organizations have developed throughout the country like the Treatment Action Campaign, Anti-Privatization Forum, Soweto Electricity Crisis Commit- tee, Anti-Eviction Campaign, and Landless People's Forum. These organizations at times coalesce and organize around certain issues, but are less coordinated than those that existed under apartheid. A union organizer and civic leader in Mpu- malanga described the ideological and practical organizational frame for these organizations:

> We do not believe in Buthelezi's Zulu nation or Mbeki's Renaissance for Africans. We believe in free basic services for all poor people. This we need for life. We believe in life. That is why we organize with the people of Chats- worth and show solidarity with the land appropriation of Bredell and the Soweto Electricity Crisis Committee.[116]

Protest has occurred around a few consistent themes – increasing poverty, increas- ing wealth for a few, decreasing welfare, increasing unemployment, high infla- tion, costly food and utilities, and frustration with corrupt leaders who appear to have abandoned policies and programs to aid and uplift the poor. Protests are not just about the delivery of services but also include inadequate housing, the quality of roads, the price of electricity and water, the state of street lighting, the lack of jobs, and corruption.[117] The DFS statement explains:

> The leaders became unrecognizable to us. Even physically. They became bloated with gravy and their faces distorted behind the dark glass of their luxury cars. They seemed to be much happier overseas groveling in front of world leaders when, not long ago, we had all shared an understanding that it was the powerful in the West and the North that had an interest in our exploitation.[118]

The Abahlali baseMjondolo community group clearly states some of these grievances in their memorandum to President Zuma:

> We are all agreed that there is a serious crisis in our country. The poor are
> being pushed out of any meaningful access to citizenship. We are becoming
> poorer. We are being forced off our land and out of our cities. The councilor
> system has become a form of top down political control. It does not take our
> voices upwards. The democracy that we won in 1994 is turning into a new
> system of oppression for the poor.[119]

The social movements of South Africa are also keenly aware of the existence
of international organizations protesting the exploitation of corporate companies.
The Trade Union movement under apartheid used international networks strategically to fight local battles. As the trade union federation COSATU is now part
of the government, some workers have even begun to organize against their own
unions. For example, VWSA (Volkswagen South Africa) is a strike committee
that organized against their own union, the National Union of Metalworkers of
South Africa (NUMSA). A statement by the chairperson of the strike committee
reflects the challenges and tensions of the current situation:

> To all NUMSA members we say: don't allow the leadership to victimize the
> fighter at VWSA – today it is us, tomorrow it will be you! To all COSATU
> members, an injury to one is an injury to all! To the VW workers across the
> world, we together produce the wealth of the company – let us stand together –
> today it is us, tomorrow who knows who will be next? To all workers every-
> where, we need your support now![120]

In sum, social movements in South Africa are beginning to mobilize against a
state that came into power through a negotiated settlement with apartheid leaders, national and international business representatives, foreign governments, and
international organizations. The type of state that was created elevated a leadership that is alienated from and distant to the rank and file.

Indian identity: closure and culture

The ANC government has employed a two-pronged strategy to address the popular
demands made by its electorate: a racial categorization that sustains apartheid era
divisions (Whites, Indians, Coloureds, Africans), and Affirmative Action effectively for Africans only. Both strategies negatively impacted Indians – as a very
small minority they have little political leverage and continue to be viewed as ethnic outsiders. Indians experienced Affirmative Action as discriminatory. One of
the reactions among the working classes and the poor has been to turn inwards, to
nurture the insularity imposed on them by apartheid, and to reinforce their cultural
and ethnic distinctiveness. Another has been to recognize the similarities of their

experiences with other racial groups – the Chatsworth community organizations have been active on this front. The large majority of Indians still live in segregated townships, albeit ones to which many Africans have moved into in recent years. To some extent this represents an extension of the apartheid system: Indians lived in Indian areas, went to Indian schools, were transported on Indian buses, shopped in Indian stores, visited families in other Indian areas, went to Indian beaches, and so on. Shopping in the Chatsworth mall for example, clearly reflects the depth of isolation and to some extent insularity of Indians – you see shop after shop of Indian foods, fashion, and religious paraphernalia with a clientele that is predominantly Indian. The market in Unit 3 is yet another space reflecting the resilience of identity. As an informant explained to me: "Anything you want, green mangoes, pickles, masalas, samosas – you will find it here. Also fresh fowls, dry fish, and vegetables. All Indian."[121]

These discourses have also affected the other classes. In their desire to consolidate Indian identity and culture, there has been renewed interest in India – its cultural offerings and its religious teachings. At the same time, as Muthal Naidoo, the vice-rector of Giyani College of Education, explains: there are those who want to go beyond the "Indian" community, and here there are many possibilities. Some have sought to

> emulate white norms, values, and customs at the expense of their inherited culture. Others have acknowledged the strong influence of the West on their socialization but do not deny their origins. Still others have asserted their rights to be called African, while acknowledging their South Asian inheritance.[122]

She herself has

> rejected the term "Indian" . . . I have a residual culture that originated in India but that is where my "Indianness" begins and ends . . . . What I try to express in my work is my South African heritage, a mixture of Western, African, and Indian influences. . .[123]

Kriben Pillay, who wrote and produced the play *Looking for Muruga* which is based on the shared experiences of social mobility among Indians, explains the reason for its popularity:

> For many Indian intellectuals today there is this middle class guilt, this sense of having to deal with something that matters, lives of flesh and blood, because we cannot come to terms with out own essentially boring and predictable lives.[124]

Another producer adds: "I've never felt more Indian than I do today – it is coming to me. I'm trying to ward it off but frankly, I don't really know how to handle it."[125] Muthal Naidoo succinctly alludes to the challenges faced by intellectuals:

> . . . I realize that many South Africans like myself, who not only reject the notion of fixed culture but also the notion of fixed identity, are caught in the

contradiction between our non-racial aspirations and the pressure to acknowledge if not assert an ethnic affiliation because race is still a major factor in our thinking in South Africa.[126]

Thomas Hansen sees a pervasive post-apartheid melancholia among all Indians, and this is expressed in theater performances, radio, and everyday jokes.[127] He sees a resurgence of the desire for news about the community (as in the "extras" – supplements for Indians, in the daily newspapers), and a general move towards more cultural programming that both elevates and derides the Indianness that prevails among the working classes and upwardly mobile. There are also more India tours catering to the middle classes – Hansen sees the relationship with India as being marked by fetishism rather than the notion of loss.[128] Stefanie Lotter emphasizes the "cultural departure" from India in that ". . . South African Indian filmmakers locate their ancestry but not their identity on the other side of the Indian Ocean, and consider themselves to be "Black South Africans" rather than hyphenated Indians."[129] However, it is clear that it is difficult to talk of an "Indian" community – class, religious and other differences matter – perhaps the only unified element is their designation as Indian.

Conclusion

In terms of the overarching thesis of the book, Indians in South Africa occupy a transnational locality – separated from India but nevertheless still categorized as an ethnic group associated with it; and at the same time deeply indigenized or Creolized. Within the larger diaspora, Indians in South Africa are most removed from India, historically and over generations, and this is reflected in their language, dress, and culture. Their minority status in the country has forced them to deal with their "Indianness" in distinctive ways: there has been a high degree of insularity and closure but also determined efforts to associate themselves with the larger African and black political struggles. This chapter argues that despite changing state formations in the country since indenture, all have relied on ethnic and racial divisions. An argument is also made against the notion of an all-encompassing Indianness but rather identities that are mainly divided along the lines of class. The transnational locality for Indians in a post-apartheid system remains as compelling as it was under apartheid, a factor that reflects the characteristics of an imposed abiding ethnic diasporic identity.

Notes

1 The category "Coloured" includes those who have a mixed racial heritage, those who identify as "Cape Malays," and those who are indigenous (San and Khoi).
2 See Loren Kruger, "Black Atlantis, White Indians, and Jews: Locations, Locations and Syncretic Identities in the Fiction of Achmat Dangor and Others," *The South Atlantic Quarterly*, Vol. 100, No. 1, (2001): p. 112.
3 The discourses surrounding this period are hotly contested. A good overview can be gleaned from Robert Shell, *Children of Bondage: A Social History of the Slave Society at the Cape of Good Hope 1652–1838*, (Hanover: Wesleyan University Press, 1994).

4 In 1856 Natal separated from the Cape colony. They joined together in 1910 to form the Union government.
5 The British took control of the Cape from the Dutch in 1795, returned the colony back to them 7 years later, and in 1806 recaptured it. In 1824 they set up a trading post in Port Natal (now Durban) and signed a treaty with Shaka, who ceded the coastal territory to them. Natal was formally annexed in 1843.
6 Maynard W. Swanson, ""The Asiatic Menace": Creating Segregation in Durban, 1870–1900," *The International Journal of African Historical Studies* Vol. 16, No. 3. (1983): pp. 401–421, on p. 404.
7 Robert A. Huttenback, "Indians in South Africa, 1860–1914: The British Imperial Philosophy on Trial," *The English Historical Review* Vol. 81, No. 319, (April 1966): p. 275.
8 See H. G. Nicholls, *South Africa in My Time*, (London: George Allen & Unwin, 1961).
9 "2011 Census," accessed October 18, 2015, www.statssa.gov.za/publications/P0302/P03022011.pdf. These were the mid-year census, 27 July 2011. Africans made up 79.5 percent; Coloureds and Whites were 9 percent each. The total population was about 50.5 million.
10 Martin Chanock, *The Making of South African Legal Culture 1902–1936: Fear, Favour and Prejudice*, (New York: Cambridge University Press, 2001), p. 19.
11 See Neilesh Bose, "New Settler Colonial Histories at the Edge of Empire: "Asiatics," Settlers, and Law in Colonial South Africa," *Journal of Colonialism and History* Vol. 15 No. 1, (2014).
12 See Lorenzo Veracini, "Settler Colonial Studies," in *Settler Colonial Studies*, Vol. 1, No. 1, (2011).
13 Ibid., p. 6.
14 Mahmood Mamdani, "Beyond Settler and Native as Political Identities: Overcoming the Political Legacy of Colonialism," *Comparative Studies in Society and History* Vol. 43, No. 4, (2001): p. 657.
15 Patrick Wolfe, "Settler Colonialism and the Elimination of the Native," *Journal of Genocide Research* Vol. 8, No. 4, (2006): p. 402.
16 Quoted in Hilda Kuper, ""Strangers" in Plural Societies: Asians in South Africa and Uganda," in *Pluralism in Africa*, ed. by Leo Kuper and M. G. Smith, (Berkeley: University of California Press, 1969), p. 246.
17 From the Clayton Commission, quoted in Hugh Tinker, *A New System of Slavery*, (Oxford: Oxford University Press, 1974), p. 331.
18 See Wragg Commission 1885–1887. A summary can be accessed online: www.sahistory.org.za/wragg-commission-1885–1887. Also see Coolie Commission of 1872.
19 Ibid., p. 26.
20 See Bill Freund, *Insiders and Outsiders: The Indian Working class of Durban, 1910–1990*, (Portsmouth: Heinemann Publishers, 1995).
21 Johannesburg *Star*, 1 March 1899, quoted in Huttenback, "Indians in South Africa," 285.
22 In 1879 after a devastating defeat at Isandlwana, the British mounted another attack and defeated the Zulus. Zululand was annexed in 1887, and was merged with Natal in 1897.
23 Rick Halpern, "Solving the 'Labour Problem': Work and the State in the Sugar Industries of Louisiana and Natal. 1870–1910," *Journal of Southern African Studies* Vol. 30, No. 1, (March 2004): 32.
24 Maynard W. Swanson, "The Asiatic Menace," p. 404.
25 Fred Alexander, "South Africa's Indian Problem," *Far Eastern Survey* Vol. 19, No. 21, (1950): p. 232.
26 Steven Howe, "Empire and Ideology," in *The British Empire: Theories and Perspectives*, ed. by Sarah Stockwell, (Milton: Blackwell Publishing, 2008), pp. 157–176, on p. 166.
27 Goolam Vahed, "Control and Repression: The Plight of Indian Hawkers and Flower Sellers in Durban, 1910–1948," *International Journal of African Historical Studies* Vol, 32, No. 1, (1999): p. 29.
28 G. Molyneux was a borough-licensing officer between 1903 and 1934. Ibid., 38.

29 Goolam Vahed, "Passengers, Partnerships, and Promissory Notes: Gujarati Traders in Colonial Natal, 1870–1920," *The International Journal of African Historical Studies* Vol. 38, No. 3, (2005): p. 469.

30 Jay Naidoo, "Clio and the Mahatma," *Journal of Southern African Studies* Vol. 16, No. 4, (1990): p. 745.

31 Quoted in Neilesh Bose, "New Settler Colonial Histories," 229.

32 Maureen Swan, "The 1913 Natal Indian Strike," *Journal of Southern African Studies* 10, no. 2 (1984): p. 240.

33 Ibid., p. 242.

34 Ibid., pp. 249–254.

35 "Natal Indian Congress Agenda Book, 1947," in *A Documentary History of Indian South Africans*, ed. by Surendra Bhana and Bridglal Pachai, (California: Hoover Institution Press, 1984), p. 193.

36 The Act made property transactions between Whites and Indians in Natal and Transvaal only possible under several conditions: Indians could purchase land in specifically defined areas, but could only sell to other races under a permit; in unexempted areas, Indians could continue to own land if they had purchased it before 21 January 1944; and they could lease land from Whites for trading purposes only. This Act disadvantaged Indians in relation to Whites and coloreds. See Gavin Maasdorp and Nesen Pillay, *Urban Relocation and Racial Segregation: The Case of Indian South Africans*, (Durban: Department of Economics, University of Natal, 1977).

37 Report of the Passive Resistance Council, Natal Indian Congress Agenda Book, 1947, from Bhana et al., *A Documentary History*, pp. 194–207.

38 The riots were reported to have begun on Thursday evening 13 January 1949, when Africans attacked a few Indian businesses, but stopped quickly with little damage done. The rioters were particularly zealous on Friday afternoon 14 January to Saturday morning 15 January.

39 "From The Forum, 29 January 1949, and Common Sense, May 1949, R. S. Nowbath Collection," in Bhana et al., *A Documentary History*, pp. 208–213.

40 For example in *Portrait of Indian South Africans*, (Durban: Avon House, 1969) Fatima Meer argues that the riots were manipulated and condoned by the state. In *An African Bourgeoisie*, (New Haven: Yale University Press), Leonard Kuper sees the rising competition between African and Indian traders as the source of tension. In "The 1949 Durban Riots – A Case Study in Race and Class," in *Working Papers in Southern African Studies*, ed. by Philip Bonner, (Johannesburg: African Studies Institute, 1978). Eddie Webster sees class-based conflicts at the underlying reason for the riots. In "Lessons of Durban Riots," *Economic and Political Weekly* Vol. 29, No. 10, (1994), T. G. Rmamurthi sees the riots as an explosion of frustrations due to urbanization, forced proletarianisation, and poverty.

41 Ian Edwards and Tim Nuttall, "Seizing the Moment: The January 1949 Riots, Proletarian Populism and the Structures of African Urban Life in Durban During the Late 1940s," History Workshop, 1990, University of Witwatersrand, 35.

42 Census figures, births and deaths are difficult to reconcile – so these numbers are an approximation. See C.A. Woods, *The Natal Indian Community: Their Economic Position*, (London: Oxford University Press, 1954).

43 See J.R. Burrows, *The Population and Labor Resources of Natal*, (Pietermaritzburg: Town and Regional Planning Commission, 1959), pp. 24–25. Quoted in Edwards and Nuttal, "Seizing the Moment," p. 4.

44 C.A. Woods, *The Natal Indian Community*, p. 1.

45 Ibid., p. 16. In 1906 the Durban Corporation had developed the "Durban System" to restrict African residences to officially approved locations.

46 See Iain Edwards, "Cato Manor: Cruel Past, Pivotal Future," *Review of African Political Economy* Vol. 21, No. 61, (1994).

47 See Ibid.

48 Quoted in Bill Freund, *Insiders and Outsiders*, p. 66.

49 R. Elphick and R. Davenport, eds., *Christianity in South Africa: A Political, Social and Cultural History*, (Cape Town: David Philip, 1997), 203.

50 Quoted in Goolam Vahed and Thembisa Waetjen, *Gender, Modernity and Indian Delights. The Women's Cultural Group of Durban, 1954–2010* (Cape Town: Human Science Research Council, 2010), p. 52.

51 Pierre L. Van Den Berghe, "Apartheid, Fascism, and the Golden Age," *Cahiers d'Études Africaines*, Vol. 2, No. 8, (1962): p. 602. Note that in the census of 1951, of the 299 Indians in Natal, 221,347 were urban and 77,675 were rural. See C.A. Woods, *The Indian Community in Natal*, p. 15.

52 There are many commentaries on the divisions and discourses that prevailed among the various white groupings under apartheid. For a comprehensive analysis, see Deborah Posel, *The Making of Apartheid, 1948–1961. Conflict and Compromise*, (Oxford: Clarendon Press, 1991).

53 Gavin Maasdrop and Nesen Pillay, *Urban relocation*, pp. 91–92.

54 Quoted in Ibid., p. 92.

55 Hilda Kuper, ""Strangers" in plural societies," p. 271.

56 Anthony Lemon, "The Political Position of Indians in South Africa," in *South Asians Overseas: Migration and* Ethnicity, ed by Colin Clarke et al., (Cambridge: Cambridge University Press, 1990), p. 136.

57 See R. Mesthrie, *Language in Indenture: A Sociolinguistic History of Bhojpuri-Hindi in South Africa*, (Johannesburg: Witwatersrand University Press, 1991).

58 Bill Freund, *Insiders and Outsiders*, p. 79.

59 Ranji S. Nowbath, a lawyer and journalist who witnessed the impact of the Act on the lives of his clients, quoted in Surendra Bhana et al., *A Documentary History*, p. 217.

60 See Bill Freund, *Insiders and Outsiders*, p. 73, Ashwin Desai, *We Are the Poors. Community Struggles in Post-Apartheid South Africa*, (New York: Monthly Review Press, 2002), p. 15.

61 See Thomas Blom Hansen, "From Culture to Barbed Wire: On Houses and Walls in South Africa," *Texas International Law Journal* Vol. 46, No. 345, (2011).

62 *90 Fighting Years 1894–1984: The Natal Indian Congress*, (Durban: Natal Indian Congress Publication, 1984).

63 Frantz Fanon, *Black Skin White Masks*, trans. by Charles Lam Markmann, (New York: Grove Press, 1967), p. 135.

64 Steve Biko, *I Write What I Like*, Selected Readings, (Chicago: University of Chicago Press, 2002), p. 29.

65 Ibid., p. 48.

66 South African Students' Association *Newsletter*, May–June 1972, quoted in Ibid., p. 121.

67 See Ibid., p. 114.

68 Frantz Fanon, *The Wretched of the Earth*, (New York: Grove Press, 1963), p. 13.

69 Ibid., 101–102.

70 Steve Biko, *I Write What I Like*, p. 149.

71 C.R.D. Halisi, "Biko and Black Consciousness Philosophy: An Interpretation," in *Bounds of Possibility: The Legacy of Steve Biko and Black Consciousness*, ed. by N. Barney Pityana, Mamphela Ramphele, Malusi Mpumlwana and Lindy Wilson, (Cape Town: David Philip, 1991), 109.

72 There is a large discourse around Inkatha. See: Movindri Reddy, *Conflicts of Consciousness: The State, Inkatha and Ethnic Violence in Natal*, (PhD diss., University of Cambridge, 1993), Gerhard Mare and Georgina Hamilton, *An Appetite for Power: Buthelezi's Inkatha and the Politics of Loyal Resistance*, (Johannesburg: Ravan Press, 1987), Courtney Jung, *Then I Was Black. South African Political Identities in Transition*, (New Haven: Yale University Press, 2000).

73 As was clearly the case in Inanda. See Heather Hughes, "Violence in Inanda, August 1985," *Journal of Southern African Studies*, Vol. 13, No. 3, (1987).
74 Forty-two Indian-owned shops and businesses, many houses, and three surgeries of Indian doctors were destroyed by fire. See Ibid, p. 351.
75 Collette Schulz-Herzenberg, "A Silent Revolution: South African Voters, 1994–2006," in *State of the Nation. South African 2007*, ed. by Sakhela Buhlungu et al., (Cape Town: Human Sciences Research Council, 2007), p. 121. By the end of 2005, 70 per cent of Indians were independents, 62 per cent of Whites, and 50 per cent of Coloureds, ibid, p. 129.
76 See Adam Habib and Sanusha Naidoo, "Race, Class and Voting Patterns in South Africa's Electoral System: Ten Years of Democracy," *Africa Development* Vol. 31, No. 3, (2006).
77 Brutus was addressing a branch of the Durban Social Forum (DSF) in Wentworth in 2001. They were preparing for a mass demonstration against ANC policies at the upcoming United Nations World Conference on Racism, Racial Discrimination, Xenophobia, and other related forms of intolerance (WCAR) Quoted in Ashwin Desai, *We Are the Poors*, p. 127.
78 See Jeff Guy, "Somewhere over the rainbow: the nation-state and race in a globalizing South Africa," *Transformation: Critical Perspectives on Southern Africa*, Vol. 56, (2004), pp. 68–89.
79 Patrick Bond, *Elite Transition. From Apartheid to Neoliberalism in South Africa*, (London: Pluto Press, 2000), 199.
80 "Obituary for Vella Pillay," *The Guardian*, August 3, 2004.
81 Alister Sparks, *Beyond the Miracle. Inside the New South Africa*, (Johannesburg: Jonathan Ball Publishers, 2003), pp. 174–175.
82 Quoted in Ibid., p. 175.
83 David Harvey, *A Brief History of Neoliberalism*, (New York: Oxford University Press, 2005), p. 2.
84 See Willie Esterhuyse, *Endgame:Secret Talks and the End of Apartheid*, (Tafelberg, 2012), pp. 22–24.
85 Bill Freund, "Swimming Against the Tide: The Macro-Economic Research Group in the South African Transition 1991–94," accessed April 13, 2015, http://afep2014.sciencesconf.org/36107/document.
86 A Working Group paper by the "RDP Council," quoted in Ibid., p. 90.
87 Brian Kahn, "Debates over IMF reform in South Africa," *Studies on International Financial Architecture*, (2000): 6, accessed April 13, 2015, http://library.fes.de/pdf-files/iez/00793.pdf.
88 John Saul, "The Hares, the Hounds, and the African National Congress: On Joining the Third World in Post-Apartheid South Africa," *Third World Quarterly* Vol. 25, No. 1, (2004).
89 Bill Freund, "Swimming Against the Tide," p. 18.
90 Ibid., p. 145.
91 Ibid., p. 150.
92 Kristin Henrard, *Minority Protection in Post-Apartheid South Africa: Human Rights, Minority Rights, and Self-Determination*, (Westpoint: Praeger Publishers, 2002).
93 Ashwin Desai and Dhevarsha Ramjettan, "The Boundaries of Sport and Citizenship in 'Liberated' South Africa," in *Racial Redress and Citizenship in South Africa*, ed. by Adam Habib and Kristina Bentley, (SA: HSRC Press, 2008).
94 Audi Klautz, *Migration and National Identity in South Africa*, (Cambridge: Cambridge University Press, 2013), p. 8.
95 Under Act No. 55 of 1998 of the Parliament of the Republic of South Africa, affirmative action measure were adopted to redress the disadvantages in employment experienced

by designated groups, these included black people, women and the disabled. Black people included Africans, Coloured and Indian.

96 Neville Alexander, "Affirmative action and the perpetuation of racial identities in post-apartheid South Africa," *Transformation: Critical Perspectives on Southern Africa*, no. 63, (2007): p. 95.

97 Richard Ballard, Adam Habib et al., "Globalization marginalization and Contemporary Social Movements in South Africa," *African Affairs*, Vol. 104, No. 417, (2004): p. 620.

98 Ibid., pp. 620–621.

99 "Quarterly Labor Force Summary, Quarter 3, 2011", accessed on October 19, 2015, www.statssa.gov.za/

100 Jeremy Seekings and Nicoli Nattrass, "Class, Distribution and Redistribution in Post-Apartheid South Africa," *Transformation: Critical Perspectives in Southern Africa* 50 (2002): p. 11.

101 Julian D. May et al., "The KwaZulu-Natal Dynamics Study (KIDS) 3rd Wave: Methods, First Findings and an Agenda for Future Research," submitted 27 January 2006, accessed on April 12, 2015, www.aae.wisc.edu/mrcarter/papers/May%20Aguero%20 Carter%20Timeaus.pdf.

102 Keith Hart and Vishnu Padayachee, "A History of South African capitalism in national and global perspective," *Transformation: Critical Perspectives on Southern Africa* Vol. 81, No. 81, (2013).

103 "Statistics South Africa," accessed on October 19, 2015, www.statssa.gov.za/publications/statskeyfindings.asp? PPN=P0211&SCH=5069

104 "Indexmundi," accessed on October 19, 2015, www.indexmundi.com/south_africa/ unemployment_rate.html

105 "Statistics South Africa," Quarterly Labor Force Summary, Quarter 3, 2011, accessed on October 19, 2015, www.statssa.gov.za/

106 Collette Schulz-Herzenberg, "A Silent Revolution," 117.

107 Adam Habib and Rupert Taylor, "Parliamentary Opposition and Democratic Consolidation in South Africa," *Review of African Political Economy* Vol. 1 No. 80, (1999): p. 263.

108 Megan Addis, "Between a Rock and A Hard Place: The Marginalization of Coloured and Indian Interests in South African Politics," *A Journal of Opinion* 27, no. 2 (1999): p. 40.

109 See Antoinette Louw, "Surviving the Transition: Trends and Perceptions of Crime in South Africa," *Social Indicators Research*, Vol. 41, No.1/3, (1997).

110 Anand Singh and Shanta Singh, "The History of Crime Among People of Indian Origin in South Africa," *Anthropologist*, Vol. 8, No. 3, (2006): p. 151.

111 Ibid. In Chatsworth there were thirty to thirty-five crimes reported per day, while in Phoenix there were 100 per day.

112 See Gerelene Pattundeen, "Missing out on Migration: "Sugars" and the Post-apartheid Youth of Chatsworth," *Journal of Social Sciences, Special Volume*, no. 10, (2008).

113 Ibid., p. 62.

114 Patrick Bond, "South Africa Tackles Global apartheid: Is the Reform Strategy Working?" *South Atlantic Quarterly*, Vol. 103, No. 4, (2004): p. 822.

115 "Durban Social Forum Declaration Statement, adopted 28 August 2001," accessed on October 19, 2015, http://monthlyreview.org/press/news/durban-social-forum-declaration/

116 Quoted in Desai, *We are the Poors*, p. 140.

117 Peter Alexander and Peter Pfaffe, "Social Relationships to the Means and Ends of Protest in South Africa's Ongoing Rebellion of the Poor: The Balfour Insurrections," *Social Movement Studies: Journal of Social, Cultural and Political Protest* (2013).

118 "Durban Social Forum Declaration."

119 "Abahlali baseMjondolo and Rural Network of KwaZulu-Natal, 23 March 2012," accessed on October 19, 2015, http://libcom.org/news/abahlali-basemjondolo-occupy-central-durban-first-time-attacks-september-last-year-23032010

120 Wilfus Ndandani, quoted in Desai, *We are the Poors*, p. 100.
121 Interview, Chatsworth, July 24, 2010.
122 Muthal Naidoo, "The Search for a Cultural Identity: A Personal View of South African "Indian" Theatre," *Theatre Journal* Vol. 49, No. 1, (1997): 30.
123 Ibid., p. 31.
124 Quoted in Thomas Blom Hansen, "Plays, Politics and Cultural Identity among Indians in Durban," *Journal of Southern African Studies* 26, no. 2 (2000): on p. 265. This was an interview conducted by the author in March 1999.
125 Ibid., pp. 266–267.
126 Muthal Naidoo, "The Search for a Cultural Identity," p. 39.
127 Thomas Blom Hansen, "Melancholia of Freedom: Humour and Nostalgia among Indians in South Africa," *Modern Drama* Vol. 48, No. 2, (2005).
128 Thomas Blom Hansen, "An Unwieldy Fetish: Desire and Disavowal of Indianness in South Africa," in *Eyes Across the Water: Navigating the Indian Ocean, (Indian Ocean Series)*, ed. by Pamila Gupta, Isabel Hofmeyr and Michael Pearson, (South Africa: Unisa Press, 2010).
129 Stefanie Lotter, "The South African Indian Film Industry: New Directions in Indian Commercial and Diasporic Cinema," in Ibid., p. 122.

6 Culture and diaspora

Figure 6.1 Narainsamy Temple, Newlands, Durban in KwaZulu-Natal

Chota Bharat (Little India – Mauritius), *girmityas* (indentured contract laborers – Fiji), *charous* (term for Indians – South Africa), *chutney soca* (music – Trinidad and Tobago) – these terms and words only have meaning in the diaspora. Living in former colonies of the British Empire for over a century and for more than five generations, Indians have become indigenized and Creolized, removed from India and rooted in their "new" birthplaces. Yet across the diaspora their categorization as "Indians" serves to eternally signify their diaspora connection, their Indianness is consistently marked as other, foreign, and outsiders to the nation and national project. The exception is Mauritius where Indo-Mauritians are in the majority, but here too, the relationship with India as the motherland is harnessed in order to maintain hegemony on the island. This chapter continues to interrogate the question of what it is to be an Indian outside India, and argues that the transnational locality inhabited by Indians is most vividly reflected in the cultural continuities and adaptations that were made. These cultural evolutions remove Indians from India indigenizing them in the diaspora simultaneously continuing the connecting thread with *Bharat Mata* (motherland).

Religious and cultural practices in the diaspora were locally based relying heavily on memories, the modification of practices from India, adaptations to local conditions, borrowing from various traditions in the new cultural mix, and the creation of new practices. Throughout the diaspora the Arya Samaj, which began its activities in the 1920s in colonies, gained considerable influence. Originally started by Dayananda Saraswati, who advocated for a movement away from image worship to an earlier form of worship around the Vedic fire alter, the Arya Samaj attracted indentured Indians who found themselves marginalized in the new social hierarchies that were developed in the colonies. In Mauritius for example, those who were categorized as "Charmār" or of lower social status joined the group in large numbers. About one quarter of Mauritian Hindus list themselves in the census as belonging to an Arya Samaj organization. In Trinidad the Arya Samaj was not as successful mainly because local leaders, including local *pandits* (who claimed Brahman caste membership), prevented more widespread recruitment. The move towards reform throughout the diaspora made the Arya Samaj an influential organization. In South Africa the spirit of reform also contributed towards the success of the Divine Life Society, the Ramakrishna Center, the Hari Krishna establishment, and the Sai Baba movement.

In Mauritius, where Indians are in the majority, various subgroups among them have recreated and established rituals, customs, and traditions that are novel to the island but nevertheless have connections, however weak, to India. This division into subgroups (like minority Tamil, Telegu, and Muslim) was made possible because of the large numbers that were indentured from specific villages and places in India, the rule whereby the few women who traveled to Mauritius were not given indentureship contracts, and the French colonial practice of centralizing operations in the estates seeing them as "organisms" with different groups playing a specified role.[1] The concept of caste, caste membership, and taboos related to caste practices, were changed. For the majority who are broadly considered Hindu and were mainly from North India, a new hierarchical system developed that combined some remnants of caste integrated into new class divisions. While the ship records reveal that about 13 per cent were Thākurs or Ksatriīyas, or people who were from the landowning class in India, in Mauritius landowners in this group adopted the title "Singh" and became defined as having high social status in the social hierarchical system. At the bottom were those who came to be defined as "Charmār" or the caste in India that makes leather goods; on ship records less than 10 per cent of indentured laborers were categorized in this way, but in Mauritius a social hierarchy between the landowning elite and the rest resulted in a large swath of society being defined in this way.[2] Furthermore, Hindus also followed Franco-Mauritian social structures when they "skillfully encouraged" a group of fellow workers to claim middle-class status by calling themselves "Vaishya" (referred to in Hindu mythology and in India as a caste that were managers in commerce and agriculture) – this replicated the social hierarchy of the French estate owners and their Franco-Creole managers.[3] In Trinidad a rudimentary caste system developed that was different to the caste ranking that indentured Indians had in India. The Trinidadian system of status was tied to wealth, upward mobility, and employment – class became associated with a pseudo-caste system.[4]

Christian mission schools played a significant role in educating the first leaders in the indentured diaspora. In Trinidad by 1900, the Canadian Presbyterian Missionary ran sixty elementary schools, several secondary schools, and three colleges. Later the Sanatana Dharma Maha Sabha, organized by the Hindu leader Bhadase Sagan Maraj, established over thirty schools to increase educational availability to Indians. In South Africa, Catholic schools were some of the first to cater to the Indian populations. They were augmented by schools built by the community; later all these schools became state-aided. Many of the leaders in South Africa were educated in these institutions. Education was valued throughout the diaspora and Mauritius, which has a majority Indian population, clearly illustrates what happens when education is prioritized. Not only is the education system very competitive, but much of the country's success is due to its ability to provide an educated workforce, sophisticated banking and computer sectors, and active economic engagement with the global arena. In Fiji, where the political system has been unstable, educated Indians have immigrated to Western countries like Australia, New Zealand, Canada, the United States, and the United Kingdom. The result is a dwindling Indo-Fijian population that has decreased from being a slight majority to a sizable minority.

The notion of being an Indian in a location outside India over multiple generations has contributed towards identities that are fluid, flexible, and dynamic. While it is possible to chart Indian diaspora progression through political, economic, and social institutions, it is more difficult to capture the spirit of "Indianness" as it has played out in diverse environments. No essentialized identity is visible, but the official categorization and subjective definitions associated with the indentured diaspora exists. In each place Indianness is clearly indigenized – localized and relevant to others in the nation. India is an imagined motherland, but daily life is embedded in the local. It is to this that we now turn. This chapter is not meant to offer an exhaustive analysis, but rather aims to highlight very few of the cultural elements that clearly reflect this indigenization.

Food

Throughout the diaspora, food maintains some continuities with the regional cuisine of India but is strongly influenced by local ingredients and culture. Food is a central component for imagining a culture – it works to resist and affirm notions of home and belonging.[5] Food is also associated with desire, desire for the imagined motherland, a "collective yearning for an authentic tradition or pure place of origin."[6] At the same time it is also about the current moment and the desire for inclusion and acceptance. Cooking is largely gendered, women are primarily the cooks in a household. Most rely on their mothers, grandmothers, aunts, cousins, and neighbors for lessons and recipes. Many also rely on cookbooks, and Appadurai recognizes that these books aim to standardize kitchen practices and culinary lore.[7] Food is a central component of the Indian diasporas struggle to survive and thrive, to gain comfort and to make progressive change, and to remember and also to forget. As Eagleton says: "If there is one sure thing about food, it is that it is never just food – it is endlessly interpretable – materialized emotion."[8] Food is often use to signify ethnic otherness – diaspora Indians are associated with chutney, masala, chai, channa, and so on. It emphasizes the connectedness to India but also recognizes their presence in a place outside India. Food works to add depth and flavor to the indentured Indian placement in the transnational locality.

In South Africa *samoosas* are delicate small flat triangular fried pastries filled with curried potatoes, vegetables or minced lamb, different to the Indian *samosas* which are much bigger, rounder, and made from thicker pastry. Rice dishes like Biryani and Pilau are popular, different to the rice dishes of India but they have similarities with Hyderabad, Tamil Nadu, and Muslim biryanis. In Trinidad *doubles* are two *bara* (like puris) filled with *channa curry* (chickpea curry), different to the *Chole Batura* of India (Punjabi origin). *Buss up shut roti* is distinctive yet similar to Indian *parathas*. Mauritius has a strong French and Creole influence, and *Dhal Puri* is one of the most popular dishes, served with curry, pickles, and salad. *Dhal Puri* is similar to Indian *Dhal Roti*, which is fried like a roti and not deep-fried as are puris. Indo-Fijian cuisine incorporates many of the island ingredients like coconut, fish, sweet potatoes, and cassava, but is also heavily reliant on meat, goat curry being very specific to Fiji. Below are some of the recipes mentioned.

Bunny-chow

A signature dish in South Africa is the *bunny-chow*, a take-out consisting of a hollowed-out whole, half, or quarter loaf of white bread filled with curry. The bread is hollowed out in one piece, which serves as a cap over the curry. Exactly why it is called "bunny" is contested, but there seems to be a connection to the Gujarati-speaking merchants who initially sold this food, known as Banya's [*baniya*][9] and *chow* is a meal. The curry fillings are peculiar to South African Indians, and are made with common spices. Here is a recipe for a mutton bunny, a popular option; beans and chicken are also favorites.

Mutton curry[10]

    1 kg mutton (leg or chump chops or shoulder)
    75 ml oil/30 g butter
    2 cloves
    2 cardamom seeds
    5 ml fine salt
    3 ml cumin powder
    5 ml *garam* masala

coriander leaves for garnishing

1 onion
1 stick cinnamon
15–25 ml mixed masala
3 ml coriander powder
5 ml crushed root ginger and garlic
1 large tomato
4–6 potatoes cut in half and + 250 ml water

Method

1   Cut meat into small cubes, wash, and drain water.
2   Heat oil and butter, add diced onions, cloves, cinnamon, and cardamom seeds.
3   Add spices, stir, and add mutton to pot. Add salt and stir all ingredients.
4   Cook on low heat for half an hour.
5   When excess water evaporates add ginger and garlic and diced tomatoes.
6   Add potatoes with +250 ml water.
7   When vegetables and meat are cooked, garnish with coriander leaves and *garam* masala.

Masala is sold in all the supermarkets and Indian chain stores (like Gorimas); popular brands include Packo's Hot Curry Powder, Rajar's Curry Powder, Haribai's Masala, and flavors for individual tastes sold in various stores and markets like mother-in-laws' tongue, Biryani Masala, fish masala, and so on. Masala is a blend of powdered spices that includes chili (the basis of the masala), coriander, cumin, pepper, cinnamon, cardamom, curry leaves, turmeric, and fennel. Bunny-Chow can be found in corner stores and fast-food shops. It is a popular lunchtime meal for all South Africans. Other popular foods include roti and kebabs (lamb and beef), samoosas, and curry and rice (meat and vegetarian curries).

Doubles

Doubles is a popular fast-food in Trinidad of two *bara* (fried flat bread) filled with *channa* (chickpea curry) and pepper sauce, *kuchela* (shredded mango chutney), and other sauces or salads. These fast-food stands can be found throughout Trinidad, operating mainly in the mornings, but some are open for lunch and late evenings.

A recipe for the *Channa*[11] filling:

2 cups dried chickpeas soaked overnight and boiled, or 1 16-ounce can
2 tbsp. oil
1 tsp. curry power
1 tsp. turmeric
1 tsp. cumin
½ onion finely chopped

salt and pepper to taste

1   Heat oil and adds all the spices.
2   Add onions and fry till golden brown.
3   Add the chickpeas with water to make a sauce.
4   Add salt and pepper to taste.

About 2 tablespoons of *channa* are placed on one *bara*. Other condiments are added such as pepper sauce, *kuchela*, cucumber, and an assortment of chutney's. The doubles are quickly wrapped up ready to go. The curry powder used in this recipe is a Trinidadian mix. Some of the ready-made mixed spices are Chatak Curry Masala (spicy), Chatak Loose Curry Powder, and Raja Jahan Special Armchar Masala. The typical ingredients are: coriander, turmeric, aniseed, mustard, cumin, fenugreek, and carom seeds. Unlike the South African variety, this masala doesn't usually include chili powder. To add heat, pepper sauce (usually made from habanero peppers) is added to the cooked food.

Mauritius *cari gros pois* (curried lima beans)[12]

1½ cup boiled Lima beans
3 finely chopped tomatoes
1 tsp. thyme
1 tsp. curry powder
½ tsp. crushed garlic
½ tsp. crushed ginger
4–5 fresh curry leaves

Fresh chopped coriander leaves salt to taste

1 tbsp. oil

1   Heat the oil in a pot and fry the ginger and garlic. Add tomatoes, curry leaves, and thyme and cook for a few minutes.
2   Add the boiled lima beans and curry powder, salt to taste, fresh coriander leaves, and cook on until beans are soft.

In Mauritius, a popular street food is *Dhal Puri* usually served with *Rougaille Mauricien* (a tomato based sauce), *cari gros pois* (curried lima beans), chutney, and pickles. A sweet version is served with *kheer* (rice pudding). Unlike the Indian version of *puri* that is deep fried, *Dhal Puri* is pan fried like roti. French, Creole, and Chinese cuisines influence Indo-Mauritian food. Cinnamon (*cannelle)* and cardamom (*cardamome*) are commonly used in savory and sweet dishes. Mauritian curries include herbs like thyme and pepper, and local produce like taro.

Fijian goat curry[13]

 10 cloves garlic, coarsely chopped
 1 red chili, de-seeded and coarsely chopped
 1 large onion, half finely chopped, half coarsely chopped
 2 strips lime zest
 3 cups (750ml) water
 1 tsp. chili powder or to taste
 1 tsp. turmeric
 2 tsp. sugar
 1 lime, juiced
 2 tsp. salt or to taste
 1 kg (2.2 lbs) goat meat (with some bone) cut into chunks
 2 cups (500ml/1 pint), sweet potato cut into 2.5 cm (1inch) chunks
 2 potatoes, peeled and cut into 2.5 cm (1inch) chunks
 1 cup coriander, leaves and stems
 2 tbsp. curry powder (like Chief Hot & Spicy Duck/Goat Curry Powder)
 ½ cup yoghurt, stirred until smooth.

1   Place the garlic, chili, the coarsely chopped onion, lime zest, and 2 cups of water into a blender jug and blend until smooth.
2   Transfer to a medium saucepan and bring to a boil. Add the chili powder, turmeric, sugar, lime juice, and salt and let the sauce simmer for 2 or 3 minutes.
3   In the meantime, place the vegetables, meat and half the coriander into a slow cooker. Pour over the hot sauce, cover, and switch onto desired setting.
4   About 40 minutes before the end of cooking, stir through the curry powder. Cook on high, uncovered, for the remainder of cooking time, stirring now and again to allow the sauce to thicken a little.
5   Stir through the remaining onion, coriander, and yoghurt just before serving.

Fijian food is generally spiced with fewer spices than are used in Mauritius or South Africa. Dishes include fish, meat, and poultry, and emphasis is placed on fresh produce. While the dishes are less complicated to prepare, the cuisine itself represents a sophisticated range of dishes based on local ingredients augmented by imported spices, legumes, rice, and flours. Kava, for example, is a common plant grown in Fiji, and its roots are used to produce a drink (called *yaqona*) traditionally imbibed for social and ceremonial purposes by indigenous Fijians, but Indo-Fijians also partake of the drink. Indo-Fijians use the leaves of the Taro plant to make "*sehna*," a savory patty made by smearing a paste of uradh dhal, chilies, onions, and spices on the leaves which are then rolled up, steamed and cut into disks that can be fried. Plantains, green bananas, cassava, and coconut are often used in curries, which are relatively mild, but spicy and tangy.

Caste and ethnicity

Throughout the diaspora, caste hierarchies as they were and are in India have, for the most part, disappeared. The exceptions are usually the Gujarati traders who were mainly free passengers, but they too do not adhere to caste practices as they operate in India. Some of the attributes of caste are endogamy (marriage within the group), occupational restrictions (some castes are associated with certain occupations), hierarchy (*varna*: Brahmins, Kshatriyas Vaishyas, and Shudras, Untouchables/outcastes, and further subdivisions into *jati*), commensality (notion of pollution with respect to eating), and hereditary membership.

Several factors militated against caste coherence and continuity. First, Indians were recruited as individuals and not as families or village members. Indian villages recognized caste membership and the commensurate hierarchies and customs. Second, Indians were recruited from a wide range of regions, and this further undermined caste membership; regional location is tied to caste designations in India. Third, there was rarely a critical mass of caste members to pursue caste practices, especially the social and economic obligations that were customarily performed.[14] Finally, the trip by ship from India to the colonies precluded caste separation and customs. The journey came to represent the place of caste pollution and ultimately caste erasure. Gujarati traders on the other hand immigrated from specific regions and with their families; this enabled them to continue with caste practices in the colonies.

With its Hindu majority, Mauritius has maintained a semblance of caste kinship. More than half the Hindus were from agricultural, shepherd, and artisan castes, considered the "clean castes" in Northern India.[15] In Mauritius some of these castes adopted a common term, Vaish, considered the middle castes as opposed to the high castes (Brahmin and Kshatriya who are about 13 per cent of all Indians) and low castes (some 27 per cent).[16] The Vaish Mukhti Sangh (Welfare Association) was established in the 1970s to further the interests of this community – to some extent they are a mix of various sub-castes, the organization provides socio-economic support with none of the religious and customary taboos practiced by caste members in India. As the largest caste and Hindu group, every prime minister has been a Vaish. Likewise, other ethnic groups have created their own socio-religious organizations, many of which have a political objective to lobby the government. However, caste identity is not rigid, it does not constrain upward or outward mobility, and other socio-economic values like occupation, education, and wealth are more salient in contemporary Mauritian society.

In Fiji, where caste lost its significance, the notion of *jahazi bhai* (boat brother) became associated with those immigrants who voyaged together; others found people from the same village in India and became *goan bhai* (village brother). These were lifelong relations that oftentimes cut across caste and religious lines.[17] These ties were so strong in some cases that upon completion of indenture, *jihazi bhai* and *goan bhai* invested jointly in sugar-cane leases, some formed joint-family households, and marriage between their children were considered tantamount to incest.[18] While caste has little resonance in Fiji, Indo-Fijians tend to practice social and marital endogamy based on the broad categories of being from North India (mainly from Uttar Pradesh, Bihar, and Central Provinces, Bhopuri-speaking) and South India (Tamil or Telugu speaking), or Muslim. About 75 per cent of indentured Indians were from North India and 25 per cent from the south.

Throughout the diaspora class has become the main source of division; it tends to trump religious affiliation and all other divisions. In South Africa, where English is the primary medium of communication, caste is largely irrelevant for the vast majority. As Kuper observed with respect to Indian South Africans: "To them caste is an embarrassing subject, irrelevant in the daily battle of existence and the surprising thing about is not that they are so ignorant of caste, but that it survives at all."[19] Class divisions are prevalent and these are determined to some extent by Western standards: education, profession, wealth, and other such accomplishments are given more significance.

Muslims are a small minority in all four countries: Fiji: 6.27 per cent (53,576 in 2007), Mauritius: 16.65 per cent (215,979 in 2000), South Africa: 1.4 per cent (738,788 in 2001), Trinidad and Tobago: 5.80 per cent (77,935 in 2000).[20] Muslims constitute a substantial percentage of the population in Mauritius, and the largest number in this diaspora is in South Africa. The identities of Muslims in both countries have been influenced by social and political circumstances, adapting and changing accordingly. In Mauritius the majority Sunni Muslims (all belonging to the Hanafi school of thought) are divided between those following the *Sunna Jamaat*, and those supporting the *Tablighi Jamaat* and the Tawheed ideology.[21] Together with the minority Ahmadiyya sect (about 4000 members) and a small group of Shiia Muslims, the various groups worship in different mosques and have different religious associations. Mainly speaking *Kreol*, with older people also speaking Bhojpuri, the majority were indentured from the same areas in India as the Hindus – eastern Uttar Pradesh and western Bihar. The community is also divided along the lines of class; a clear division between indentured Muslims and those who settled in the country as merchants, the Kutch Memons and the Surtees (from Surat in Gujarat) who live in the cities. There is little intermarriage among the various groups, and each tends to specialize in different professions. For example, many Ahmadiyyas are educated and middle class working as clerks, doctors, lawyers, and government administrators. Trade remains the most favored profession and the various associations work diligently to offer financial and other support to its members. In this respect, Muslims have been able to maintain a high degree of coherence and religious awareness.

Unlike Mauritius, in South Africa about 45 per cent of the Muslim population is of East Indian (Malaysia), Indian, and African origin, first entering Dutch dominated Cape Town as slaves from 1658. A similar percentage is of Indian origin entering the country during the period of indenture (a small percentage as indentured workers, the large majority as free passenger traders) in the nineteenth Century, and an even smaller percentage is indigenous. Divisions between Memon-speaking and Gujarati-speaking Muslims have resulted in separate mosques and religious associations.

Dangor proposes that Muslim identification with India (in tandem with other Indians) changed from 1960 to identification with the Muslim world.[22] Organizations like the *Tabligh Jama'ah* with its reform ideology pivoted on the precepts of the Prophet, increasing access to Muslim thinkers from the Arab world, and closer ties with Saudi Arabia, distanced South African Muslim identity from India.[23] In post-apartheid South Africa, the presence of Muslims from Pakistan and other Arab countries has introduced more traditional practices into the country – veiled women are now common where previously they were rare, the favored style was mostly western dress for younger Muslims and a Salwar Kameez (long tunic over narrow pants and a long neck/head scarf) for older women. Race still matters among Muslims. African Muslims have accused Indian Muslims of racism towards them, coveting funds and leadership positions in major organizations. Muslim identity is once again undergoing changes, impacted in part by the new political system, globalization, and increasing integration into the global Muslim community (*umma*). But for all this, South African Muslims are indigenized – they speak English, they have an African allegiance, they actively participated in the struggles against apartheid, and during the many decades of isolation from the rest of the world, their sense of identity became local, national, and rooted in the country. Muslims in South Africa have made a distinctive mark in terms of their philanthropy and commitment to the uplifting of all Indians. Prominent families have initiated (directly funded or partly funded) the development of schools, juvenile hostels, institutions for the disabled, tertiary educational facilities like M. L. Sultan Technikon and the University of Durban-Westville, and clinics and hospitals (R. K. Khan Hospital in Chatsworth, 1969). They have played an influential role in anti-Apartheid resistance organizations and currently are prominent in the post-Apartheid administration.

In Trinidad despite the construction of a largely homogenous Hindu community, Brahmins still play an important role. The majority of indentured Indians came from Northeast India (mainly Bihar and Eastern Uttar Pradesh) and once in Trinidad, a standardization and homogenization of religion occurred with a Creolized "plantation Hindi" (based largely on Bhojpuri) becoming the *lingua franca*. The Hinduism that emerged was one that recognized a smaller pantheon of sanskritic deities (including Vishnu, Shiva, Ganesha, and Hanuman), emphasis on "Vaishnava devotionalism (bhakti)," the elevation of the Ramanyan (by Tulsidas), and acceptance of the "ritual authority of Brahmans."[24] The latter have retained their high positions despite the dilution of cast hierarchy at all other levels. As van der Veer et al. observe, Brahmans took on multiple roles as teachers, spiritual guides, family priests, temple priests, funeral priests, astrologers, healers, exorcists, and so on.[25] In Trinidad the "Brahmin elite, especially through their control of Hindu institutions, has played a significant part in the political mobilization of Indians abroad, as well as in the refinement and routinization of doctrinal matters and ritual forms."[26]

Temples and rituals

In South Africa despite the disappearance of caste division and the Creolization of identity, the rituals associated with Indian traditional practices have been meticulously preserved even though the mythology has been lost.[27] South Africa is distinctive for its majority Tamil population (45 per cent, with 18 per cent Telugus, 30 per cent Hindi speakers, and 7 per cent Gujarati), 95 per cent of all Indians speak

English as their first language and few have any real knowledge of Tamil.[28] For Tamils, worship to the Dravidian *Amman* (Mother) Goddesses is most visible and popular – public and elaborate festivals include the Draupadi firewalking festival, the Mariammam "Porridge" prayer, and the Gengaiammam festival. Kavadi (held twice yearly) is a festival in honor of Muruga/Soobramonier.[29] These festivals are held in temples dedicated to the various deities, a large number of them dedicated to Mariamman, the most-widely worshipped Goddess in KwaZulu-Natal. Diesel contends that public rituals in South Africa reflect a remarkable degree of preservation; for example the Draupadi firewalking ceremony corresponds closely with the way it is practiced in South India.[30] For 10 to 18 days, devotees participate in various rituals and dramas depicting Draupadi's story, ending with the firewalking ritual (walking barefoot over burning coals). The Goddess is believed to lead the way cooling the coals; walking on the hot coals unscathed affirms ones purity and devotion, and is simultaneously empowering. The ritual is also believed to facilitate healing. Such worship has increased steadily in South Africa; it is probably associated with the uncertainty of political transitions, the increasing marginalization of Indians, their increasing insularity, and rising poverty, health risks, and other maladies. In some ways, firewalking plays an important psychological role in allaying the fears and traumas of the Indian diaspora experience in South Africa.

Temples in South Africa reflect a process of "Sanskritization," or social and religious reforms that move away from rituals associated with villages towards those that use the Sanskrit language and texts.[31] This affected the style of temples that were built; the first few temples were very much like those in South India, Shakti temples or goddess temples of Mariyamman or Draupadi. Given that the largest number of indentured laborers came from this region, and among South Indians there is no Brahmin leadership, temples were built in this style. Many of the early temples were made with reeds, wood-and-iron, or wattle-and-daub – these were temporary structures replaced later by more sturdy structures. There are many Mariamman temples in former sugar estates, like one in Mount Edgecombe which is a simple structure built around a sacred anthill. One of the most popular venues for Mariamman worship is the Isipingo Rail Temple, where animal sacrifices still occur.

The "sanscritization" of temples is reflected in the Umgeni Road temple (or Shree Vaithyanathan Easwar Alayam) dedicated to an orthodox style of Siva worship in the form of a *linga* housed inside a *garbha griha* or inner sanctorum. Younger observed that the orthodox style of Saiva worship is similar to that found in the towns of Kaveri River in South India "where the Velala landlords were primarily responsible for the temple traditions."[32] He sees the effort to establish this kind of temple worship as a way to "upgrade the goddess tradition that had arrived with the earliest South Indian workers."[33] The temple compound also includes two separate temples for Vishnu and Mariamman, and has a well-maintained garden for large festivals and prayer meetings. It is frequented regularly by people wishing to bless their new cars, which is particularly poignant given that the walled temples are located on the busy Umgeni Road surrounded by auto-workshops and businesses.

The Ganesha Temple in Mount Edgecombe was one of the first temples built by Kistappa Reddy in 1898.[34] Reddy was indentured in 1898 from North Arcot near Madras in South India, and upon his arrival he was commissioned to build the temple. Mikula et al. make the following observation regarding his skills: "There is about this building a feeling of competence and a measure of skill which indicate that Reddy was definitely no beginner."[35] The temple is a brick building with teak beams, brick corbelled domes and arches, and moldings and figures built with plaster directly on the structure. The Narainsamy Temple at Newlands, built in 1906, reflects a more mature style and familiarity with the local materials. Dedicated to Vishnu but also used by Shivites, the temple also has *Nandi* with two bodies linked with one head, a trademark of Reddy's temples.[36] Reddy was part of the 'Sanskritizing" movement of the day – his temples are dedicated to Gods and Goddesses that were considered to be associated with early forms of Hinduism. Like his fellow architect Kothenar Ramaswamy Pillai, Reddy's buildings included certain structures and emblems representative of South Indian temple architecture, but they also suited the reformist tendencies that prevailed among Indian South Africans. Many of these temples remain the locus of festivals and more frequent worship among Indians. By 1916 Reddy also owned one of the first vernacular printing presses in Natal (Ganesen Printing Press), the first bus service that ran from Cato Manor (a district outside the city center where many former indentured Indians settled) to Durban, a taxi service, a grocery store and tearoom, and a large dairy farm. Besides these temples dedicated to South Indians, there are North-Indian style temples, mosques, and places of worship dedicated to reform religious groups like the Ramakrishna Center, the Divine Life Society, and the Hari Krishna Center.

With the majority of Trinidad's descendants from Northern India the temples of Trinidad are distinctively different to those in South Africa. Moreover, numerous new temples were constructed in the 1950s, reflecting a renewed interest in India and *bhakti* devotion.[37] Epitomizing the Creolization of Indian identity, the architecture of these temples represented a mix of Christian churches and traditional Hindu temples, with the aesthetics being peculiarly Trinidadian. These temples have long halls filled with rows of benches, a raised stage-like area in front, and an external dome to signify the sanctum for deities. Services are held mainly on Sundays, and include listening to a sermon and singing hymns, worship that is modeled on Christian services.

The strength of the twice-migrated Fijian diaspora contributed towards building a temple in Nadi in Fiji. Opened in 1994, the Sri Siva Subramaniya Swami Temple was designed by the well-known Indian temple architect V. Ganapati Sthapati. Indo-Fijians who had emigrated to Canada after the 1987 coup, contributed towards rebuilding the temple; the original temple was founded by Ramaswami Pillai in 1913 on land leased from indigenous Fijians. This ornate and imposing building has priests trained in the most elaborate Brahmanical rituals; the signs in front of the temple warn patrons of the strict dress code and code of conduct: "STRICTLY NO SMOKING, NO ALCOHOL, NO GROG." Following all the traditional agamic scriptures of South India, this is one of only a few orthodox temples outside India. A priest from India dedicated the temple over a period of 50 days with rituals in accord with the Kumara Tantra. Hindu orthodox priests are reticent to cross the ocean to another country for fear of losing caste, but this priest said that the prohibition was only in the Dharma Shastras and not the Agamas (considered the higher authority) and "the prohibition is against sailing and going to meleccha (non-Hindu) countries, not places with large Hindu populations."[38]

Most of the oldest temples in Fiji were established by the South Indian community and dedicated to many Goddesses, especially Mariamman. Similar to such temples in South Africa, the Mariamman temple on Howell Road in Suva has an annual firewalking puja. There are also North Indian temples dedicated to a Vaishnavite deity (Vishnu-Luxmi, Ram, or Hanuman) or a Shaivaite deity (Shiva-Parvati, Ganesh).[39] As is true throughout the diaspora, there is little division between North and South Indian devotees, and both worship at any of these temples. The cornerstone of Hinduism and reformism in Fiji is the central place given to Goswami Tulsidas' Ramanyana, (or the *Ramcaritmanas* in Hindi, which was translated by Valmiki), and the Brahmins who orchestrate these regular performances (weekly recitals). Indo-Fijians mainly practice bhakti worship, actively participating in devotional songs (*bhajan*) and kirtans (leader-led devotional hymns). The text forms the basis of the conservative Sanatan Dharm position, serving to inform individual practice and to provide moral instruction for the community – it is the basis of Hinduism in Fiji. The main organization that claims to represent the majority of Hindus in Fiji is the Shri Sanatan Dharm Pratinidhi Sabha of Fiji, but other groups are also influential like the TISI Sangam, Arya Samaj, and Gujarat Samaj.

Festivals and ceremonies

Thousands of Indo-Trinidadians perform the epic *Ramleela* (or Ramdilla) every year around October in over thirty venues throughout the island. Based on Goswami Tulsidas' *Ramcharitmanas* (or *manas*), each episode focuses on key events in the life of Lord Rama (Vishnu's seventh avatar). Hundreds of villagers attend and participate in the festivities which are held over 3–10 days and usually ending with the burning of an effigy of the multi-headed *Ravan*. Milla Riggio suggests that the "*manas* had replaced the Sanskrit *Bhagavata Purana* and *Bhagavat Gita* well before independence from the British in 1962."[40] The story of Sri Ram is particularly relevant for Indo-Trinidadians, most of whom came from Bihar and Uttar Pradesh in the home state of Varanasi (Benares); this is the place where Tulsidas wrote the *manas* in Avadhi, a language that is similar to Bhopuri. Sung in verse and easily chanted, this epic play was portable and resonated with the diaspora experience. The notion of Ram's exile in the forest and his triumphant return is clearly reflected in the experiences of indentured labor.

One particular episode that speaks directly to this experience is the *staapana* ceremony of the *Baal Ramdilla* held in Enterprise. Here in tandem with the Ramayana, the aggressive recruitment and violent separation from India of indentured Indians is depicted. "Kidnapped" from Varanasi (the home of Tulsidas and the

Ramayana) and receiving a message from the heavens that they were to live by and follow the teachings of the *Ramanyana*, they began to recite in earnest verses from the *manas* smuggled from India. Riggio sees this as the way in which Indo-Trinidadians appropriated, yet continued to enact, the fundamental tenets of the *Ramanyana* in Trinidad.[41]

In Fiji too, the vast majority of Hindus following the Sanatan Dharm form of Hinduism that entered Fiji in 1920s to counter the influence of purified Vedic Hinduism propagated by the Arya Samaj, which emphasizes the Ramanyana of Thusidas as a preeminent text. But unlike Indo-Trinidadians, Indo-Fijians have moved away from ending the Ram Lilas (as they are spelled there) with the ritual lighting of giant effigies of the demon king Ravan. Instead, the focus is more straightforward, the most popular being the story of Ram's birth; these readings are well attended, but do not have the pomp and ritual associated with the Ram-leelas of Trinidad. John Kelly relates this to the changing status of Indo-Fijians as they moved out of indenture and became more urbanized, and increasingly formed and joined trade unions and political parties.[42] These changes were reflected in their forms of worship.

There has also been a marked movement away from celebrating Holi as the principle religious festival, to a celebration of Diwali. Kelly sees this as enacting a "transformation of devotional attitudes, from a transcendence – to a perfection-oriented devotionalism."[43] Brahmins still retain some caste status because of their ability to perform religious rituals, but they have limited social and political power. Holi is a public festival that entails the splashing of colored powder, singing, and other festivities. Class and social status are irrelevant; the splashing of the powders covers the body, hiding such distinctions.[44] Diwali is a more private affair, with individual families lighting lamps, preparing sweetmeats, holding private prayers, and dressing up in finery to celebrate the end of the Ram's exile and to welcome Lakshmi (Goddess of wealth and prosperity) into their homes.

Kelly sees the shift in worship as indicative of the shift in the status and position of Indians in Fiji. From being subjects under colonialism to citizens after independence, Indo-Fijians have shifted their style of worship from Holi and elaborate Ram Lila festivals that epitomized their low and powerless social status, to more sedate and streamlined Ram Lilas and private Diwali. This paralleled the situation whereby Indians became more embedded in Fiji and more active in local and global capitalist networks.[45] Hence the move away from a transcendent devotionalism to a more duty and perfection oriented one.

The volatile nature of Fijian politics, due in part to the level of ethnic tension in the country, has also impacted the kind of worship that has evolved. There has been an obvious shift to more private and quieter events, together with a steep incline in belief systems and rituals that provide solace against the uncontrollable aspects of life in Fiji. These include tensions associated with Fijian politics, the fear of being attacked by Indigenous Fijians, frustrations associated with the feeling that affirmative action (and hence jobs and university admittance) discriminates against them, the general feeling of powerlessness, and the constant anxiety associated with work/visa/immigration applications to the West.[46]

In Mauritius, the Night of Siva or *Sivarthri* held annually has become a week-long national celebration. The significance of the Indian River Ganga was substituted in Mauritius by water taken out of the Grand Bassin, a crater in the Southwest which fills with rainwater. Over time, the place came to be known as Ganga Talao. During *Sivarathri* devotees build colorful and elaborated shrines (called *kawer*) and carry it on foot to Ganga Talao to get the holy water for their temples. Throughout the week, approximately one third of the population participates in the pilgrimage, while others (including non-Hindus) provide refreshments and commodities, and some devotees stay in the temples and prepare for the reception of returning pilgrims. The festival is televised with regular coverage of the pilgrims, the songs and prayers that are chanted, and interviews – the Prime Minister goes to some of the prominent temples for worship. Special tours are conducted during this period; they are packaged to visiting South Africans and Indians.

Music

Chutney music is intrinsic to Trinidad reflecting the Creolization of Indo-Trinidadian culture; peculiar to the island but retaining some continuities with the *mathkor* tradition in India. *Mathkor* is a pre-wedding ritual performed by women that involves dances that are sexually explicit, a sanctioned religious ritual that prepares the bride for her life as a married woman. But *chutney* is not a derivative of *mathkor*; it is influenced by Indian film and folk songs, religious music (*bhajans*), calypso, and rap.[47]*Chutney* then is wholly Trinidadian. Unlike *mathkor*, which is mainly for women (male musicians are allowed) and is a private ritual, *chutney* is a public performance with male and female participants. It openly challenges gender stereotypes, and the sexually provocative dance styles and lyrics reflect the sexual independence of women and the lack of 'traditional' authority that men have over women.[48] But here too it is the lesser of two evils – a woman's participation in *chutney* might prevent her from participating in carnival and *calypso* events with Afro-Trinidadians; thus *chutney* becomes a place that prevents Creolization.[49] *Chutney* shares some aspects with *mathkor*, but it is novel, dynamic, and contemporary.

On the contrary, in South Africa the "downward diffusion of bourgeois culture and ideology linked to the massive urbanization and industrialization of the late thirties," disrupted the earlier folk and village musical and dance traditions that were practiced.[50] The *ta'zia* processions, Moharrem tiger dance, the *natchania* (sung in Bhojpuri Hindi dialect), and the *tirukuttu* (South Indian six-foot-dance), were practiced during the early years of indenture but soon stopped being performed.[51] The Sufi *qawwali*, on the other hand, is one of the few genres that has an unbroken tradition from the earliest times, and attracts a wide and dedicated audience. *Bhajans* and *kirtans* are sung at prayer gatherings strongly influenced by the Arya Samaj, which originated in India in 1875 and was introduced to South Africa in 1905. The neo-Vedanta institutions that developed from the 1940s included the Ramakrishna Center (1946), the Divine Life Society (Swami Sahajananda started the first ashram in 1949), and the Hare Krishna (ISKON) movement (started by the founder Swami Bhaktivedanta Prabhupada in 1975). Dance bands like the Dukes Combo (the oldest), the Jazz Pirates, Buxson, The Raiders, El Ricas Band, and Kreme, were popular western oriented Indian bands that represent a trans-formation from "indic to Eurocentric South Africa."[52]*Chutney* music and Indian movie tracks are also popular.

From the four cases studied in this book Fiji most clearly reflects a culture of displacement. Indians in Fiji experience a marginalization that doesn't exist to the same extent in other parts of the diaspora; despite Indo-Fijians once constitut-ing more than half of the population and currently making up a large minority, Fijian culture has distinctive features associated with home and homeland. For the majority[53] home is Fiji, this is clearly expressed by Usha Sundar-Harris who left after the first coup:

> I have often pondered about the place called home. Home is not a place where we can be arbitrarily told to belong or not belong. Home is that favourite tree in the schoolyard, or that bend in the river, or that lonely hill beyond – places of our childhood deeply etched in the memory. Chiefs and coup leaders in Fiji may tell the world Indians don't belong in Fiji, but we know that Fiji belongs to us.[54]

But relations between the two main ethnic groups are fraught with tension, espe-cially relevant during elections and various coups that have occurred (1987, 2000, 2006). The indigenous Fijian community is not a united and coherent one either, and this has been an important contributing factor to the coups. Although Indo-Fijian cultural adaptations have been complex and nuanced, their insularity has been significant. The two main ethnic groups (indigenous and Indians) have decidedly different cultures: a strong communal ethnic versus a more individu-alistic one, a commitment to a social hierarchical system versus the breakdown of caste hierarchy (a distinction between Brahmans and all others), the abiding significance of land for Indigenous-Fijian ethnic identity versus the fact that Indo-Fijians do not own land, an Indigenous-Fijian culture that emphasizes communal sharing, equality and current well-being versus an Indo-Fijian emphasis on indi-vidual success and planning for the future. In sum it is noticeable that there is an Indigenous valuing of a communal/socialist cultural aesthetic that is opposed to the capitalist ethnics that brought Indo-Fijians to Fiji in the first place. Indo-Fiji-ans have created group coherence around socio-cultural values like a commitment to education, work, and worship.

Misra defines the culture established by the newly freed (after completion of their indentured contracts) as the "old Indian diaspora of exclusivism as dis-tinguished from the new Indian diaspora of the border," the latter a product of globalization and modernity.[55] Like their counterparts in other parts of the dias-pora, Indo-Fijians celebrated holi and *tazia*. Tazia is a Shi'a festival that laments the martyrdom of Imam Hussain with elaborately decorated portable tombs and mausoleums. Given that the majority of Indo-Fijians were Hindus, and from among the small Muslim minority the percentage of Shia was even smaller, it is remarkable that tazia was celebrated by *all* Indians. The elaborate models used in these celebrations reflected a space of contestation against the harsh reality of labor, it was more of an "aesthetic-expressive-political practice" than a religious one, and it represented a "potential social arrangement" that was integrated and unhampered by social hierarchies and divisions.[56] Its decline over time (it was practiced regularly during 1879–1920) paralleled the development of a society that was more impacted by capitalism, modernity, and globalization.

The feeling of displacement remains relevant for Indo-Fijians, particularly following the implications of each of the coups on the group sense of self and identity. Despite the social and political divisions that exist in Fiji, Indo-Fijians did not flock to India when their place in Fiji was being contested. It is estimated that nearly one-third of all Indo-Fijians have emigrated since independence in 1970. Almost everyone I met either had a family member living abroad or was planning to get younger members of the family out of the country. The main destinations are Australia, the United States, Canada, and New Zealand; communication among this diaspora is maintained through Fiji-based websites and blogs. The diaspora finds that they have less in common with Indians from the subcontinent but more in common with others from the indentured diaspora.

Conclusion

The objective in this chapter was to provide a window into the cultural hybridity and localization of members of the indentured diaspora. There are numerous parts of this subject that I haven't covered including musical forms, wedding, and other life changing ceremonies, language, and dress. The diaspora is culturally, ethically, and religiously diverse and defies any generalizations. What is clear from this chapter is the distinctiveness of each ethnic group in terms of its localized and hybridized identities. From the food consumed to the festivals and places of worship, the indentured diaspora has defined a place in the nation within every nation that they reside. Over more than five generations and having to consciously and actively battle to determine their place in the nation, the indentured Indian diaspora is far removed from India, but forever tied to it. The sameness they all share is their categorization as the ethnic-Indian other. They are assumed never to be Creolized or indigenized; their identity is tied to India and continues to dilute ties of belonging to the nation. This chapter highlighted belonging and separation from the Indian motherland. While imagining India as pure, authentic, and sacred, Indians in the diaspora have invested in defining their local status and in creating a culture that is wholly local. They have navigated their placement in the transnational locality by alluding to India whenever it suited them, especially with respect to food, Gods, and music, but they have also chosen to ignore the modernity, neoliberalism, and global capitalist voracity that that come to define India. The indentured diaspora is unique and local, they were constituted through a former era of global capitalism and they were products of that system. Their strong sense of individuality and competitiveness had enabled them to be upwardly mobile in the diaspora and equally competitive in the Western developed world. Twice migration to the West is common throughout the diaspora – the off-spring of indentured Indians are adaptable and are more Westernized than many in the Indian motherland. Their ties to India will always have some degree of relevance, but their sense of home is definitively placed in their current nation-states.

Notes

1 Paul Younger, *New Homelands: Hindu Communities in Mauritius, Guyana, Trinidad, South Africa, Fiji, and East Africa*, (New York: Oxford University Press, 2010), 27.
2 Ibid., p. 32.
3 Ibid., p. 52.
4 See Morton Klass, *East Indians in Trinidad: A Study of Cultural Persistence*, (New York: Columbia University Press, 1961).
5 See Anita Mannur, *Culinary Fictions: Food in South Asian Diasporic Culture*, (Temple University Press, 2009).
6 Sunaina Maira, *Desis in the House: Indian American Youth Culture in New York City*, (Philadelphia: Temple University Press, 2002), p. 194.
7 Arjun Appardurai, "How to Make a National Cuisine: Cookbooks in Contemporary India," *Comparative Studies in Society and History* 30, (January 1988): p. 6.
8 Terry Eagleton, "Edible Ecriture," in *Consuming Passions: Food in the Age of Anxiety,"* ed. by Sian Griffiths and Jennifer Wallace, (Manchester: Manchester University Press, 1998), p. 204.
9 See Rajend Mesthrie, *A Lexicon of South African Indian English*, (Yorkshire: Peepal Tree Press, 1992), p. 4.
10 Adapted from Kanthie Iyer, *Easy to Cook Indian Recipes*, (1991), 25.
11 Recipe adapted from Trinidadian informants.
12 Recipe adapted from Mauritian informants.
13 Recipe adapted from Bharti Ben Patel, Fiji (2006).
14 See Elizabeth M. Grieco, "The Effects of Migration on the establishment of Networks: Caste Disintegration and Reformation among the Indians of Fiji," *International Migration Review*, Vol. 32, No. 3, (1998).
15 Oddvar Hollup, "The Disintegration of Caste and Changing Concepts of Indian Ethnic Identity in Mauritius," *Ethnology*, Vol. 33, No. 4, (1994): p. 301.
16 Ibid. 60 per cent of all Indians came from eastern Uttar Pradesh and Western Bihar, 33 per cent came from southern India, and 7 per cent from Maharashtra.
17 Elizabeth M. Grieco, "The Effects of Migration on the Establishment of Networks: Caste Disintegration and Reformation among the Indians in Fiji," *International Migration Review*, Vol. 32, No. 3, (1999): p. 722.
18 Ibid. Also see C. Jayawardena, "The Disintegration of Caste in Fiji Indian Rural Society," in *Anthropology in Oceania: Essays Presented to Ian Hogbin,"* ed. by L. Hiatt and C. Jayawardena, (Melbourne: Angus and Robertson, 1971), A.C. Meyer, *Peasants in the Pacific: A Study of Fiji Indian Rural Society*, (Berkeley: University of California Press, 1961).
19 Hilda Kuper, "Changes in Caste of the South African Indians," *Race Relations Journal* 22 (1955): p. 24.
20 Houssain Kettani, "2010 World Muslim Population," *Proceedings of the 8th Hawaii International Conference on Arts and Humanities*, Honolulu, Hawaii, (January 2010): 12–16.

21 See Oddvar Hollup, "Islamic Revivalism and Political Opposition among Minority Muslims in Mauritius," *Ethnology*, Vol. 33, No. 4 (1996).
22 S. E. Dangor, "Negotiating Identities: The Case of Indian Muslims in South Africa," in *South Asians in the Diaspora. Histories and Religious Traditions*, ed. by Knut A. Jacobsen and P. Pratap Kumar, (Leiden: Koninklijke Brill, 2004).
23 Ibid., 252–256. There are an estimated 400 mosques and 400 Muslim organizations in South Africa.
24 Peter van der Veer and Steven Vertovec, "Brahmanism Abroad: On Caribbean Hinduism as an Ethnic Religion," *Ethnology*, Vol. 30, No. 2, (1991): pp. 153–154.
25 Ibid., p. 157.
26 Ibid., p. 163.
27 See Alleyn Diesel, "Hinduism in KwaZulu-Natal, South Africa," in *Culture and Economy in the Indian Diaspora*, ed. by Bhikhu Parekh et al., (London: Routledge, 2003).
28 Ibid., 34. Also see Bill Freund, *Insiders and Outsiders: The Indian Working Class of Durban*, (Pietermaritzburg: University of Natal, 1995), p. 86.
29 Diesel, "Hinduism in KwaZulu-Natal," pp. 42–43.
30 Ibid., p. 43. Also see A. Hiltebeitel, *The Cult of Draupadi. Vol. 1. Mythologies from Gingee to Kuruksetra*, (Chicago: Chicago University Press, 1988).
31 See Paul Younger, *New Homelands*.
32 Ibid., 142.
33 Ibid.
34 Kistappa Reddy, considered a master architect of temples in South Africa, built 10 temples between 1898 and 1937; he died in 1941.
35 Paul Mikula, Brian Kearney and Rodney Harber, *Traditional Hindu Temples in South Africa*, (Durban: Hindu Temple Publications, 1982), p. 14.
36 Ibid., pp. 32–33.
37 See Martin Baumann, "Becoming A Color of the Rainbow: The Social Integration of Indian Hindus in Trinidad, Analysed along a Phase Model of Diaspora," in *South Asians in the Diaspora. Histories and Religious Traditions*, ed. by Knut A. Jocobsen and P. Pratap Kumar, (Leiden: Koninklijke Brill, 2003).
38 "Largest Temple in Fiji Opens. Fijian Hindus Celebrate a New National Temple," *Hinduism Today*, accessed May 21, 2015, www.hinduismtoday.com/modules/smartsection/item.php?itemid=3328.
39 Kevin Christopher Miller, *A Community of Sentiment: Indo-Fijian Music and Identity Discourse in Fiji and its Discourses*, (PhD diss., University of California, Los Angeles, 2008), 155.
40 Milla Cozart Riggio, "Reforms in the Lap of the Feet of God: Ramleela in Trinidad, 2006–2008," *The Drama Review* 54, no. 1 (2010): pp. 106–149, on p. 112.
41 Ibid., 142.
42 John D. Kelly, "From Holi to Diwali in Fiji: An Essay on Ritual and History," *Man*, (New Series) 23, no. 1 (1998): 40–55.
43 Ibid., 40.
44 Holi is associated with the myth of Prahlad (devotee of Vishnu), whose devotion saved him from death and led to the death of an evil king. Everyone played in the ashes of the dead king demonstrating their equality. It is also related to the playful Krishna, who played with colored powders with his *gopis* (female devotees). See Ibid.
45 Ibid.
46 This was gleaned from my own observations. I do not have data to prove any of this.
47 Tina K. Ramnarine, "Historical Representations, Performance Spaces, and Kinship Themes in Indian-Caribbean Popular Song Texts," *Asian Music* 30, no. 1 (1998–99): p. 9.
48 See Ibid. From my own observations, dancing associated with *chutney* is awe-inspiring and challenging for both men and women. What might have been relegated to the private domain is openly flaunted in public – heightened levels of sexuality challenge societal norms and taken-for-granted traditions.

49 Ibid., p. 16.
50 Melveen Jackson, "Popular Indian South African Music: Division in Diversity," *Popular Music*, Vol. 10, No. 2, (1991): 179.
51 Ibid., pp. 178–179.
52 Ibid., p. 183.
53 Between 1879 and 1911, 60,000 Indians were indentured to Fiji. A large majority remained.
54 Usha Sundar-Harris, "Outcasts of the People," in *Coup: Reflections on the political crisis in Fiji*, ed. by Brij V. Lal and Michael Pretes, (Canberra: The Australia National University, 2008), 59.
55 Sudesh Mishra, "TAZIA FIJI! The Place of Potentiality," in *Transnational South Asians. The Making of a Neo-Diaspora*, ed. by Susan Kosay and R. Radhakrishnan, (Oxford: Oxford University Press, 2008), p. 73.
56 Ibid., p. 77.

Conclusion

The main argument throughout is that the transnationality intrinsic to diaspora identities *marks* them as others in the nation-state, and simultaneously *separates* them from the homeland/motherland, thus displacing them from both states and situating them in a *transnational locality*. This space is objectively and subjectively defined and includes the interplay of at least three dimensions. At the transnational level, diasporas have identities that are associated with like communities dispersed from the same point of origin, and who share similar cultural foundations regarding language, religion, and customs. At the trans-state level, by maintaining (or presuming to retain) an association with a motherland (as myth or reality), they are distinguished as having dual identities. At the level of the nation-state, diasporic identities are localized, indigenized through generations, but nevertheless continue to represent difference, an otherness that contributes towards definitions of nationhood, but which also challenges it. The significance of each level on diasporic identities is dependent on factors such as the reasons for leaving the motherland/homeland (economic, political, social, through coercive means, or voluntarily), the generational depth of each diaspora, the degree of acceptance and assimilation in the host-lands, the character of relations with the motherland/homeland, and the strength of connections among the diaspora. The *transnational locality* encapsulates their indigenization *and* transnationality, their sense of belonging and their displacement, and their sense of identity as national and transnational.

This study interrogates the home-host trope that is generally alluded to in defining diasporas. It is argued that a focus on the dual-state identity undermines the transnational aspect of diasporas and the ambivalences associated with being displaced from multiple states (especially if they have twice-migrated) but also having a localized and indigenized identity associated with their new home-nations. The home-host model also underplays the dynamic changes that occur through time, memories of the 'homeland' become part of the mythology associated with identities that are frozen in a space and time that has long passed. In many diasporas identities are constructed with respect to the new home-nation, especially after several generations, and connections with the state of origin get weaker through each generation. Placement in a transnational locality allows for more flexibility with respect to understanding the identity constructions of multiple generations and identities that are composed of elements from national and transnational spaces.

The Indian indentured diaspora has been indigenized through the generations, their identities are localized and Creolized representing the multicultural mix that prevails in each of the former colonies. The perspective taken in this book is that these are plural societies where different ethnic groups meet in the market place, but operate as separate and discreet entities in their neighborhoods.

In international relations the notion of state sovereignty is assumed to be integral to definitions of a state; it offers a sense of certainty, physical distinctiveness, and internal coherence. The presence of diasporas and immigrants, migrant workers, guest workers, and illegal residents, undermines this notion of sovereignty. The transnationality that is intrinsic to diasporas challenges these notions of sovereignty – state borders appear to be more elastic and state sovereignty becomes less clearly defined. Furthermore, the hybrid identities of diasporas challenge the underlying logic of nationhood. One of the main objectives of a nation is to develop a coherent narrative of nationalist history, culture, and identity. The presence of diasporas and other groups that confuse and destabilize these linear narratives present serious challenges to the concept of nationhood. In Fiji for example, contestation over definitions of the nation has resulted in political instability. In South Africa xenophobic attacks against African immigrants reflect tensions at various levels of the state and define the post-apartheid nation.

Global capitalist networks and the international hegemony of neoliberal economics also impact the character of social movements in the global south. In some instances, as in South Africa, the country transitioned to democracy and simultaneously adopted a neoliberal regime. The increasing integration of the global south into global capitalist networks creates similar societal schisms and divisions throughout the region. These include increasing wealth disparities, unemployment and underemployment, gender and racial inequalities, and a host of other maladies associated with shrinking state expenditure and increasing privatization. New social movements have to contend with global business enterprises and lowered national protections. Hence even though social movements in the global south are nationally focused (on local issues), they are transnationalized because of the international companies they have to contend and bargain with. Diasporas are caught in this web especially if they were historically and continue to be associated with the global movement of labor. In the current period it was argued that rather than an exclusive focus on political opportunities (in terms of social movement theories), it is also expedient to focus on economic inequalities that seriously affect many diasporas.

Indian indenture was introduced immediately following the Slavery Abolition Act 1833, and the structural institutions and ideologies that undergirded slavery made indenture possible. It was argued in Chapter 1 that the main points of intersection in England that tied indenture to slavery were the central role played by the West Indian capitalist and plantation elite in British politics, and the agendas, ideologies, and characteristics of the anti-slavery movements. The strength of the British Empire at the time, and its role in the global capitalist market, contributed towards racism and notions of superiority with respect to the "non-White" and non-Western other. These underlying assumptions also influenced the anti-slavery movements whereby the agenda to abolish slavery did not include a call for free-dom, rights, equality, and citizenship for former slaves or all people of color, nor did it call for restitution and justice, or abolition of all types of bonded labor.

Social movements that mobilized against indenture were likewise burdened by several factors. Indenture was positioned midway between slavery and free labor – indentured workers were under fixed and finite contracts. The agendas of these social movements were circumscribed by the rhetoric of plantation and other capitalist interests, as well as the political primacy given to sustaining the Empire from other competitive European powers – this gave rise to calls for checks and balances, protections, and oversight over the indentured system rather than a con-certed effort to abolish it. Importantly, indenture was as system that was histori-cally developed in England; husbandry was a common practice whereby young poor individuals entered into contracts with wealthier families for small salaries, food, and lodging. Furthermore, a system of indenture was also practiced in Brit-ish America with English men and women entering contracts of 1 to 7 years in lieu of payment for the transatlantic journey; about half to one-third of White immigrants to the American colonies went under indentured servitude. Europe-ans were also indentured to the Caribbean and included Irish servants, German redemptioners, and English convicts. During this period of extensive colonialism and global capitalist expansion, bonded labor was used fairly frequently in Europe and in the colonies, it was wage labor that was the "odd institution." One of the factors that distinguished Indian indenture from these previous institutions, was the place of Indians in the social and economic hierarchy of colonialism – Indians were "non-White" and colonial subjects.

The structural positioning of indentured Indians in the colonies engendered racial suspiciousness and divisions among the working peoples. Much like scab labor, Indians were consciously used to undermine the bargaining position of freed slaves or indigenous peoples by providing a new source of cheap labor. Indians were separated from each other and from former slaves and indigenous peoples; they were housed in separate quarters and their movement was strictly monitored. Once the indentured contracts were over they were subject to segregationist and other racist legislation. Social movements among them were initially focused only on local issues reflecting their social and political isolation; this pattern of resist-ance and organization was to become the hallmark of their social movements. This diaspora has not activated transnational networks, but focus on India as the source of their identity; there is little dialogue among members of this diaspora with weak awareness of their similar experiences. Instead they have relied on those members who have twice-migrated to assist with finances and media cover-age for their organizational objectives. The local and parochial character of social movements among indentured Indians, together with their cultural recognition of India as the motherland, illustrates how their positioning in the transnational locality has affected their identities and allegiances.

Fiji and Trinidad are similar in terms of their colonial and post-colonial histori-cal experiences, yet their political outcomes are very different. Fiji has experienced four coups since independence from British colonialism in 1970, in contrast Trini-dad has held consistent democratic elections since independence in 1962 (despite an attempted coup in 1990). Both Trinidad and Fiji were British colonies integrated into the imperial economy through the production of cash crops. Trinidad was colonized in 1797 and joined by Tobago in 1888. Ruled directly until 1925, it became independent in 1962. Fiji came under British rule via a Deed of Cession signed by leading ethnic Fijian chiefs in 1874, and became independent in 1970. About half of the population of each country is Indian, indentured during colonialism to replace emancipated slave labor in Trinidad, and to provide a new source of labor in Fiji. In Trinidad, 134,183 Indians were indentured from 1845 to 1917. By 1946 Indians accounted for about 35 per cent of the population.[1] In Fiji 60,000 Indians were indentured between 1879 and 1916, and by 1945 they outnumbered Fijians. Both countries are islands with roughly the same size population.

In Chapter 3 in this book I argue that constitutional engineering (which was instituted in Fiji in 1997, and electoral reform in 1999) cannot overcome the political tensions in Fiji because of several systemic conditions that exist. Indigenous Fijians make a generational claim on land and by extension, the nation. This has given them priority in the nation, and in the process Indo-Fijians have been positioned as outsiders and temporary residents. In Trinidad, both Indo-Trinidadians and Afro-Trinidadians were immigrants, laborers under colonialism through slavery and indenture respectively. This has created the situation whereby ethnic claims have to be bargained for even though Afro-Trinidadians have claimed a higher degree of indigeneity and hence nationhood. The Fijian hierarchical chiefly institutions that structure indigenous Fijian society substantiates the claim on nationhood and ethnic coherence. In Trinidad, a more hybrid and distinctively Trinidadian culture has evolved in music, carnival, language, food, intermarriage, and racial mixing. These are visible public spaces for the contestation of identity; the sparring that occurs over ethnic stereotyping during carnival, for example, brings such discourses out in the open. Ultimately the Westminster system, despite being problematic in plural societies, has proven to be quite malleable. Hence the reasons for continued instability needs to be sought elsewhere; in the more intangible factors pertaining to nationalism, citizenship, and identity, matter.

The position taken with respect to Mauritius is that like indentured Indians throughout the diaspora, Indo-Mauritians have an ambiguous relationship, in terms of identity, with the motherland (India) and their homeland (Mauritius). It is argued that Indo-Mauritian identity is as much about the minority Creole peoples as it is about diaspora connections to India. Indo-Mauritians have strengthened their relations with India to bolster their position in the state, but also to increase their status and position in the nation. The legacies of slavery and indenture under three European powers (Dutch, French, and English) left structural and institutional memories of racism, Whiteness, social and cultural hierarchies, and social divisions of difference variously defined in terms of race, ethnicity, religion, language, gender, generation, and class. These histories continue to define the Mauritian state and conceptions of nation and citizenship. Colonial administrations in tandem with global capitalism created institutional structures that met their needs for labor; these new centralized administrations were unchallenged by precolonial structures (of which there were none) or of aboriginal social systems.

Indo-Mauritians underplay evidence of their indigenous/Creolized/hybridized identities even though the majority among them speak Mauritian-Kreol and about a quarter of the population speaks Mauritian-Bhojpuri. They claim purity against Creole hybridity by drawing on their historical connection to India, specifically its ancient cultural and religious roots. In this endeavor the move to make "ancestral" languages part of the core in national examinations elevates these languages over the *lingua franca* (Mauritian Kreol) of the land and the language that a sizable portion of Hindus speak, Bhojpuri (a local version of the languages spoken by various groups in Northern India, and considered sub-par to Hindi). Even though they try to distance themselves from Creoles, Indo-Mauritians are themselves Creolized – they speak the local language and their Indianness is Creolized and mixed with strong influences from local Creole and French cultures. Mauritian Creoles are considered a marginal ethnic group that has not made similar strides in economic, political, and social terms as have Indo-Mauritians. The reasons for *Le Creole Malaise* are debated; the structures of colonialism with its emphasis on French Kreol, the violence of slavery, and the implications of the apprenticeship system, are some of the reasons put forth. In terms of resistance, what has been called a problem can be looked on as a means through which Creoles have survived and thrived within the capitalist system – Creoles have retracted from mainstream society, interacting when necessary but creating alternative community-oriented groups in remote and isolated parts of the country.

Mauritius is unique in the economic model it has pursued, actively and successfully engaging with the global neoliberal regime while maintaining some degree of state intervention. Its relations with India have been particularly strong as the subcontinent has itself moved towards a more robust neoliberal global engagement. Mauritius has been used as a conduit for direct investment in India (it is protected by a taxation agreement) and it is a robust site for offshore banking and efficient and open foreign investment. With its low tariffs and taxation laws, weak trade unions, educated labor force, and technological efficiency, Mauritius has thrived. But Creoles have been further marginalized despite state spending on welfare; low-level ethnic tensions persist as Indo-Mauritians make more gains and become more mobile and internationally engaged. Social movements among Creoles have not been strong and neither are they among Indo-Mauritians.

In post-apartheid South Africa, the ruling tripartite alliance of the African National Congress (ANC), the Congress of South African Trade Unions (COSATU) and the South African Communist Party (SACP), chose not to reclassify Indians as African or Afro-Indian or Indo-African, but to keep their classification as Indian. Indians are *ethnically* seen as "Coolie"(named as such during indenture and used pejoratively), Asiatic (another colonial category that included Indians, Arabs, Malays, and Chinese), and Indian (a colonial, apartheid and post-apartheid category). The rest of South Africa is classified in terms of race: Black African, White, Coloured.

The post-apartheid state has had to deal with several compelling challenges. It had to meet the needs of the Black majority, the basis of their support. At the same time the state had to ensure that White capitalist flight did not adversely affect the economy. Lastly, it had to create structures to enable the country to actively participate in the global neoliberal economic system. From its adoption in the mid-1990s, the neoliberal economic frame of reference has generally failed to effectively redistribute income to the lower levels of society. The increase in protests and resistance a decade later reflect growing discontent among the poor. While affirmative action programs ensure that the middle classes grow, ethnic and racial classifications continue to divide the population, maintaining low-level tensions and competition among the various groups. In other words, by keeping the racial classifications of apartheid, the post-apartheid state also kept the narratives of racism that had been propagated under 42 years of apartheid (1948–1990) and 130 years of colonial and settler self-rule (1814–1947).

The implications for Indians are twofold. First, a majority of them are poor due to unemployment, under-employment, low wages, weak social services, inadequate welfare programs, and underfunded education facilities. Second, even though Indians and Coloureds[2] are officially included in affirmative action programs, they are practically excluded. Despite majority rule, state functions are still dependent on racial divisions; voting rosters, access to government programs, affirmative action programs, educational, and other services are facilitated through racial classification. Indians have experienced this state from the perspective of a small minority divided along the lines of class and ethnicity (religion and regional origin from India are still relevant). As they are not officially considered African (in terms of South Africa) or Indian (in terms of India), Indians occupy the *transnational locality*, neither wholly belonging to South Africa nor to India. They are designated as the ethnic other and structurally excluded from the post-apartheid state. The discourses on race put forth by this system do not interrogate the constructs of race, on the contrary, it has re-emphasized them while at the same time re-instituting new levels of class disparities across all ethnic and racial groups.

This analysis is based on a structural argument; despite the powerful mobilization and action by social movements in the country, the manner and terms of the negotiations leading up to the democratic transition, as well as the characteristics of the post-apartheid system, were decided upon by elites far removed from the masses. Global and local capitalists, national and international government elites, and the exiled, detained, and national leadership of social movements facilitated the transition to a post-apartheid system. The social movements among Indians responded to the various state systems in myriad ways: during colonialism Indians formed many political organizations focused on rights, during apartheid they allied with the broader anti-apartheid movements or joined organizations that concentrated on local demands, in the post-apartheid system Indians have been active in local level movements dealing with social and political issues. Indians were active in social movements from the early periods of indenture yet have been unable to influence structural shifts at the state level. Their ethnicity and diaspora identities have been constantly used to marginalize, subjugate, and separate them from the Black majority. Social movement theories shift attention to agency – to the people that actively participate in organizations to increase their rights with respect to the state. I show that despite the action of Indians over the duration of their settlement in South Africa, the various states have reacted by giving Indians rights but ultimately falling back on ethnic definitions to control and marginalize them. By employing this ethnic category these states have also used Indians to divide the majority and to undermine united action – during colonialism they were seen as scab labor and outsiders whose relative upward mobility came to be resented by the Black proletariat; during apartheid they were used as a buffer between Whites and Blacks (both figuratively and in geographical and political segregation), and in post-apartheid they have been sidelined and isolated from mainstream politics, denied upward mobility, and treated as "outsiders." It is my contention that an emphasis on structures rather than agency is the most compelling way of understanding the plight of Indians in South Africa today.

The notion of being an Indian in a location outside India over multiple generations has contributed towards identities that are fluid, flexible, and dynamic. While it is possible to chart Indian diaspora progression through political, economic and social institutions, it is more difficult to capture the spirit of "Indianness" as it has played out in diverse environments. No essentialized identity is visible, but the official categorization and subjective definitions associated with the indentured diaspora exists. In each place Indianness is clearly indigenized – localized and relevant to others in the nation. India is an imagined motherland, but daily life is embedded in the local. The analysis in Chapter 6 is not meant to be an exhaustive overview, but aims to highlight a few of the cultural elements that clearly reflect this indigenization.

In this diaspora, class has become the most important indicator of status. Diaspora members are Westernized, adept at actively engaging with capitalism while being physically and mentally separate from India. From the food they consume to their festivals and places of worship, the indentured diaspora has defined a place in the nation. They are, however, never considered to have indigenized identities in the nation-states that they call home; Indians from the subcontinent also view them as being marginal, if not irrelevant, to India. They belong to and are separate from the India. While imagining India as pure, authentic, and sacred, Indians in the diaspora have constructed a culture that is wholly national and local. In terms of their food, music, the character of worship that has evolved, the languages they speak, and the religions they follow, the culture of indentured Indians is unique in each state. Few generalizations can be made, the common element is their historical connection to India.

The indentured Indian diaspora is best understood from its placement in the transnational locality. Viewed as neither fully belonging to the nation-states they call home, nor the nation-state from which their forefathers left behind, the diaspora experiences identity in terms of both belonging and displacement. Like other diasporas, the placement in the transnational locality has, through the generations, also led to subjective moves to isolate themselves. A high degree of insularity is visible throughout the diaspora in terms of marriage, celebratory events, politics, and economic endeavors. Transnational bodies that connect with the ambivalences associated with diaspora are likely to gain support. Transnational Muslim groups, for example, have gained support because of the alienation that some of its members feel in the nation-state. Diasporas play a significant role in the current international system. The role of transnational movements in creating both security and insecurity has become more salient. With the current global economic system that is transnational in its operation (in that state borders have less relevance), the placement of diasporas enables them to actively articulate with this economy. Diaspora Indians for example, are well placed to take advantage of the transnational moment, their skills are in demand and they are highly mobile. Every country in which this diaspora resides has experienced the migration of the younger generation to the West. The pull of transnational social movements is well known; the growth of fundamentalist groups that have a global reach has added new levels to international security. Integration into a state requires structural changes as well as an expansion of nationhood to include diasporas and transnational identities. While this is not an argument for or against state sovereignty or the integrity of states, it does suggest that in line with the transnationalism that exists in terms of the global economy and the movement of labor, it is not far-fetched to imagine state based nations as being more flexible and open to multiple identities. The placement of diasporas in a transnational locality because of the demands of state-driven definitions of belonging, serves to undermine notions of state and nations, and drives diasporas to look for belonging elsewhere, especially in the transnational arena.

Notes

1   Bridget Brereton, *Race Relations in Colonial Trinidad, 1870–1900*, (Cambridge: Cambridge University Press, 1979), 9.
2   The category "Coloured" includes those who have a mixed racial heritage, those who identify as "Cape Malays," and those who are indigenous (San and Khoi).

Bibliography

Abdulhadi, Rabab. "The Palestinian Women's Autonomous Movement: Emergence, Dynamics, and Challenges." *Gender and Society* 12.6(1998): 649–673.

Adam, Barry D. *The Rise of a Gay and Lesbian Movement*. New York: Twayne Publishers, 1995.

Addis, Megan. "Between a Rock and A Hard Place: The Marginalization of Coloured and Indian Interests in South African Politics." *A Journal of Opinion*, 27.2(1999): 37–41.

Alexander, Fred. "South Africa's Indian Problem." *Far Eastern Survey* 19.21(1950): 230–232.

Alexander, Neville. "Affirmative Action and the Perpetuation of Racial Identities in Post-Apartheid South Africa." *Transformation: Critical Perspectives on Southern Africa* 63(2007): 92–108.

Alexander, Peter and Peter Pfaffe. "Social Relationships to the Means and Ends of Protest in South Africa's Ongoing Rebellion of the Poor: The Balfour Insurrections." *Social Movement Studies: Journal of Social, Cultural and Political Protest*, 13.2(2014): 204–221.

Allen, Richard. Slaves, Freedmen, and Indentured Laborers in Colonial Mauritius. Cambridge: Cambridge University Press, 1999.

Anderson, Benedict. *Imagined Communities: Reflections on the Origins and Spread of Nationalism*. London: Verso, 1991.

Appadurai, Arjun. "Grassroots Globalization and the Research Imagination." *Public Culture* 12.1(2000): 1–19.

Appadurai, Arjun. *Modernity at Large: Cultural Dimensions of Globalization*. Minneapolis: University of Minnesota Press, 1996.

Appardurai, Arjun. "How to Make a National Cuisine: Cookbooks in Contemporary India." *Comparative Studies in Society and History* 30(1988): 2–13.

Armitage, David. *The Ideological Origins of the British Empire*. Cambridge: Cambridge University Press, 2000.

Aumeerally, N. L. "'Tiger in Paradise': Reading Global Mauritius in Shifting Time and Space." *Journal of African Cultural Studies*. 17.2(2005): 161–180.

Ayres, Jeffrey M. *Defying Conventional Wisdom: Political Movements and Popular Contention Against North American Free Trade*. Toronto: University of Toronto Press, 1998.

Ballantyne, Tony. "Colonial Knowledge." In *The British Empire: Themes and Perspectives*. Edited by Sarah Stockwell, 177–197. Victoria, Australia: Blackwell Publishers, 2008.

Ballard, Richard, Adam Habib, Imraan Valodia, and Elke Zuern. "Globalization, Marginalization and Contemporary Social Movements in South Africa." *African Affairs*, 104.417(2005): 615–634.

Bangura, Yusuf. "Introduction: Ethnic Inequalities and Public Sector Governance." In *Ethnicity Inequalities and Public Sector Governance*. Edited by Yusuf Bangura, 1–30. New York: Palgrave Macmillan, 2006.

Barry, Brian. "Political Accommodation and Consociational Democracy." *British Journal of Political Science* 5.4(1975): 477–505.

Basch, Linda, Nina Glick Schiller, and Blanc Cristina Szanton. *Nations Unbound: Transnational Projects, Postcolonial Predicaments, and Deterritorialized Nation-states.* London: Routledge, 1993.

Baumann, Martin. "Becoming A Color of the Rainbow: The Social Integration of Indian Hindus in Trinidad, Analysed along a Phase Model of Diaspora." In *South Asians in the Diaspora. Histories and Religious Traditions*. Edited by Knut A. Jocobsen and P. Pratap Kumar, 77–96. Leiden, The Netherlands: Koninklijke Brill, 2003.

Bayley, Susan. *Caste, Society and Politics in India from the Eighteenth Century into the Modern Age*. Cambridge: Cambridge University Press, 1999.

Beaton, Rev. Patrick. *Creoles and Coolies. Five Years in Mauritius*. New York and London: Kennikat Press, 1859.

Beinin, Joel and Fréderic Vairel. Editors. *Social Movements, Mobilization, and Contestation in the Middle East and North Africa*. Stanford: Stanford University Press, 2011.

Bhabha, Homi. *The Location of Culture*. London: Routledge, 1994.

Bhana, Surendra and Bridglal Pachai. Editors. *A Documentary History of Indian South Africans*. Stanford, CA: Hoover Institution Press, 1984.

Biersteker, Thomas J. and Cynthia Weber. *State Sovereignty as a Social Construct*. Cambridge: Cambridge University Press, 1996.

Biko, Steve. *I Write What I Like*, Selected Readings. Chicago: University of Chicago Press, 2002.

Bill Freund, Bill. "Swimming Against the Tide: The Macro-Economic Research Group in the South African Transition 1991–94." http://afep2014.sciencesconf.org/36107/document.

Blackburn, Robin. *The Overthrow of Colonial Slavery 1776–1848*. London, New York: Verso, 1988.

Bond, Patrick. "South Africa Tackles Global Apartheid: Is the Reform Strategy Working?" *South Atlantic Quarterly* 103.4(2004): 817–839.

Bond, Patrick. *Elite Transition: From Apartheid to Neoliberalism in South Africa*. London: Pluto Press, 2000.

Bose, Neilesh. "New Settler Colonial Histories at the Edge of Empire: "Asiatics," settlers, and law in colonial South Africa." *Journal of Colonialism and History* 15.1(2014).

Boswell, Boswell. "Unraveling Le Malaise Créole: Hybridity and Marginalization in Mauritius." *Identities: Global Studies in Culture and Power* 12.2(2005): 195–221.

Boswell, Rosabelle. "Heritage Tourism and Identity in the Mauritian Villages of Chamarel and Le Morne." *Journal of Southern African Studies* 31.2(2005): 283–295.

Boswell, Rosabelle. *Le Malaise Créole: Ethnic Identity in Mauritius*. New York: Berghahn Books, 2006.

Brah, Avtar and Annie E. Coombes. *Hybridity and Its Discontents: Politics, Science, Culture*. London: Routledge, 2000.

Bräutigam, Deborah. "Institutions, Economic Reform, and Democratic Consolidation in Mauritius." *Comparative Politics* 30.1(1999): 45–62.

Braziel, Jana Evans and Anita Mannur. *Theorizing Diaspora: A Reader*. Malden, MA: Blackwell Publishing Ltd., 2003.

Brecher, Jeremy, Tim Costello, and Brendan Smith. *Globalization from Below: The Power of Solidarity*. Boston: South End, 2000.

Brenneis, Donald. "Grog and Gossip in Bhatgaon: Style and Substance in Fijian Indian Conversation." *American Ethnologist* 11.3(1984): 487–506.

Brereton, Bridget. *Race Relations in Colonial Trinidad, 1870–1900*. Cambridge: Cambridge University Press, 1979.

Buechler, Steven M. "New Social Movement Theories." *The Sociological Quarterly* 36.3(1995): 441–464.

Buechler, Steven M. *Women's Movements in the United States: Woman Suffrage, Equal Rights, and Beyond*. New Brunswick, NJ: Rutgers University Press, 1990.

Burrows, J. R. *The Population and Labor Resources of Natal*. Pietermaritzburg: Town and Regional Planning Commission, 1959.

Buzan, Barry and Lene Hansen. *The Evolution of International Security Studies*. Cambridge: Cambridge University Press, 2009.

Carter, Marina. *Voices of Indenture. Experiences of Indian Migrants in the British Empire*. London and New York: Leicester University Press, 1996.

Castells, Manuel. *The Information Age: Economy, Society and Culture*, Vol. 2, *The Power of Identity*. Oxford UK: Blackwell, 1977.

Chandrasekhar, S. "Growth and Characteristics of Population – The Island of Mauritius: 1767–1987." *Population Review* 32.1–2(1988): 11–40.

Chanock. Martin. *The Making of South African Legal Culture 1902–1936: Fear, Favour and Prejudice*. New York: Cambridge University Press, 2001.

Charlton, James I. *Nothing About Us Without Us: Disability Oppression and Empowerment*. Berkeley: University of California Press, 1998.

Clarke, Colin G. "Residential Segregation and Intermarriage in San Fernando, Trinidad." *Geographical Review* 61.2(1971): 198–218.

Clifford, James. "Diasporas." *Cultural Anthropology* 9.3(1994): 302–338.

Cohen, Robin. "Diasporas and the Nation-State: From Victim to Challengers." *International Affairs* 72.3(1996): 507–520.

Cohen, Robin. *Global Diasporas: An Introduction*. Seattle: University of Washington Press, 1997.

Cohn, Bernard S. *Colonialism and Its Forms of Knowledge: The British in India*. Princeton: Princeton University Press, 1996.

Colley, Linda. *Britons, Forging the Nation 1707–1837*. New Haven: Yale University Press, 2009.

Collier, George with Elizabeth Lowery Quaratiello. *Basta! Land and the Zapatista Rebellion in Chiapas*. Oakland, CA: Food & Development Policy, 1994.

Connor, Walker. "The Impact of Homelands Upon Diasporas." In *Modern Diasporas in International Relations*. Edited by Gabriel Sheffer, 16–46. London: Croom Helm, 1986.

Connor, Walker. *Ethnonationalism: The Quest for Understanding*. Princeton NJ: Princeton University Press, 1994.

Craton, Michael, James Walvin and David Wright. *Slavery, Abolition and Emancipation: Black Slaves and the British Empire. A Thematic Documentary*. London and New York: Longman, 1976.

Croucher, Sheila L. "Perpetual Imagining: Nationhood in a Global Era." *International Studies Review* 5.1(2003): 1–24.

Daalder, Hans. "The Consociational Democracy Theme." *World Politics* 26.4(1974): 604–621.

Dangor, S. E. "Negotiating Identities: The Case of Indian Muslims in South Africa." In *South Asians in the Diaspora: Histories and Religious Traditions*. Edited by Knut A. Jacobsen and P. Pratap Kumar, 243–268. Leiden, The Netherlands: Koninklijke Brill, 2004.

Davis, David Brian. *Slavery and Human Progress*. Oxford: Oxford University Press, 1984.

Davis, David Brian. *The Problem of Slavery in the Age of Revolution*, 1770–1823. Oxford: Oxford University Press, 1984.

Davis, David Brian. *The Problem of Slavery in Western Culture*. Ithaca: Cornell University Press, 1973.

Dawes, Robyn M., Anthony J. C. Van de Kragt, and John M. Orbell. "Not Me or Thee But We: The Importance of Group Identity in Eliciting Cooperation in Dilemma Situations; Experimental Manipulations." *Acta Psychologica* 68(1989): 83–97.

della Porta, Donatella and Mario Diani. *Social Movements: An Introduction*. UK: Blackwell, 1999.

Desai, Ashwin and Dhevarsha Ramjettan. "The Boundaries of Sport and Citizenship in 'liberated' South Africa." In *Racial Redress and Citizenship in South Africa*. Edited by Adam Habib and Kristina Bentley, 289–313. South Africa: HSRC Press, 2008.

Desai, Ashwin. *We are the Poors: Community Struggles in Post-Apartheid South Africa*. New York: Monthly Review Press, 2002.

Diesel, Alleyn. "Hinduism in KwaZulu-Natal, South Africa." In *Culture and Economy in the Indian Diaspora*. Edited by Bhikhu Parekh et al., 33–50. London: Routledge, 2003.

Dinan, Monique, Vidula Nababsing, and Hansraj Mathur. "Mauritius: Cultural Accommodation in a Diverse Island Polity." In *The Accommodation of Cultural Diversity: Case Studies*, edited by Crawford Young. New York: St. Martin's Press, 1999.

Dirks, Nicholas B. *Castes of Mind*. Princeton: Princeton University Press, 2001.

Doty, Roxanne Lynn. "Sovereignty and the Nation: Constructing the Boundaries of National Identity." In *State Sovereignty as Social Construct*. Edited by Thomas J. Biersteker and Cynthia Weber, 121–147. Cambridge: Cambridge University Press, 1996.

Drescher, Seymour. "Eric Williams: British Capitalism and British Slavery," *History and Theory* 26.2(1987): 180–196

Drescher, Seymour. *Econocide: British Slavery in the Era of Abolition*. Pittsburgh: University of Pittsburgh Press, 1977.

Du Bois, W. E. B. *The Souls of Black Folk*. Edited by Henry Louis Gates Jr., and Tern Hume Oliver. New York: Norton and Company, 1999.

Dufoix, Stéphane. *Diasporas*. Berkeley: University of California Press, 2008.

Durutalo, Alumita. "Defending the Inheritance: The SDL and the 2006 Elections." In *From Election to Coup: The 2006 Campaign and its Aftermath*. Edited by Jon Fraenkel and Stewart Firth, 78–88. Canberra, Australia: ANU Press, 2007).

Eagleton, Terry. "Edible Ecriture." In *Consuming Passions: Food in the Age of Anxiety*. Edited by Sian Griffiths and Jennifer Wallace, 203–208. Manchester: Manchester University Press, 1998.

Edelman, Marc. "Social Movements: Changing Paradigms and Forms or Politics." *Annual Review of Anthropology* 30(2001): 285–317.

Edelman, Marc. *Peasants Against Globalization: Rural Social Movements in Costa Rica*. Stanford: Stanford University Press, 1999.

Edwards, Iain. "Cato Manor: Cruel Past, Pivotal Future." *Review of African Political Economy* 21.61(1994): 415–427.

Edwards, Ian and Tim Nuttall. "Seizing the Moment: The January 1949 Riots, Proletarian Populism and the Structures of African Urban Life in Durban During the Late 1940s." History Workshop. 1990. University of Witwatersrand.

Eisenlohr, Patrick. "Register Levels of Ethno-National Purity: The Ethnicization of Language and Community in Mauritius." *Language in Society* 33.1(2004): 59–80.

Eisenlohr, Patrick. "The Politics of Diaspora and the Morality of Secularism: Muslim Identities and Islamic Authority in Mauritius." *The Journal of the Royal Anthropological Institute* 12(2) (2006): 396–412.

Eisenlohr, Patrick. *Little India, Diaspora, Time, and Ethnolinguistic Belonging in Hindu Mauritius*. Berkeley, University of California Press, 2006.

Eller, Jack and Reed Coughlan, "The Poverty of Primordialism: The Demystification of Ethnic Attachments." *Ethnic and Racial Studies* 16.2(1993): 183–202.

Elphick, R. and R. Davenport. Editors. *Christianity in South Africa: A Political, Social and Cultural History*. Cape Town: David Philip, 1997.

Eltis, David and Stanley L. Engerman. "The Importance of Slavery and the Slave Trade to Industrializing Britain." *Journal of Economic History* 60.1(2000): 123–144.

Eltis, David. "Slavery and Freedom in the Early Modern World." In *Terms of Labor: Slavery, Serfdom, and Free Labor*. Edited by Stanley L. Engerman, 25–49. Stanford: Stanford University Press, 1999.

Eriksen, Thomas Hylland. *Common Denominations: Ethnicity, Nation Building and Compromise in Mauritius*. Oxford, UK: Berg, 1998.

Erikson, Thomas Hylland. "Creolization in Anthropological Theory and in Mauritius." In *History, Ethnography, Theory*. Edited by Charles Stewart, 153–177. Walnut Creek, CA: Left Coast Press, 2006.

Esman, Milton, J. "Diasporas and International Relations." In *Modern Diasporas in International Politics*. Edited by Gabriel Sheffer, 16–46. New York: St. Martins, 1986.

Esterhuyse, Willie. *Endgame: Secret Talks and the End of Apartheid*. Tafelberg, Cape Town, 2012.

Falk, Richard. "The Making of Global Citizenship." In *Global Visions: Beyond the New World* Order. Edited Jeremy Brecher, John Brown Childs, and Jill Cutler, 39–50. Montreal, Canada: Black Rose Books, 1993.

Fanon, Frantz. *Black Skin White Masks*. Translated by Charles Lam Markmann. New York: Grove Press, 1967.

Field, Michael. "The Media and the Specter of the 2000 Coup." In *From Election to Coup: The 2006 Campaign and its Aftermath*. Edited by Jon Fraenkel and Stewart Firth, 174–184. Canberra, Australia: ANU Press, 2007.

Fireman, Bruce and Steven Rytina. *Encounters with Unjust Authority*. Homewood, IL: Dorsey Press, 1982.

Foweraker, Joe. *Theorizing Social Movements*. London: Pluto, 1995.

Fox, Jonathan A. "Assessing Binational Civil Society Coalition: Lessons from the Mexico-US Experience." Paper presented at the *Latin American Studies Association*. Miami Florida. 2000. http://lasa.international.pitt.edu/Lasa2000/Fox.PDF

Fox, Jonathan D. and David L. Brown. *The Struggle for Accountability: The World Back, NGOs, and Grassroots Movements*. Cambridge: MIT Press, 1998.

Fraenkel, Jon and Bernard Grofman. "Does the Alternative Vote Foster Moderation in Ethnically Divided Societies?" *Comparative Political Studies* 39(2006): 623–651.

Fraenkel, Jon and Bernard Grofman. "The Failure of the Alternative Vote as a Tool for Ethnic Moderation in Fiji: A Rejoinder to Horowitz." *Comparative Political Studies* 39(2006): 663–666.

Fraenkel, Jon and Bernard Grofman. "The Merits of Neo-Downsian Modeling of the Alternative Vote: A Reply to Horowitz." *Public Choice* 133.1–2(2007): 1–11.

Fraenkel, Jon. "Melanesia in Review: Issues and Events, 2007: Fiji." *The Contemporary Pacific* 20.2(2008): 450–460.

Fraenkel, Jon. "Multiparty Cabinet and Power-Sharing: Lessons from Elsewhere." In *From Election to Coup in Fiji: The 2006 Campaign and its Aftermath*. Edited by Jon Fraenkel and Stewart Firth, 368–378. Canberra, Australia: ANU Press, 2007.

Fanon, Frantz. *The Wretched of the Earth*. New York: Grove Press, 1963.

Freund, Bill. *Insiders and Outsiders: The Indian Working Class of Durban, 1910–1990*. Portsmouth, NH: Heinemann Publishers, 1995.

Furnivall, J. S. *Colonial Policy and Practice: A Comparative Study of Burma and Netherlands India*. Cambridge: University of Cambridge Press, 1948.

Galenson, David. *White Servitude in Colonial America: An Economic Analysis*. New York: Cambridge University Press, 1981.

Gamson, William A. and David Meyer. "Framing Political Opportunity." In *Comparative Perspectives on Social Movements*. Edited by Doug McAdam, John McCarthy, and Mayer Zald, 275–290. New York: Cambridge University Press, 1996.

Gandhi, M. K. *Satyagraha in South Africa*. Ahmedabad: Navajivan Publishing House, 1928 (reprint 2008)

Geertz, Clifford. "The Integrative Revolution." In *Old Societies and New States*. Edited by Clifford Geertz, 105–157. New York: Free Press, 1963.

Gilroy, Paul. *The Black Atlantic: Modernity and Double Consciousness*. Cambridge, MA: Harvard University Press, 1993.

Goodwin, Jeff and James M. Jasper. "Caught in a Winding, Snarling Vine: The Structural Bias of Political Process Theory." *Sociological Forum*, 1999, 14.1(1999): 27–54.

Goolam Vahed, "Passengers, Partnerships, and Promissory Notes: Gujarati Traders in Colonial Natal, 1870–1920," *The International Journal of African Historical Studies* 38.3 (2005): 449–479.

Green, William. *British Slave Emancipation: The Sugar Colonies and the Great Experiment 1830–1865*. Oxford: Clarendon Press, 1976.

Grieco, Elizabeth M. "The Effects of Migration on the Establishment of Networks: Caste Disintegration and Reformation among the Indians of Fiji." *International Migration Review* 32.3(1998): 704–736.

Grosby, Steven. "The Verdict of History: The Inexpungible Tie of Primordiality – A Response to Elle and Coughlan." *Ethnic and Racial Studies* 17.1(1994): 164–171.

Gupta, Akhil. *Postcolonial Developments: Agriculture in the Making of Modern India*. Durham: Duke University Press, 1998.

Guy, Jeff. "Somewhere Over the Rainbow: The Nation-State and Race in a Globalizing South Africa." *Transformation: Critical Perspectives on Southern Africa* 56(2004): 68–89.

Habib, Adam and Rupert Taylor. "Parliamentary Opposition and Democratic Consolidation in South Africa." *Review of African Political Economy* 1.80(1999): 261–267.

Habib, Adam and Sanusha Naidoo. "Race, Class and Voting Patterns in South Africa's Electoral System: Ten Years of Democracy." *Africa Development* 31.3(2006): 81–92.

Halisi, C. R. D. "Biko and Black Consciousness Philosophy: An Interpretation." In *Bounds of Possibility. The Legacy of Steve Biko and Black Consciousness*. Edited by N. Barney Pityana, Mamphela Ramphele, Malusi Mpumlwana, and Lindy Wilson, 100–110. Cape Town: David Philip, 1991.

Hall, Stuart and David Morley. *Critical Dialogues in Cultural Studies*. London: Routledge, 1997.

Hall, Stuart. "Race, Articulation and Societies Structured in Dominance." In *Sociological Theories, Race and Colonialism*. Edited by UNESCO, 305–345. Paris: UNESCO, 1980.

Hall, Stuart. *Culture, Globalization and World System. Contemporary Conditions for the Representation of Identity*. Minneapolis: University of Minnesota Press, 1977.

Halpern, Rick. "Solving the "Labour Problem": Work and the State in the Sugar Industries of Louisiana and Natal. 1870–1910." *Journal of Southern African Studies* 30.1(2004): 19–40.

Hannerz, Ulf. *Transnational Connections: Culture, People, Places*. London and New York: Routledge, 1996.

Hansen, Thomas Blom. "An Unwieldy Fetish: Desire and Disavowal of Indianness in South Africa." In *Eyes Across the Water: Navigating the Indian Ocean (Indian Ocean Series)*. Edited by Pamila Gupta and Isabel Hofmeyr, 109–121. South Africa: Unisa Press, 2010.

Hansen, Thomas Blom. "From Culture to Barbed Wire: On Houses and Walls in South Africa." *Texas International Law Journal* 46.345(2011): 345–353.

Hansen, Thomas Blom. "Melancholia of Freedom: Humour and Nostalgia among Indians in South Africa." *Modern Drama* 48.2(2005): 297–315.

Hansen, Thomas Blom. "Plays, Politics and Cultural Identity among Indians in Durban." *Journal of Southern African Studies* 26.2(2000): 255–269.

Harewood, Jack and Ralph Henry. *Inequality in a Post-Colonial Society: Trinidad*. Trinidad: Institute of Economic and Social Research, University of West Indies, 1985.

Hart, Keith and Vishnu Padayachee. "A History of South African Capitalism in National and Global Perspective." *Transformation: Critical Perspectives on Southern Africa* 81.81(2013).

Harvey, David. *A Brief History of Neoliberalism*. New York: Oxford University Press, 2007.

Harvey, Neil. *The Chiapas Rebellion: The Struggle for Land and Democracy*. Durham, NC: Duke University Press, 1988.

Hazareesingh, K. "The Religion and Culture of Indian Immigrants in Mauritius and the Effect of Social Change." *Comparative Studies in Society and History* 8.2(1966): 241–257.

Hempel, Lynn M. " Power, Wealth and Common Identity: Access to Resources and Ethnic Identification in a Plural Society." *Ethnic and Racial Studies*, 32.3(2009): 460–489.

Henrard, Kristin. *Minority Protection in Post-Apartheid South Africa: Human Rights, Minority Rights, and Self-Determination*. Westpoint, Connecticut: Praeger Publishers, 2002.

Hiltebeitel, A. *The Cult of Draupadi. Vol. 1. Mythologies from Gingee to Kuruksetra*. Chicago: Chicago University Press, 1988.

Hochschild, Adam. *Bury the Chains. Prophets and Rebels in the Fight to Free an Empire's Slaves*. Boston and New York: Houghton Mifflin Company, 2005.

Hollup, Oddvar. "Islamic Revivalism and Political Opposition among Minority Muslims in Mauritius." *Ethnology* 33.4(1996): 285–300.

Hollup, Oddvar. "The Disintegration of Caste and Changing Concepts of Indian Ethnic Identity in Mauritius." *Ethnology* 33.4(1994): 297–316.

Horowitz, Donald L. "Electoral Systems: A Primer for Decision Makers." *Journal of Democracy* 14.4(2003): 115–127.

Horowitz, Donald L. "Where Have All the Parties Gone? Fraenkel and Grofman on the Alternative Vote – Yet Again." *Public Choice* 133.13(2007): 13–23.

Howe, Steven. "Empire and Ideology." In *The British Empire. Theories and Perspectives*. Edited by Sarah Stockwell, 157–176. Australia: Blackwell Publishing, 2008.

Hughes, Heather. "Violence in Inanda, August 1985." *Journal of Southern African Studies* 13.3(1987): 331–354.

Hunt, Margaret R. *The Middling Sort: Commerce, Gender, and the Family in England 1680–1780*. Berkeley: University of California Press, 1996.

Hurwitz, Edith F. *Politics and the Public Conscience. Slave Emancipation and the Abolitionist Movement in Britain.* London: George Allen & Unwin Ltd., 1973.

Huttenback, Robert A. "Indians in South Africa, 1860–1914: The British Imperial Philosophy on Trial." *The English Historical Review* 81.319(1966): 273–291.

Iyer, Kanthie. *Easy to Cook Indian Recipes.* 1991.

Jackson, Melveen. "Popular Indian South African Music: Division in Diversity." *Popular Music* 10.2(1991): 175–188.

James, C. L. R. *Black Jacobins: Toussicont L'Overture and the San Domingo Revolution,* 2nd ed. New York: Vintage Books, 1989.

Jayawardena, C, "The Disintegration of Caste in Fiji Indian Rural Society." In *Anthropology in Oceania: Essays Presented to Ian Hogbin.* Edited by L. Hiatt and C. Jayawardena. Melbourne: Angus and Robertson, 1971.

Jayawardena, Chandra. "Culture and Ethnicity in Guyana and Fiji." *Man, New Series* 15.3(1980): 430–450.

Jung, Courtney. *Then I Was Black: South African Political Identities in Transition.* New Haven: Yale University Press, 2000.

Kahn, Brian. "Debates over IMF Reform in South Africa." *Studies on International Financial Architecture/IMF Special – No.* 6 (2000) http://library.fes.de/pdf-files/iez/00793.pdf.

Kale, Madhavi. ""When the Saints Came Marching In": The Anti-Slavery Society and Indian Indentured Migration to the British Caribbean." In *Empire and Others: British Encounters with Indigenous Peoples, 1600–1850.* Edited by Martin Daunton and Rick Halpern, 325–344. Philadelphia: University of Pennsylvania Press, 1999.

Kale, Madhavi. "Projecting Identities: Empire and Indentured Labor Migration from India to Trinidad and British Guiana, 1836–1885." In *Nations and Migration: The Politics of Space in the South Asian Diaspora.* Edited by Peter van der Veer, 74–92. Philadelphia: University of Pennsylvania Press, 1995.

Kale, Madhavi. *Fragments of Empire. Capital, Slavery, and Indian Indentured Labor Migration in the British Caribbean.* Philadelphia: University of Pennsylvania) Press, 1998.

Kalra, Virindar, Raminder Kaur, and John Hutnyk. *Diaspora and Hybridity: Theory, Culture and Society.* UK: Sage Publications Ltd., 2005.

Kasfir, Nelson. "Explaining Ethnic Political Participation." *World Politics* 31.3(1979): 365–388.

Katzenstein, Peter, Robert Keohane, and Stephen Krasner. "International Organization and the Study of World Africa." *International Organizations* 52.4(1998): 645–685.

Katzenstein, Peter. Editor. *The Culture of National Security: Norms and Identity in World Politics.* New York: Columbia University Press, 1996.

Keck, Margaret E. and Kathryn Sikkink. *Activists Beyond Borders. Advocacy Networks in International Politics.* Ithaca: Cornell University Press, 1998.

Kelly, John D. "Fiji Indians and "Commoditization of Labor."" *American Ethnologist* 19.1 (2002): 97–207.

Kelly, John D. "From Holi to Diwali: An Essay on Ritual and History." *Man, New Series* 23.1(1988): 40–55.

Kelly, John D. "Threats to Difference in Colonial Fiji." *Cultural Anthropology* 10.1(1995): 64–84

Kettani, Houssain. "Proceedings of the 8th Hawaii International Conference on Arts and Humanities," Honolulu, Hawaii, January 2010, www.pupr.edu/hkettani/papers/HICAH2010.pdf

Khan, Aisha. "What is 'a Spanish'? Ambiguity and 'Mixed' Ethnicity in Trinidad." In *Trinidad Ethnicity*. Edited by Kevin A. Yelvington, 180–207. Knoxville: The University of Tennessee Press, 1993.

King, Anthony D. Editor. *Culture, Globalization and World-System. Contemporary Conditions for the Representation of Identity*. Minneapolis: University of Minnesota Press, 1977.

Klandermans, Bert, Hanspeter Kriesi, and Sidney Tarrow. *From Structure to Action: Comparing Social Movement Research Across Cultures, International Social Movement Research, Vol. 1*. Greenwich, Conn: JAI, 1988.

Klass, Morton. *East Indians in Trinidad: A Study of Cultural Persistence*. New York: Columbia University Press, 1961.

Klautz, Audi. *Migration and National Identity in South Africa*. Cambridge: Cambridge University Press, 2013.

Koopmans, Ruud. "A Failed Revolution, But a Worthy Cause." *Mobilization* 8(2003): 116–119.

Kruger, Loren. "Black Atlantis, White Indians, and Jews: Locations, Locations and Syncretic Identities in the Fiction of Achmat Dangor and Others." *The South Atlantic Quarterly*. 100.1(2001): 111–143,

Kuper, Hilda. ""Strangers" in Plural Societies: Asians in South Africa and Uganda." In *Pluralism in Africa*. Edited by Leo Kuper and M. G. Smith, 246–282. Berkeley and Los Angeles: University of California Press, 1969.

Kuper, Hilda. "Changes in Caste of the South African Indians." *Race Relations Journal* 22 (1955): 18–26.

Kuper, Leo and M. G. Smith. Editors. *Pluralism in Africa*. Berkeley and Los Angeles: University of California Press, 1969.

Kuper, Leonard. *An African Bourgeoisie*. New Haven: Yale University Press.

Laitin, David. "South Africa: Violence, Myth, and Democratic Reform." *World Politics* 39.2 (1987): 258–279.

Laitin, David. *Hegemony and Culture. Politics and Religious Change among the Yoruba*. Chicago: University of Chicago Press, 1986.

Lal, Brij V. *A Vision for Change: A.D. Patel and the Politics of Fiji*. Canberra, Australia: The Australian National University, E Press, first edition 1977, 2011.

Lal, Brij V. *Islands of Turmoil. Elections and Politics in Fiji*. Canberra, Australia: Australian National University Press, 2006.

Lapid, Yosef and Friedrich V. Kratochwil, *The Return of Culture and Identity in IR Theory*. Boulder: Lynne Rienner, 1996.

Lapid, Yosef. "Culture's Ship: Return and Departures in International Relations Theory." In *The Return of Culture and Identity in International Relations Theory*. Edited by Yousef Lapid and Friedrich Kratochwil, 3–20. Boulder: Lynne Rienner, 1996.

Larson, Piers M. "Enslaved Malagasy and 'Le Travail De La Parole' in the Pre-Revolutionary Mascarenes." *The Journal of African History* 48.3(2007): 457–479.

Lawson, Stephanie. "The Myth of Cultural Homogeneity and Its Implications for Chiefly Power in Fiji." *Comparative Studies in Society and History* 32.4(1990): 795–821.

Lawson, Stephanie. *The Failure of Democratic Politics*. Oxford: Clarendon Press, 1991.

Lemon, Anthony. "The Political Position of Indians in South Africa." In *South Asians Overseas: Migration and* Ethnicity. Edited by Colin Clarke, Cere Peach, and Steven Vertovec. 131–148. Cambridge: Cambridge University Press, 1990.

Lijphart, Arend. "Consociation and Federation: Conceptual and Empirical Links." *Canadian Journal of Political Science* 12.3(1979): 499–515.

Lijphart, Arend. *Democracies in Plural Societies: Comparative Exploration.* New Haven: Yale University Press, 1977.

Lincoln, David. "Beyond the Plantation: Mauritius in the Global Division of Labor." *The Journal of Modern African Studies* 44.1(2006): 59–78.

Look Lai, Walton. "Chinese Diaspora: An Overview." *Caribbean Quarterly* 50.2(2004): 1–14.

Look Lai, Walton. *Indentured Labor, Caribbean Sugar. Chinese and Indian Migrants to the British West Indies, 1838–1918.* Baltimore, London: The Johns Hopkins University Press, 1993.

Loomba, Ania. *Colonialism/Postcolonialism.* London and New York: Routledge, 1998.

Lotter, Stephanie. "The South African Indian Film Industry: New Directions in Indian Commercial and Diasporic Cinema." In *Eyes Across the Water*, 122–139. COMPLETE

Louw, Antoinette. "Surviving the Transition: Trends and Perceptions of Crime in South Africa." *Social Indicators Research* 41.1/3(1997): 137–168.

Lustick, Ian S. "Lijphart, Lakatos, and Consociationalism." *World Politics* 50.1(2007): 88–117.

Lutz, Jessie G. "Chinese Emigrants, Indentured Workers, and Christianity in the West Indies, British Guiana and Hawaii." *Caribbean Studies*, 37.2(2009): 133–154.

Maasdorp, Gavin and Nesen Pillay. *Urban Relocation and Racial Segregation. The Case of Indian South Africans.* Durban: Department of Economics, University of Natal: 1977.

Maira, Sunaina. *Desis in the House: Indian American Youth Culture in New York City.* Philadelphia: Temple University Press, 2002.

Major, Andrea. *Slavery, Abolition and Empire in India, 1772–1843.* Cambridge: Cambridge University Press, 2012.

Malik, Yogendra K. "Socio-Political Perceptions and Attitudes of East Indian Elites in Trinidad." *The Western Political Quarterly* 23.3(1970): 552–563.

Mamdani, Mahmood, "Beyond Settler and Native as Political Identities: Overcoming the Political Legacy of Colonialism." *Comparative Studies in Society and History* 43.4(2001): 651–664.

Manderville, Peter. *Transnational Muslim Politics: Reimagining the Umma.* New York: Routledge, 2001.

Mani, Lata. "Cultural Theory, Colonial Texts: Reading Eye-Witness Accounts of Widow Burning." In *Cultural Studies.* Edited by L. Grossberg, C. Nelson and P. Treichler, 382–405. London: Routledge, 1992.

Mannur, Anita. *Culinary Fictions: Food in South Asian Disaporic Culture.* Temple University Press, 2009.

Mare, Gerhard and Georgina Hamilton. *An Appetite for Power: Buthelezi's Inkatha and the Politics of Loyal Resistance.* Johannesburg: Ravan Press, 1987.

Margadant, Ted. *French Peasants in Revolt: The Insurrection of 1851.* Princeton: Princeton University Press, 1979.

Marshall, P. J. "The Moral Swing to the East: British Humanitarianism in India and the West Indies." In *East India Company Studies: Papers Presented to Professor Sir Cyril Philips.* Edited by Kenneth Ballhatchet and John Harrison, 60–96. Hong Kong: Asian Research Service, 1986.

Maurice Agulhon, Maurice. *The Republic in the Village. The People of the Var from the French Revolution to the Second Republic.* Translated by Janet Lloyd. Cambridge and New York: Cambridge University Press, 1982.

McAdam, Doug Sidney Tarrow, and Charles Tilly. *Dynamics of Contention.* New York: Cambridge University Press, 2001.

McAdam, Doug. "Recruitment to High-Risk Activism: The Case of Freedom Summer." *American Journal of Sociology* 92.1(1986): 64–90.

McAdams, Doug. "Tactical Innovation and the Pace of Insurgency." *American Sociological Review* 48.6(1983): 735–754.

McAdams, Doug. *Freedom Summer*. New York: Oxford University Press, 1988.

McCarthy, John D. and Mayer N. Zald. "Resource Mobilization and Social Movements: A Partial Theory." *American Journal of Sociology* 82.6(1977): 1212–41.

Mearsheimer, John. "Disorder Restored." In *Rethinking America's Security*. Edited by G. Allison and G. F. Treverton, 213–237. New York: W. W. Norton, 1992.

Meer, Fatima. *Portrait of Indian South Africans*. Durban: Avon House, 1969.

Meighoo, Kirk and Peter Jamadar. *Democracy and Constitutional Reform in Trinidad and Tobago*. Kingston: Ian Randle Publishers, 2008.

Meighoo, Kirk. *Politics in a Half Made Society: Trinidad and Tobago 1925–2001*. Oxford: James Currey Publishers, 2003.

Meisenhelder, Thomas. "The Developmental State in Mauritius." *The Journal of Modern African Studies* 35.2(1997): 279–297.

Melucci, Alberto. *Nomads of the Present: Social Movements and Individual Needs in Contemporary Society*. Edited by John Keane and Paul Mier. Philadelphia: Temple University Press, 1989.

Menard, Russell R. *Migrants, Servants and Slaves. Unfree Labor in Colonial British America,*. Burlington, Vermont: Ashgate Publishing Company, 2001.

Mesthrie, R. *Language in Indenture: A Sociolinguistic History of Bhojpuri-Hindi in South Africa*. Johannesburg: Witwatersrand University Press, 1991.

Mesthrie, Rajend. *A Lexicon of South African Indian English*. Yorkshire, England: Peepal Tree Press, 1992.

Meyer, A. C. *Peasants in the Pacific: A Study of Fiji Indian Rural Society*. Berkeley: University of California Press, 1961.

Midgley, Clare. *Women Against Slavery. The British Campaigns, 1780–1870*. London and New York: Routledge, 1992.

Mikula, Paul, Brian Kearney, and Rodney Harber. *Traditional Hindu Temples in South Africa*. Durban, South Africa: Hindu Temple Publications, 1982.

Miles, William F. S. "The Creole Malaise in Mauritius." *African Affairs* 98(1999): 211–228.

Miles, William F. S. "The Politics of Language Equilibrium in a Multilingual Society: Mauritius." *Comparative Politics* 32.2(2000): 215–230.

Miller, Kevin Christopher. *A Community of Sentiment: Indo-Fijian Music and Identity Discourse in Fiji and its Discourses*. Dissertation submitted for a Ph.D. in Ethnomusicology. University of California Los Angeles, 2008,

Mills, John Stuart. *Considerations on Representative Government*. New York: Liberal Arts Press, 1958.

Milne, Robert Stephen. *Politics in Ethnically Bipolar States: A Comparative Exploration*. New Haven: Yale University Press, 1977.

Mintz, Sidney W. *Sweetness and Power. The Place of Sugar in Modern History*. US: Penguin Books, 1985.

Mishra, Sudesh. "TAZIA FIJI! The Place of Potentiality." In *Transnational South Asians. The Making of a Neo-Diaspora*. Edited by Susan Kosay and R. Radhakrishnan, 71–94. Oxford: Oxford University Press, 2008.

Misra, Sudesh. *Diaspora Criticism*. Edinburgh: Edinburgh University Press, 2006.

Morris, Aldon and Carol McClurg Mueller. Editors. *Frontiers of Social Movement Research*. New Haven and London: Yale University Press, 1992.

Munasinghe, Viranjini. "DOUGLA LOGICS. East Indians, Miscegenation, and the National Imaginary." In *Transnational South Asians. The Making of a Neo-Diaspora.* Edited by Susan Koshy and R. Radhakrishnan, 181–214. Oxford: Oxford University Press, 2008.

Munasinghe, Viranjini. "Nationalism in Hybrid Spaces: The Production of Impurity out of Purity." *American Ethnologist* 29.3(2002): 663–692.

Munasinghe, Viranjini. "Theorizing World Culture Through the New World: East Indians and Creolization." *American Ethnologist* 33.4(2006): 549–562.

Munasinghe, Viranjini. *Callaloo or Tossed Salad? East Indians and the Cultural Politics of Identity in Trinidad.* Ithaca: Cornell University Press, 2001.

Naidoo, Jay. "Clio and the Mahatma." *Journal of Southern African Studies* 16.4(1990): 741–750.

Naidoo, Muthal. "The Search for a Cultural Identity: A Personal View of South African "Indian" Theatre." *Theatre Journal* 49.1(1997): 29–39.

Nash, June. "The Fiesta of the World: The Zapatista Uprising and Radical Democracy in Mexico." *American Anthropology* 99.2(1997): 261–274.

Nave, Ari. "The Institutionalisation of Communalism: The Best Loser System." In *Consolidating the Rainbow: Independent Mauritius, 1968–1998.* Edited by Marina Carter, 19–26. Port Louis, Mauritius: Center for Research on Indian Ocean Studies, 1998.

Nelson, Bernard H. "The Slave Trade as a Factor in British Foreign Policy 1815–1862." *Journal of Negro History* 27.2(1942): 192–209.

Newland, Lynda. "The Role of the Assembly of Christian Churches in Fiji in the 2006 elections." In *From Election to Coup. The 2006 Campaign and its Aftermath.* Edited by Jon Fraenkel and Stewart Firth, 300–314. Canberra, Australia: ANU Press, 2007.

Nicholls, H. G. *South Africa in My Time.* London: George Allen & Unwin, 1961.

Northrup, David. "Free and Unfree Labor Migration, 1600–1900: An Introduction." *Journal of World History* 14.2(2003): 125–130.

Norton, Robert. "Epilogue. Understanding Fiji's Political Paradox." In *From Election to Coup: The 2006 Campaign and its Aftermath.* Edited by Jon Fraenkel and Stewart Firth, 403–419. Canberra, Australia: ANU Press, 2007).

Nwulia, Moses D. E. "The "Apprenticeship" System in Mauritius: Its Character and Its Impact on Race Relations in the Immediate Post-Emancipation Period, 1839–1879." *African Studies Review* 21.1(1978): 89–101.

Nwulia, Moses D. E. *The History of Slavery in Mauritius and the Seychelles, 1810–1875.* New Brunswick, Associated University Press, 1981.

O'Flynn, Ian. "Review Article: Divided Societies and Deliberative Democracy." *British Journal of Political Science* 37(2007): 731–751.

O'Hanlon, Rosalind and David Washbrook. "After Orientalism, Culture, Criticism, and Politics in the Third Word." *Comparative Studies in Society and History,* 34.1(1992): 141–167.

Offe, Claus. "New Social Movements: Challenging the Boundaries of Institutional Politics." *Social Research* 52.4(1985): 817–867.

Oxaal, Ivar. *Race and Revolutionary Consciousness: A Documentary Interpretation of the 1970 Black Power Revolt in Trinidad.* Cambridge, Massachusetts: Schenkman Publishing Company, 1971.

Pattundeen, Gerelene. "Missing out on Migration: "Sugars" and the Post-Apartheid Youth of Chatsworth." *Journal of Social Sciences, Special Volume* 10(2008): 61–71.

Plotke, David. "Representation is Democracy," *Constellations* 4.1(1997): 19–34.

Pollock, Sheldon. "Deep Orientalism? Notes on Sanskrit and Power Beyond the Raj." In *Orientalism and the Postcolonial Predicament: Perspectives on South Asia*. Edited by Carol A. Breckenridge and Peter van der Veer, 76–133. Philadelphia: University of Pennsylvania Press, 1993).

Porter, Dale H. *The Abolition of the Slave Trade in England 1784–1807*. US: Archon Books, 1970.

Posel, Deborah. *The Making of Apartheid, 1948–1961: Conflict and Compromise*. Oxford: Clarendon Press, 1991.

Prakash, Gyan. *Bonded Histories: Genealogies of Labor Servitude in Colonial India*. Cambridge: Cambridge University Press, 1990.

Prasad, Jonathan. "The Role of Hindu and Muslim Organizations During the 2006 Election." In *From Election to Coup: The 2006 Campaign and its Aftermath*. Edited by Jon Fraenkel and Stewart Firth, 315–336. Canberra, Australia: ANU Press, 2007.

Premdas, Ralph R. "Ethnic Conflict, Inequality and Public Sector Governance in Trinidad and Tobago." In *Ethnicity Inequalities and Public Sector Governance*. Edited by Yusuf Bangura, 98–119. New York: Palgrave Macmillan, 2006.

Rabushka, Alvin and Kenneth A. Shepsle. *Politics in Plural Societies: A Theory of Democratic Instability*. Columbus, CO: Charles E. Merrill Publishing Company, 1972.

Ragatz, Lowell J. *The Fall of the Planter Class in the British West Indies, 1763–1833*. New York: Octagon Books, 1928, reprinted in 1963.

Ramamurthi, T. G. "Lessons of Durban Riots." *Economic and Political Weekly* 29.10 (1994): 543–546,.

Ramnarine, Tina K. ""Indian" Music in the Diaspora: Case Studies of "Chutney" in Trinidad and London." *British Journal of Ethnomusicology* 5(1996): 133–153.

Ramnarine, Tina K. "Historical Representations, Performance Spaces, and Kinship Themes in Indian-Caribbean Popular Song Texts." *Asian Music* 30.1(1998–99): 1–33.

Ratuva, Steven. "The Pre-Election "Cold War."" In *From Election to Coup in Fiji: The 2006 Campaign and its Aftermath*. Edited by Jon Fraenkel and Stewart Firth, 26–45. Canberra, Australia: ANU Press, 2007).

Ravuvu, Asesela. *The Façade for Democracy: Fijian Struggles for Political Control*. Suva: Reader Publishing House, 1991.

Reddy, Movindri. "Challenging Democracy: Ethnicity in Post-Colonial Fiji and Trinidad." *Journal of Nationalism and Ethnic Politics* 17.2(2011): 182–202.

Reddy, Movindri. "Ethnic Conflict and Violence: South Africa and South Asia." In *Ethnicity and Governance in the Third World*. Edited by John Mukum Mbaku, Pita Ogaba Agbese, and Mwangi S. Kimenyi, 295–326. Farnham: Ashgate Publishing Company, 2001.

Reddy, Movindri. *Conflicts of Consciousness: The State, Inkatha and Ethnic Violence in Natal*. University of Cambridge, Ph. D. Thesis, 1993.

Riggio, Milla Cozart. "Reforms in the Lap of the Feet of God: Ramleela in Trinidad, 2006–2008." *The Drama Review* 54.1(2010): 106–149.

Risse-Kappen, Thomas. Editor. *Bringing Transnational Relations Back In: Non-State Actors, Domestic Structures and International Institutions*. Cambridge: Cambridge University Press, 1995.

Ritchie, Mark. "Cross-Border organizing." In *The Case Against the Global Economy and for a Turn toward the Local*. Edited by Jerry Mander and Edward Goldsmith, 494–500. San Francisco: Sierra Club, 1996.

Rohlehr, Gordon. *Calypso and Society in Pre-Independent Trinidad*. Port of Spain: Trinidad, 1990.

Ruggie, John G. *Multilateralism Matters: The Theory and Praxis of an Institutional Form.* New York: Columbia University Press, 1993.

Rutz, Henry J. "Capitalizing on Culture: Moral Ironies in Urban Fiji." *Comparative Studies in Society and History* 29.3(1987): 533–557.

Ryan, Selwyn. *Race and Nationalism in Trinidad and Tobago. A Study of Decolonization in a Multicultural Society.* Toronto: University of Toronto Press, 1972.

Safran, William and Jean A Laponce. *Language, Ethnic Identity, and the State.* Philadelphia, PA: Cass, Taylor & Francis Group, 2004.

Safran, William. "Diasporas in Modern Societies: Myths of Homeland and Return.*" Diaspora* 1.1(1991): 83–99.

Sandbrook, Richard and David Romano, "Globalization, Extremism and Violence in Poor Countries." *Third World Quarterly* 25.6(2004): 1007–1030.

Sandbrook, Richard. "Origins of the Democratic Developmental State: Interrogating Mauritius." *Canadian Journal of African Studies* 39.3(2005): 549–581.

Sassen, Saskia. *Territory, Authority, Rights: From Medieval to Global Assemblages.* Princeton: University of Princeton Press, 2006.

Saul, John. "The Hares, the Hounds, and the African National Congress: On Joining the Third World in Post-Apartheid South Africa." *Third World Quarterly* 25.1(2004): 73–86.

Schulz-Herzenberg, Collette. "A Silent Revolution: South African Voters, 1994–2006." In *State of the Nation. South African 2007.* Edited by Sakhela Buhlungu, John Daniel, Roger Southall, 114–145. Cape Town: Human Sciences Research Council, 2007.

Scobell, Andrew. "Politics, Professionalism, and Peacekeeping: An Analysis of the 1987 Military Coup in Fiji." *Comparative Politics* 26.2(1994): 187–201.

Scott, James. *Weapons of the Weak: Everyday Forms of Peasant Resistance.* New Haven, CT: Yale University Press, 1985.

Scott, James. *Weapons of the Weak. Everyday Forms of Peasant Resistance.* New Haven: Yale University Press, 1987.

Seekings, Jeremy and Nicoli Nattrass. "Class, Distribution and Redistribution in Post-Apartheid South Africa." *Transformation: Critical Perspectives in Southern Africa* 50 (2002): 1–30.

Sen, Sudipta. *Empire of Free Trade: The East India Company and Making of the Colonial Marketplace.* Philadelphia: University of Pennsylvania Press, 1998.

Shain, Yossi and Aharon Barth. "Diasporas and International Relations Theory." *International Organizations* 57.3(2003): 449–479.

Shell, Robert. *Children of Bondage: A Social History of the Slave Society at the Cape of Good Hope 1652–1838.* Hanover: Wesleyan University Press, 1994.

Shils, Edward. "Primordial, Personal, Sacred and Civil Ties: Some Particular Observations on the Relationships of Sociological Research and Theory." *British Journal of Sociology.* 8.2 (1957): 130–145.

Shorter, Edward and Charles Tilly. *Strikes in France, 1830–1968.* Cambridge: Cambridge University Press, 1974.

Shukla, Sandhya. "Locations for South Asian Diasporas." *Annual Review of Anthropology* 30(2001): 551–572.

Singh Anand and Shanta Singh. "The History of Crime Among People of Indian Origin in South Africa." *Anthropologist* 8.3(2006): 147–156/

Smith, Adam. *Wealth of Nations,* [first published in 1776]. Thrifty Books, 2009.

Smith, Jackie, Charles Chatfield, Ron Pagnucco. *Transnational Social Movements and Global Politics: Solidarity Beyond the State.* Syracuse: Syracuse University Press, 1997.

Snow, David A., Louis A. Zurcher Jr., and Sheldon Ekland-Olson. "Social Networks and Social Movements: A Microstructural Approach to Differential Recruitment." *American Sociological Review* 45.5(1980): 787–801.

Soysal, Yasemin. *Limits of Citizenship: Migrants and Postnational Membership in Europe.* Chicago: University of Chicago, 1994.

Spadafora, David. *The Idea of Progress Eighteenth-Century Britain.* New Haven: Yale University Press, 1990.

Sparks, Alister. *Beyond the Miracle. Inside the New South Africa.* Johannesburg and Cape Town: Jonathan Ball Publishers, 2003.

Srebrnik, Henry. ""Full of Sound and Fury": Three Decades of Parliamentary Politics in Mauritius." *Journal of Southern African Studies* 28.2(2002): 277–289.

Strange, Susan. "Political Economy and International Relations." In *International Relations Theory Today.* Edited by Ken Booth and Steve Smith, 154–174. Pennsylvania: The Pennsylvania State University Press, 1995.

Sundar-Harris, Usha. "Outcasts of the People." In *Coup: Reflections on the political crisis in Fiji.* Edited by Brij V. Lal and Michael Pretes, 56–59. Canberra, Australia: The Australia National University, 2008.

Swaminathan, Srividhya. *Debating the Slave Trade. Rhetoric of British National Identity, 1759–1815.* (Burlington, VT: Ashgate Publishing Company, 2009.

Swan, Maureen. "The 1913 Natal Indian Strike," *Journal of Southern African Studies* 10.2(1984): 239–258.

Swanson, Maynard W. ""The Asiatic Menace": Creating Segregation in Durban, 1870–1900." *The International Journal of African Historical Studies* 16.3(1983): 401–421.

Swidler, Ann. "Culture in Action: Symbols and Strategies." *American Sociological Review* 51.2(1986): 273–286

Tarrow, Sidney. *Democracy and Disorder: Protest and Politics in Italy, 1965–1975.* New York: Oxford University Press, 1989.

Tarrow, Sidney. *Power in Movement.* Cambridge: Cambridge University Press, 1994.

Tarrow, Sidney. *The New Transnational Activism.* Cambridge: Cambridge University Press, 2005.

Thompson, E. P. *The Making of the English Working Class.* England: Penguin Books, 1963.

Tilly, Charles and Lesley J. Wood. *Social Movements, 1768–2012*, 3rd Edition. Boulder and London: Paradigm Publishers, 2013.

Tilly, Charles. *The Contentious French.* Cambridge, MA: Harvard University Press, 1986.

Tinker, Hugh. "Between Africa, Asia and Europe: Mauritius: Cultural Marginalisation and Political Control." *African Affairs* 76.304(1997): 321–338.

Tinker, Hugh. "Into Servitude: Indian Labour in the Sugar Industry, 1833–1970." In *International Labour Migration: Historical Perspectives.* Edited by Shula Marks, 76–89. Middlesex, Great Britain: Maurice Temple Smith Limited, 1984.

Tinker, Hugh. "Mauritius: Culture and Political Control." *African Affairs*, 76.304(1997): 321–338,

Tinker, Hugh. *A New System of Slavery: The Export of Indian Labour Oversees. 1830–1920.* London: University of Oxford Press, 1974.

Tölölyan, Khachig. "The Contemporary Discourse of Diaspora Studies." *Comparative Studies of South Asia, Africa, and the Middle* East 27.3(2007): 647–655.

Toren, Cristina. "Making the Present, Revealing the Past: the Mutability and Continuity of Tradition as Process." *Man, New Series* 23.4(1988): 696–717.

Touraine, Alain. *Can We Live Together? Equality and Difference.* Stanford, CA: Stanford University Press, 2000.

Touraine, Alain. *Return of the Actor: Social Theory in Postindustrial Society*. Translated by M. Godzich. Minneapolis: University of Minnesota Press, 1988.

Traugott, Mark. "Recurrent Patterns of Collective Action." In *Repertoires and Cycles of Collective Action*. Edited by Mark Traugott, 1–14. Durham, NC: Duke University Press, 1995.

Trnka, Susanne. *State of Suffering: Political Violence and Community Survival in Fiji*. Ithaca: Cornell University Press, 2008.

Tuimaleali'ifano, Morgan. "Indigenous Title Disputes: What it Meant in the 2006 Election." In *From Election to Coup: The 2006 Campaign and its Aftermath*. Edited by Jon Fraenkel and Stewart Firth, 261–271. Canberra, Australia: ANU Press, 2007.

Tylor, Verta and Nancy E. Whittier. "Collective Identity in Social Movement Communities: Lesbian Feminist Mobilization." In *Frontiers in Social Movement Theory*. Edited by Aldon D. Morris and Carol McClurg Mueller, 104–130. New Haven, CT: Yale University Press, 1992. PAGE NUMBERS

Vahed, Goolam and Thembisa Waetjen. *Gender, Modernity and Indian Delights. The Women's Cultural Group of Durban, 1954–2010*. Cape Town: Human Science Research Council, 2010.

Vahed, Goolam. "Control and Repression: The Plight of Indian Hawkers and Flower Sellers in Durban, 1910–1948," *International Journal of African Historical Studies* 32.1(1999): 19–48.

Vahed, Goolam. "Passengers, Partnerships, and Promissory Notes: Gujarati Traders in Colonial Natal, 1870–1920." *The International Journal of African Historical Studies* 38.3(2005): 449–479.

Van Den Berghe, Pierre L. "Apartheid, Fascism, and the Golden Age." *Cahiers d'Études Africaines* 2.8(1962): 598–608.

Van Den Berghe, Pierre L. "Ethnicity and the Sociological Debate." In *Theories of Race and Ethnic Relations*. Edited by John Rex and David Mason, 246–263. Cambridge: Cambridge University Press, 1988.

Van Den Berghe, Pierre L. *The Ethnic Phenomenon*. New York: Elsevier North-Holland, 1979.

van der Veer, Peter and Steven Vertovec. "Brahmanism Abroad: On Caribbean Hinduism as an Ethnic Religion." *Ethnology* 30.2(1991): 149–166.

Van der Veer, Peter. *Nations and Migration: the Politics of Space in the South Asian Diaspora*. Philadelphia: University of Philadelphia, 1995.

Varadarajan, Latha. *The Domestic Abroad: Diasporas in International Relations*. Oxford: Oxford University Press, 2010.

Veracini, Lorenzo. "Settler Colonial Studies." *Settler Colonial Studies* 1.1(2011): 1–12.

Vertovec, Steven. *Hindu Trinidad. Religion, Ethnicity and Socio-Economic Change*. London: Macmillan Education, 1992.

Vertovec, Steven. *Transnationalism*. London and New York: Routledge, 2009.

Walker, R. B. J. "International Relations and the Concept of the Political. In *International Relations Theory Today*." Edited by Ken Booth and Steve Smith, 306–327. Pennsylvania: The Pennsylvania State University Press, 1995.

Walker, R. B. J. *Inside/Outside: International Relations as Political Theory*. Cambridge: Cambridge University Press, 1993.

Wallerstein, Immanuel. "The National and the Universal: Can There Be Such a Thing as World Culture?" In *Culture, Globalization and World-System: Contemporary Conditions for the Representation of Identity*. Edited by Anthony D. King, 91–106. Minneapolis: University of Minnesota Press, 1977).

Waterman, Peter. *Globalization, Social Movements and the New Internationalisms.* Routledge, 2004.

Webster, Eddie. "The 1949 Durban Riots – A Case Study in Race and Class." *Working Papers in Southern African Studies* (1979): 1–54.

Wendt, Alexander. "Constructing International Politics." *International Security* 20.1(1995): 71–81,

Werbner, Pnina and Tariq Modood. *Debating Cultural Hybridity: Multi-cultural Identities and the Politics of Anti-racism.* London: Zed, 1997.

Williams, Eric. "The Golden Age of the Slave System in Britain." *Journal of Negro History.* 25.1(1940): 60–106.

Williams, Eric. *Capitalism and Slavery.* Chapel Hill: The University of North Carolina Press, 1994.

Williams, Eric. *From Columbus to Castro: The History of the Caribbean, 1942–1969,* New York: Vintage Books, 1984 (1970 first edition)

Williams, Patrick. "What Shall We do Without Exile?: The Contradiction of 'Return' in the Palestinian Diaspora." In *Comparing Postcolonial Diasporas.* Edited by M Keown, D. Murphy, and J. Procter. Palgrave Macmillan, 2009.

Wilson, Kathleen. *A New Imperial History: Culture, Identity and Modernity in Britain and the Empire. 1660–1840.* Cambridge: Cambridge University Press, 2004.

Wilson, Kathleen. *The Sense of the People: Politics, Culture and Imperialism in England, 1715–1785.* Cambridge: Cambridge University Press, 1998.

Wolfe, Patrick. "Settler Colonialism and the Elimination of the Native." *Journal of Genocide Research* 8.4(2006): 387–409.

Womack, John Jr. *Rebellion in Chiapas: An Historical Reader.* New York: The New Press, 1999.

Woods, C. A. *The Natal Indian Community. Their Economic Position.* London: Oxford University Press, 1954.

Yang, Anand A. "Bandits and Kings: Moral Authority and Resistance in Early Colonial India," *Journal of Asian Studies,* 66(4) 2007: 881–896.

Yelvington, Kevin. "Ethnicity at Work in Trinidad." In *The Enigma of ETHNICITY: An Analysis of Race in the Caribbean and the World.* Edited by Ralph R. Premdas, 99–122. Trinidad and Tobago: University of West Indies, 1993.

Younger, Paul. *New Homelands: Hindu Communities in Mauritius, Guyana, Trinidad, South Africa, Fiji, and East Africa.* New York: Oxford University Press, 2010.

Index

Page numbers for figures are in italics.

transnationalism 61–2, 102–5
transnational locality 12, 45–76, 97, 123–4, 145, 172–3, 177–9
Transvaal 22
Transvaal Indian Congress (TIC) 129–30, 133
Treaty of Paris (1814) 106
Tricameral Parliament (South Africa) 69, 132–3, 136
Trinidad 5–6, 11, 27; caste system in 154; cuisine of 155–7; culture of 84–5, 164–5; economy of 85–7; elections in 78, 174; ethnicity in post-colonial 77–95; indenture in 2, 14, 30, 175; language in 85, 161; music in 166–7; political system of 88–90; populations of 28, 79–80, 83–4, 160–1; religion in 84, 153–4, 163; slavery in 80
Trinidad Workingmen's Association 89
Trnka, S. 84–5, 85
Tuimaleali'ifano, M. 88
Tulsidas, G.: *Ramcharitmanas* 164–5
2000 Census (Trinidad) 83–4
2007 Census (Fiji) 83, 86

UDF (United Democratic Front) 5, 69, 133–6
uitlanders (outsiders) 131
Umgeni Road temple 162
Umlazi township, South Africa 131–2
UNC (United National Congress) 89–91
unemployment 56, 123–4, 139–41, 140
Union of Creole Organizations/*Rassemblement Organization Creoles* 106
Union of the Working Classes, The 25
Unitarians 23
United Democratic Front (UDF) 5, 69, 133–6
United Fiji Party (Soqosoqo Duavata ni Lewenivanua Party; SDL) 88, 91
United Labor Front 89
United National Congress (UNC) 89–91
United States 27, 34
Urdu language 98, 114

Vahed, G. 128
Vaish 159
Vaish Mukhti Sangh (Welfare Association) 159

Vaishya 153–4
Van Den Berghe, P. 80–1, 131
Varadarajan, L.: *The Domestic Abroad: Diasporas in International Relations* 9
Veer, P. van der 55, 58, 161
Vertovec, S. 8
Vishnu Hindu Parishad (World Hindu Council) 114
vulagi 85

wage labor 15
Walker, R. 51, 61
Wallerstein, I. 103
Ward, W. 19–20
Waterman, P. 66
Welfare Association (Vaish Mukhti Sangh) 159
Wendt, A. 51
Werbner, P. 58
West India Committee 22
West Indian Commission (1897) 33
West Indies 21–2, 26–8, 34–5
Westminster system 78–9, 82, 88–91, 175
white settlers (Natal) 125–33
widow-burning 19
Wikileaks 120n62
Wilberforce, W. 19–20, 23
Williams, E. 21–4, 88–9
Wilson, K. 19
Woods, C. 130
working classes 19, 25, 129, 133
World Bank 100, 109, 139
World Economic Forum 138
World Hindu Council (Vishnu Hindu Parishad) 114
World Trade Organization 67

xenophobia 59, 91, 173

Yang, A. 22
Yelvington, K. 86
Younger, P. 162; *New Homeland. Hindu Communities in Mauritius, Guyana, Trinidad, South Africa, Fiji, and East Africa* 9

Zulu Kingdom 28, 125
Zuluness 136
Zuma, J. 143

For Product Safety Concerns and Information please contact our EU
representative GPSR@taylorandfrancis.com
Taylor & Francis Verlag GmbH, Kaufingerstraße 24, 80331 München, Germany

www.ingramcontent.com/pod-product-compliance
Lightning Source LLC
Chambersburg PA
CBHW050435280326
41932CB00013BA/2120

9 781138 592957